For Some, the Dream Came True

For Some, the Dream Came True

The Best From 50 Years of Fortune Magazine

Selected and edited by
DUNCAN NORTON-TAYLOR

LYLE STUART INC.   *Secaucus, N.J.*

Queries regarding rights and permissions
should be addressed to:
Lyle Stuart Inc.
120 Enterprise Ave., Secaucus, N.J. 07094

Published by Lyle Stuart Inc.
Published simultaneously in Canada by
Musson Book Company
A division of General Publishing Co. Limited
Don Mills, Ontario.

Manufactured in the United States of America.

Articles reprinted with the permission of *Fortune* Magazine.

Library of Congress Cataloging in Publication Data
Main entry under title:

For some, the dream came true.

   1. United States—Economic conditions—1918-
1945—Addresses, essays, lectures.   2. United
States—Economic conditions—1945-   —Addresses,
essays, lectures.   3. United States—Commerce—
Addresses, essays, lectures.   4. Businessmen—
United States—Biography—Addresses, essays, lec-
tures.   5. Capitalism—Addresses, essays, lectures.
I. Norton-Taylor, Duncan.   II. Fortune.
HC106.F64   330   81-9034
                    AACR2

Contents

5

The Fifties   113

Contents

Acknowledgments

My thanks to those former colleagues of mine in the editorial, art and business departments of *Fortune* who helped me in so many ways in the compilation of this book. I am grateful to Robert Lubar, who presided as managing editor over the 50th Anniversary issue, from which this book developed. And I am especially grateful to Rosalind Berlin. When I had to assemble and cull through 634 back issues, she was my indefatigable provider and researcher.

–D.N.-T.

For Some, the Dream Came True

Preface

To walk through a picture gallery is to sense the essence of an era. *For Some, the Dream Came True* is a gallery of pictures in words that evoke an extraordinary era in American Capitalism, extending from the Depression to 1980. In the gallery are portraits of businesses, geniuses, heroes, rogues; landscapes of industrial achievement, and wreckage; artifacts of industry's handmaidens, science and technology. Some of the pictures are comic, some tragic; all of them are instructive.

The word-pictures are digests and excerpts of articles that first appeared in *Fortune* magazine. To celebrate Henry R. Luce's somewhat reckless launching of a luxurious and expensive business magazine a few months after the Wall Street Crash of 1929, *Fortune*'s editors brought out a 50th Anniversary issue in February 1980, and it was my pleasure—having once been managing editor—to compile out of back numbers the articles to run in that issue, and then to gather up many more to include in a book, which thus becomes an extended celebration. *Fortune*'s staff, which embraced poets, scholars, and many writers of otherwise considerable talent, produced a unique body of business literature over those years. *The Best from Fifty Years of Fortune*—well, I selected what I thought *best* told the story of an era; another editor might have come up with different choices (*Fortune* published some 6,000 articles in the fifty years).

Each story bears the date when it appeared. They are not, however, arranged in the book in the order of their appearance but more according to the events they described, or to fit them together into certain themes. The notes I have appended to each decade will indicate what each room of the gallery is going to hold up to view.

The title, *For Some, the Dream Came True*, could be a summation of American Capitalism, for dreams are part of its dynamics–and some come true and some don't. Running through the history that unfolds in the background are the writers' commentaries: always implicit is what they thought American Capitalism ought to be; i.e., better than it was. It is not what it used to be 50 years ago; it

13

would hardly be recognized by its practitioners of the early Twentieth Century. Changes have been wrought by the centrifugal forces of politics, war, science, and by novel ideas of men who have worked within its system. No one can deny an improvement in its morals and its social consciousness. It presents today, however, a picture of some uncertainty.

But this may be due to miscalculations of its practitioners; it can be argued that its future depends not on intervention of government, as is so often proposed, but on the ability of the practitioners to overcome their own difficulties. American society is organized around Capitalism and no better system has yet been invented. What Capitalism has working for it is the philosophy that man is eager to work if he is rewarded.

The gallery will stir memories of things past—of tourist cabin camps at the end of the day's journey, voices of doom coming over radio sets, of the first blast-off into outer space—and, in Capitalism's ever changing world, provoke wonderment at things to come.

—D.N-T.

The Thirties

The scenes are not propitious. Before the Crash of 1929 capitalists could be perceived as men dancing on the edge of an earthquake. When some of them disappear, people begin to realize the depth of the fissure which the Crash has opened up.

Actually it is remarkable how few people are affected. "The only thing we have to fear is fear itself," the newly elected President says, lifting the line from Thoreau. It is, on the whole, still a lively landscape. Business that is sound (e.g., A & P) continues to function very well and profitably. A good society is still evident. Families enjoy their new love, the automobile, which Capitalism has provided, and even enjoy such exotic entertainment as popularly priced cruises to the Caribbean.

But seven years after the Crash, almost 11 million people find themselves out of work, and some of them are white collar workers, tokens of Capitalism's failures. The Thirties become the Great Depression, the efforts of government and the New Deal notwithstanding. The years are marked by growing chasms of poverty, even starvation, and the labor leader, John Lewis, scowls from the walls, showing his determination to rescue those who have been deprived of the system's benefits. Capitalism is in bad repair in the Thirties. It will take a war to restore it.

The Times Were Right for Ivar Kreuger

By ARCHIBALD MacLEISH

The stair smelled as it had always smelled of hemp and people and politeness—of the decent bourgeois dust. Mr. Kreuger breathed it softly as he went down around the caged-in column of the *ascenseur*. At the bottom of the stair he pushed the glass-paned door.

Mr. Kreuger, in all his years on the Avenue Victor-Emmanuel III, had never walked. There had always been a car at the door, a taxi waiting. But the distance was not long. He had seen the gun-store windows often. There was a sign in front like a target with the words "Tir Gastinne-Renette." There were rifles in the windows and dueling pistols hung in pairs and English guns. It was a few steps in the gathering dusk.

A clerk received him in the lighted shop. "Monsieur desires . . . ?" "An automatic—a revolver—it makes no difference which." Monsieur was very calm, in no way excited, nothing to make a man suppose . . . "Perhaps the 6.35-mm. Browning?" The 6.35 mm. Browning was too small. "The army type? The 9-mm.?" Yes, the army type. He gave his name and address: Mr. Ivar Kreuger, Numéro Cinq Avenue Victor-Emmanuel III, and dropped the heavy package in his pocket.

That evening Mr. Kreuger did not eat. He was suffering from a heavy cold, one of those colds which a March crossing of the Atlantic and a drafty train and a Paris chill can give a man. He would not admit even to Jeanette his housekeeper that he was ill, and sat alone playing solitaire . . . .

Saturday, March 12, 1932, was a sunless, white-skied, pale spring morning. From Numéro Cinq Avenue Victor-Emmanuel you could see the raw light on the roof of the Grand Palais and the open ground with its gravel and its plane trees and the new buds swelling on the trees. Jeanette had gone to do her marketing. Mr. Kreuger drew the bedroom blinds, smoothed the unmade bed-clothes and lay down. Looking up he saw the fat, gold stucco cherubs in the ceiling corners of the room. Odd witnesses! He snapped a cartridge in the army type, the 9-mm., and placed his feet together neatly.

Jeanette returned from marketing a little before twelve. She told Monsieur Krister Littorin, Mr. Kreuger's friend, calling from the Hôtel du Rhin that Mr. Kreuger had gone out—then later that Mr. Kreuger was asleep. Monsieur kept calling. Mr. Kreuger was expected at the hotel. Would someone go and waken him? Jeanette had called him but he did not wake.

At one, Monsieur Littorin drove up. The room was dark and Littorin, groping toward the bed, put out his hand. Jeanette heard him cry: "*Il est mort.*" She pulled the blinds back. His feet together neatly on the spread, his left hand on his abdomen with the thumb cocked upward, his right arm straight against his side, a little blood, a very little blood, below his heart, Mr. Kreuger lay along the unmade bed.

Headlines ran the world. "IVAR KREUGER DÖD"..."MORT DE M. IVAR KREUGER"..."KREUGER'S LETZTE TAGE."

In Stockholm the Swedish Parliament convened hurriedly at midnight on Sunday night. In Warsaw there was a run on Kreuger's Polish American Bank.

The days passed. Kreuger stocks fell. Kreuger companies tottered. Kreuger's name went back and forth over the cables of the Atlantic and the Pacific. People asked one another about Kreuger in subway trains and on the porches of Riviera hotels. The act of his death, like a chemical thrown into a solution, had precipitated facts unknown even to his closest friends. The central story was clear enough. Born in 1880 of a bourgeois German family in the little Swedish town of Kalmar on the Baltic, Kreuger had worked through grammar school and technical college, emigrated to America at the age of twenty, tried real estate and wire stringing. He worked on a bridge in Vera Cruz and on the Flatiron Building, Macy's, the Metropolitan Life Building in New York. He toured the Far East, swung back to the States, worked on the Syracuse Stadium, and ended up in Sweden in 1907 with an ambition to rebuild the city of Stockholm.

The rest was one of the great success stories of the age. At thirty he joined forces with a young Swedish engineer named Toll, and ran away with the building business in Stockholm. He extended his interests into Finland, Russia, and Germany, and ran his capital from one million kronor up to six million. He turned to the match business in 1913, formed Swedish Match in 1917, and at the age of thirty-seven in the face of enormous difficulties, restored to

Sweden her predominance in match production lost during the War. He extended his operations into every European country except Spain, Russia, and France and to sixteen non-European countries, and bought or built 250 match factories. He set up subsidiaries in America, acquired absolute monopolies in fifteen countries, *de facto* monopolies in nine, and market dominance in ten more, associated with himself the great banking names of Europe and America, and lent almost $400 million to fifteen countries including France and Germany. His interests touched the world at every point. His telephone company, the Ericsson, had factories in twelve countries and concessions in five. His newspapers included the *Svenska Dagbladet*, one of the best papers of Scandinavia. His Boliden Mining Co. controlled the gold fields of northern Sweden. He strode the world, the Scandinavian world at least, like a colossus.

People talked of his penthouse at 791 Park Avenue, Manhattan, where the bedroom was like a lady's bedroom in a French house and the bath was walled in pink marble with a sea-bottom scene above; of his apartment in Berlin on the Pariser Platz; of his monogrammed silk underwear in shades of tan; of his dinner parties with antique gold snuffboxes for place cards; of dancers, whores, prima donnas, other men's wives, desks full of gold handbags and diamond brooches, photographs inscribed "to darling Ivar," thousand-kronor notes handed to women on the street, and other similar fancies. In New York, in his dining room draped like a Tennysonian barge, he took what Hilda Åberg cooked for him and little enough of that—only a second helping of dessert—although he could drink bottle after bottle of Veuve Cliquot without visible effects. Sweets overmastered him. Once at dinner he had gulped an entire bowl of chocolates before the soup was served.

Ivar Kreuger's face faded out of memory. No one seemed able to recall his eyes—only his big-boned Swedish frame filling a doorway and the porous pallid skin of his face strangely fat above so gaunt a body. What survived was not a head but a manner—an embarrassing trick of talking with the mouth drawn back in a kind of canine grin, a way of twisting the neck, a gracious, gentle courtesy in speech; a man who could talk figures in the four languages of the world—whom the French bankers had called *l'oiseleur,* the charmer of birds.

He would amuse himself on the *Train Bleu* writing down the

Ivar Kreuger in 1896, a lad of sixteen with a passion for cherries, a contempt for money and no particular brilliance in the studies he had just completed at the Kalmar Grammar School in Sweden.

AMERICAN-SWEDISH NEWS EXCHANGE, INC.

Kreuger in British militia uniform during his restaurant- keeping interlude in South Africa in 1904.

AMERICAN-SWEDISH NEWS EXCHANGE INC

*Kreuger (seated left) and his partner
Toll (standing) during the
early days of his career as a builder
in Stockholm.*

Kreuger leaving the U.S. in 1930.

quotations on a given stock for a year and making only fractional mistakes. His calmness was incredible—no one had ever heard him raise his voice. His secrecy was a tradition.

On Tuesday the twenty-second day of March, gentlemen from all parts of Europe, from England, from America, drove to the Crematorium of the North Cemetery outside the city of Stockholm. The great of European industry, they took their seats in a chapel banked with orchids, and sat there while the double door swung open—while eight tall chauffeurs in the uniform of the Match Trust bore in the light wood coffin with its load of lilies of the valley, and saw the coffin sink to the furnaces below. They filed out through the chapel door with solemn, grief-touched faces. It was very sad. And very, very strange. So great a man, so rich a man. Why should a man so rich and great have died by his own will?

Donald Durant of the firm of Lee, Higginson & Co., bankers, had much to think of as he left the crematorium. He had met Kreuger in 1922, had arranged for the flotation of his American issues, dined with him, entertained him over ten profitable years. It was not easy, Ivar being dead, to estimate the future. Lee, Higginson, and he himself and his partners and their families held upward of eight millions of the dead man's stocks and bonds.

The Investigating Commission, appointed by the government, met and retained Price, Waterhouse & Co. as accountants. Their report was read in the Second Chamber of the Riksdag. The phrases were colorless and dry: the December 31, 1930, balance sheets of Kreuger & Toll "grossly misrepresent the true financial position of the company," the fraudulent entries were made "under the personal direction of the late Mr. Kreuger"; Continental Investment, the vital organ of Kreuger's U.S. International Match Corp., was in the same condition; profit-and-loss accounts had been cooked for years. . . .

Accountants and bookkeepers and lawyers and creditors and financiers piled into Stockholm on every train. Lee, Higginson, International Match, Banque de Paris, Crédit Lyonnais, British Match, International Telephone & Telegraph filled the Grand Hotel with their representatives.

And while they were finding their way along the quays and picking up enough Swedish to order a beer, the police were rummaging through Kreuger's apartment in the Villagatan, and the Investigating Commission was sending the Minister of Justice down to Rome with a package of forty-seven bonds amounting to some £28,668,500 issued by the Italian Match Monopoly with a guaranty by the Italian Government, and Mussolini was explaining to the Minister of Justice with some heat that the signatures on the bonds were forgeries. The great financier, the creditor of governments, the floater of $250 million more or less of American issues through American bankers was not only a suicide and not only a bankrupt but a common and a very clumsy forger of bad bonds.

Hell, in the expressive phrase, broke with that news. Within a week the suicides were coming in—a municipal clerk who had owned Kreuger & Toll stock was found with his wrists cut; another clerk, his savings wiped out, dead in the Humlegarden. And with the suicides came the arrests. A certain Bror Bredberg was dragged up from Zurich charged with manipulating the books of Kreuger companies of which no one had heard. An individual named Victor Holm was pulled out of Holland for entering on the books of something called *Dutch* Kreuger & Toll a deposit in a bank which did not exist. Finally brother Torsten Kreuger himself was charged with falsification and offenses against the bankruptcy act.

The whole structure of the state was shaken. Prime Minister Ekman was forced to resign because of his denial of the receipt by his party of gifts from Kreuger shortly before Kreuger was granted an important credit by the Swedish Riksbank. Many of the richest men of the country were bankrupt. The King's brother Carl, father of the Crown Princesses of Norway and Belgium, moved into humble quarters. Old Ernst Kreuger left his apartment on the Strandvägen because his telephone rang so continually with curses for his son.

In Manhattan the Irving Trust was appointed receiver for International Match, Kreuger's great holding company in New York, and International Match filed a voluntary petition in bankruptcy.

Price, Waterhouse through the summer and fall of 1932 engaged on one of the longest chronicles of industrial dynasties ever undertaken. In the Swedish Match Co. palace with its lovely *Diana* by Milles and its exquisite paneling, thirty men with a dozen calculating machines and hundreds of ledgers and great stacks of correspondence and 150 sacks of waste paper saved at the last moment from Mr. Kreuger's office collaborated in the writing of fifty-seven fact-finding reports which would tell a story which not even Kreuger's closest banking associates had previously guessed.

Kreuger's career in the years from 1911 to 1923 or 1924 had been approximately what the world believed it to be.

Kreuger & Toll was without doubt the most successful building company in Scandinavia. The same thing was true of the beginnings of the Match Trust. Sweden prior to the War had been the great match-producing country of the world. During the War it had lost its markets rapidly due in part to tariffs and in part to the unfair competition of other nations such as Japan which was manufacturing matches "made in Tidaholm, Sweden" and swamping the East. A price war was on and only by standardizing Swedish matches so as to force out imitations and only by building factories back of tariff walls could the Swedes regain their control of the industry. This Kreuger accomplished. Kreuger & Toll was turned into a holding company, and took over about one-fourth of the stock of Swedish Match (120,000 shares) and Swedish Match was incorporated with a capital of 45 million kronor and 61.74 million kronor of reserves. Swedish Match at once began purchasing chemical factories, timberland, and factories abroad until it had run the number of the latter up into the hundreds. Swedish exports which had at one time fallen to 49 percent as of 1913 rose to approximately 95 percent of 1913 while the Swedish Match Trust alone made and sold about two-thirds of the world's matches. Enormous Kreuger & Toll profits were not all made out of matches. A part was made out of such speculations as Kreuger's 1917 dollar purchases on which he is said to have netted 10 million kronor by 1920. But it is nevertheless true that Kreuger was in 1924 a great industrialist, that he had inaugurated one industry and rehabilitated another, and that his companies were approximately what they represented themselves to be.

Price, Waterhouse began its investigations of that period with the three central beams of the Kreuger house, which were as open as the columns of a Greek porch: Kreuger & Toll, a super-holding company owning Swedish Match; Swedish Match, a holding company owning match factories in various parts of the world, and also International Match of New York; and International Match, founded in 1923, in turn a holding company owning other and numerous match factories in other and numerous countries of the earth. All that seemed clear enough. But the accountants had not gone very far before they began to find that, close-to, the beams were caught, like the timbers of a dusty barn, in a mesh and tangle of spider-web subsidiaries. Some of these subsidiaries were real, some were a set of books, some were a name; but name, books, or reality the entries spun back and forth, the debit and credit items tangled from roof to wall.

It was discovered, first of all, that most of these companies had been set up by Kreuger agents whose simple duty was to keep their books as Kreuger should direct them. Bror G. B. Bredberg, for example, was a clerk and stockbroker who had been sent down to Zurich in March, 1923; there, with two checks for 1.5 million Swiss francs and one million Swiss francs he registered a company called the Finanzgesellschaft. A few days later brother Torsten Kreuger appeared and he and Bredberg moved east to Vaduz, capital of the minute principality of Liechtenstein where, with the same checks used to register Finanz, they registered the Union Industrie A.G. with Bredberg as board of directors, managing director, and accountant. After which creative act Torsten Kreuger removed 2,450,000 francs of the company's capital for the purpose, as he said, of acquiring match factories in Poland and Czechoslovakia.

Continental was formed by Kreuger personally. That company, which was eventually to bleed American investors through International Match of $88 million, was founded in Zurich in 1923 by Kreuger and his Swiss-American secretary Hoffman with a capital of 60 million francs, of which sum one million francs was in cash, nine million in checks, and 50 million in a guaranty of Swedish Match executed by Kreuger himself. Once the company was registered, Kreuger and Hoffman left Switzerland with its capital in their briefcases and eventually Continental was transferred to Liechtenstein where the Prince's finance minister obligingly made a deal to limit the company's taxes.

Entering the same asset on the books of several companies, crediting one company without charging another, omitting from the balance sheet amounts borrowed, entering the purchase of nonexistent securities backed by a certificate from another corporation that the securities in question were deposited there, entering as an asset on the books of a parent company a claim against a subsidiary which was in reality Kreuger himself or of which the only asset was a claim against Kreuger—thus Kreuger spun his webs. About 425 million kronor of assets shown on Kreuger & Toll's 1930 balance sheet were created by fictitious gains shown over a period of years by such methods, and more than half the company's net profit for that year was the product of bookkeeping not match selling.

But fake companies and glib bookkeeping were not enough to sell fifteen issues of shares and bonds, with some issues amounting to $50 million over a period of nine years. There must also be expansion, industrial conquest—something to spread across the annual statements to capture the public imagination. The enormous loans to governments in return for match concessions played a large and spectacular part. By the simple mechanism of tying his loan to the grant of a match monopoly and making the royalties on the match monopoly (which he was to pay the borrowing government) security for the service of the debt (which the borrowing government was to pay him) he put it in his own power to pay himself. And thus provided not only for a banker's profit on the loan and a match maker's profit on the concession but for complete security for both. In addition, he advertised himself and his companies. His success in supplanting J.P. Morgan & Co. as banker to the French made him for a time the unquestioned leader in world finance. After all it is no small thing for a private individual to lend $384 million to fifteen countries including a loan of $75 million to France.

But it was also necessary to expand in industry itself. And beginning in 1926 and 1927 when the great offerings of Kreuger & Toll and Swedish Match and International Match were made in New York and in Europe, Kreuger began to buy into iron and pulp and telephones and newspapers, and sulphite and sulphate, and the Boliden gold fields. And in 1930 he secured his hold upon L.M. Ericsson Telephone Co. which he had begun to buy in 1925. Meanwhile through his Federal Match and Vulcan Match companies in the U.S., and by such devices as the fake Commercial & Industrial Properties Corp. he was secretly buying the Ohio Match Co. and the Union Match Co.—And through his agents he was acquiring 350,000 shares of Diamond Match.

His match industry made relatively small advances. But between 1923 and 1931 Kreuger's companies sold a variety of shares, debentures, bonds; $250 million worth in America alone.

What Kreuger was playing was the old Ponzi game—paying dividends out of capital, and trusting to more capital to make good the loss. The only question was how long disaster could be deferred.

By the year 1928 Kreuger had himself begun to guess how long. He had pledged his personal credit for unsubscribed balances on four stock issues of Kreuger & Toll. And in addition he had engaged at great cost to himself and to his companies in supporting operations to maintain the market for each issue as it had appeared.

In the fall of 1929 with 101,738,000 kronor of capital shortages on, or rather under, his companies' books, Kreuger undertook to lend the German government (which was in ill odor among international bankers, thanks to the rise of Adolf Hitler) the enormous sum of $125 million. Nothing in Kreuger's career was more amazing than this loan made in the shadow of the Great Depression to a nation with impaired credit by a man whose securities would not sell. But only by an act of desperate courage capable of restoring his slipping prestige could Kreuger hope to extricate himself.

But not even vast sums which he appropriated from his five principal companies would supply the money promised Germany. Millions had gone into supporting other operations. Millions more were being poured into old borrowings to expand the shrinking collateral. Millions had been paid out in dividends, thrown into unsound investments, and tied up in long-term loans. Short of a miracle he couldn't produce the first installment of the German loan.

Kreuger performed the miracle. And out of the emptiest hat. Or rather out of the Italian coat-of-arms on the flap of an old envelope he found in a desk drawer; and forty-six embossed and printed sheets; and a little ink. He had the sheets with the coat-of-arms on them printed up by a Stockholm printer. And the ink Kreuger himself applied, laboriously and clumsily forging the signatures of two of Mussolini's ministers to £28,668,500 of worthless Italian bonds. Nine million pounds of these bonds were wedged into the statement of Kreuger & Toll for 1930, a loan was arranged with the Skandinaviska Kredit A.B.—And the German installment was delivered.

The crisis was past. But another crisis immediately replaced it—July dividends. Kreuger went to America in the summer of 1931. There he arranged for an exchange of stock between I.T.&T. and Ericsson Co., and the payment by the former of $11 million and, in August, borrowed $4 million more from the National City, The Bankers Trust, the Union Trust of Pittsburgh, and the Continental Illinois for his immediate needs. From New York he returned to Stockholm. Kreuger & Toll must have 40 million kronor. There was no collateral—only stock in the Boliden gold mines and that stock was already pledged to Skandinaviska. There was only one way out, to "borrow" $50 million of the German bonds covering the loan, pledge them with Skandinaviska, free the Boliden stock, pledge the Boliden stock with the Riksbank, tell the Riksbank that Kreuger & Toll was in danger, and force the Riksbank to lend him the 40 million kronor. And that he did. The "borrowing" of the German bonds was covered by £19 million of the forged Italian bonds. And the public was told that Kreuger & Toll's indebtedness would be down $20 million in September.

But danger now threatened in New York. I.T.&T. was threatening to send auditors to Stockholm to check the Ericsson books. On December 22, 1931, Kreuger reappeared in New York. Boliden was the card. Largely out of his own head and without reference to the books he dictated the annual report of Kreuger & Toll for 1931, painting a picture of the Boliden mines which was calculated to sweep another score of New York millions into his empty tills. But New York in January, 1932, was in no mood whatever to respond. And while he waited, while he listened, while he talked, I.T.&T.'s auditors in Stockholm discovered that an asset item of 27 million kronor cash on the books of Ericsson was really only a claim against Kreuger companies in that amount. I.T.&T. called on Kreuger to explain. There was no adequate explanation.

The catastrophe was complete, for Kreuger had not only squeezed the last sponge of credit dry. He had been playing the market for two years, using the funds of Kreuger & Toll and the services, under one name or another, of most of the brokerage houses of New York.

On the twenty-first of February, Kreuger was in New York, his credit gone, his Ericsson contract rescinded, his reputation impugned, and losing millions on a falling Stock Exchange. He borrowed a last feeble $1.2 million from Swedish banks to pay interest on debentures, and pledged 350,000 shares of Diamond Match to extend a $4-million loan from National City Bank.

In his Park Avenue apartment the telephone was going day and night. Hilda Åberg, the housekeeper, was setting an alarm clock to waken him for transatlantic calls past midnight. People were coming in to see him at all hours. He began smoking—lighting cigarettes rather—and playing solitaire at his desk. One day he came in with a package forty inches long and stood it in a corner in his bedroom.

He was telephoning and telegraphing and sending messengers with wrong addresses and saying, "What is it? What is it?" At two-thirty one morning Hilda woke up and the lights were on and he had gone out. When she went in to wake him at eight, there was some candy on the table in a box—some candy from a night-owl tearoom on Lexington Avenue, and Kreuger was lying on the bed fully dressed, only his coat off and his shoes beside him on the blankets. When he came out to breakfast there was shaving cream smeared on his tie. Hilda went in to make his bed when he was gone. There was a slip of paper on the table by the bed. It said: "I am too tired to continue." At 3:30 he came home and asked if she had packed his things. He had said nothing about packing. "Hurry," he said. "The boat sails at six." The next day when he was gone Hilda opened the tall package forty inches long. It was a loaded rifle.

Kreuger sailed the fourth of March on the *Île de France*. The bankers let him go. Why they let him go, why they did not suspect him, why for eight years they had not suspected him, they themselves have never said.

On Thursday the tenth the *Île de France* made Le Havre. The early boat train reached Paris at noon on Friday and in the afternoon, Krister Littorin, Victor Holm of Dutch Kreuger & Toll, and Bergenstråhle, Wendler, and Hennig, his accountants, met in Kreuger's apartment. Kreuger's mind appeared to wander. Hennig, who had never dared to question Kreuger's will, finally screwed up his courage to say that there were some who could not understand where the money for the Italian bonds had come from. Kreuger made no reply. Hennig, desperate, pushed the question: "Are they authentic?" Kreuger walking absently up and down the room. "Yes," he said. . . .

At 3:45 Kreuger and Littorin drove to the Hôtel Meurice and went to the room of Oscar Rydbeck, head of the Skandinaviska bank. Rydbeck asked if the Italian bonds might not serve as basis for a loan. No, for Kreuger had bound himself neither to sell nor pledge them. . . . But would not the Italian government buy them in? . . . Kreuger would have to go to Rome for that himself. . . . Then why not go? . . . It would take so long a time. . . . All the more reason then to start at once. . . . The subject was dropped.

At five Littorin drove Kreuger to the Avenue Victor-Emmanuel and left him there in the salon in the gathering dusk.

It was then, after Littorin had gone, that Kreuger went downstairs and down the street to the gun shop.

How had Ivar Kreuger taken in half the investment bankers and most of the brokerage houses in Wall Street, and hoodwinked a board of directors seating some of the most impressive names in America?

Approximately $250 million is in default due to the most flagrant swindle perpetrated upon any body of American investors in our time. Three-fifths of that amount was invested in issues of the International Match Corp. whose directors were Frederic W. Allen, director in thirty-one corporations including Otis Elevator, Chase Bank, and I.T.&T.; Donald Durant, of Lee Higginson, director in seven corporations including Continental Securities; Henry O. Havemeyer, director in thirteen corporations including Chase Bank and Kennecott Copper; Francis L. Higginson, director in thirteen corporations including General Electric and International Paper & Power; Adrian H. Larkin, senior partner in Larkin, Rathbone & Perry, lawyers, and director in six corporations including U.S. Industrial Alcohol; John McHugh, chairman of the executive committee of Chase Bank, the world's largest bank, and director in seventeen corporations; Samuel F. Pryor, director in thirty-one corporations including Chase Bank and Air Reduction; and Percy A. Rockefeller, nephew of John D. Rockefeller and director in forty-nine corporations including Bethlehem Steel, Consolidated Gas of New York, and National City Bank.

The entire $250 million of shares and debentures, both International Match and Kreuger & Toll, was marketed either directly or indirectly through Lee, Higginson & Co., a private banking house formed in Boston in 1848, leader in railroads in the great period of rail expansion, prominent in Calumet & Hecla in the copper age, instrumental in building American Telephone & Telegraph and General Electric, powerful in the reorganization of General Motors, the possessor, down to the publication of the Kreuger audits, of one of the most honored reputations in American banking history.

Underlying these $250 million of debentures and shares were the corporate statements of Kreuger & Toll and International Match, the latter signed by Ernst & Ernst, one of the best-known firms of chartered accountants in New York.

They had all *relied* on Kreuger. Lee, Higginson generally accepted without question the information Ivar Kreuger gave. When Lee, Higginson issued its International bond statements on "information and belief" the "information" was the information supplied by Kreuger. And when Kreuger in 1931 supplied Lee, Higginson with a "confidential memorandum" on match concessions in which were listed investments of $28,979,577 in "X country" and $27,830,600 in "Y government" and $9.5 million in "Z," Lee, Higginson solemnly accepted and conscientiously guarded the weighty secret together with its code explanation that "X" was Italy and "Y" was Spain and "Z" was the Diamond Match. That there was no Italian concession and no Spanish concession the bankers never learned, any more than they learned by independent report the state of the match factories International was supposed to own.

It is true that Mr. Kreuger was a charming man. It is true that when Mr. Pryor went to Stockholm in 1930, everyone spoke beautifully of Mr. Kreuger—so beautifully that Mr. Pryor had "never heard a man more beautifully spoken of by everyone." But charm, although it may explain mistaken marriages, New York mayors, and a few Presidents of the U.S., will not, in all serious-ness, serve to explain how a Stockholm match manufacturer was able over nine years to dupe the international financiers of New York and walk off with $250 million of the country's cash.

Price, Waterhouse & Co., the accountants, say of the Kreuger & Toll reports: "We do not think more need by said about these published accounts except that the manipulations were so childish that anyone with but a rudimentary knowledge of bookkeeping could see the books were falsified."

In a period of relaxed moral standards and weakened respect for law only the crass and obvious will be noticed as a deviation from probity. In the decade of the 1920's the general measure of conduct was "good business." If a maneuver "paid" it was sound. If a corporate device yielded profits it was above reproach. And if a banker's client paid his interest and piled up his dividends there was nothing suspicious to catch the banker's eye. It was quite understood that taxes would be avoided wherever possible.

The application of the morality of the 1920's to Ivar Kreuger is too apparent to require proof. Everything in the New York scene was made to Kreuger's hand. By and large the New York bankers of the period were law-abiding and honest, if romantic, men. But their boom-year complacence with regard to the dodging of certain laws, the laws specifically of taxation, gave Kreuger the tool he needed. Tax laws like prohibition laws were laws you dodged if you could. It was apparently enough for Kreuger to explain to Lee, Higginson or to the directors of International Match that some secret and mysterious deal or some darkling subsidiary had been put through or set up "to avoid taxes." They asked no further questions. Mr. Durant understood that the reason for the arbitrary quarterly earnings of International Match (which were just large enough to cover dividend requirements) was that "by not bringing the earnings into the parent corporation each time, but keeping them in the subsidiaries, it was not necessary to pay income tax on earnings which were not brought into the country." Mr. Pryor "assumed" that there was a reason why International's Vulcan Match Co. barely kept out of the red year after year and that the reason was "possibly taxation." And everyone having to do with Kreuger understood that the whole reason for the existence of Dutch Kreuger & Toll was the evasion of Swedish imposts. It is old wisdom that if you can get a man to wink with you he will not see.

And there was more in the New York scene in the 1920's than mere complacence about tax devices. There was also an arbitrary free-and-easiness in the disposition of corporation funds. There was, for instance, the now well-known example of the National City Bank which, while closing out the accounts of its old customers during the crash, lent $2.4 million (of which only 5 percent had been paid back) to its own officers to support their market commitments. And there was also the bonus of $3.4 million over and above salary paid by the same bank and the National City Co. to Charles Mitchell in 1927 and 1928 and 1929. The use of Transamerica money by Mr. Amadeo P. Giannini in 1929 to support the company's stock is equally notorious.

And there was also complacence about the sale of securities. The National City Co. underwrote in September, 1929, in conjunction with J. Henry Schroeder & Co. of London, an issue of $8 million of bonds of the Brazilian state of Minas Geraes. The underwriters knew that the state of Minas Geraes had defaulted on $42 million of its bonds marketed in London and Paris from 1907 to 1916. They presumably knew that George F. Train of National City's foreign department had written in April, 1927, a letter, stating that "the laxness of its [Minas Geraes's] finances is almost fantastic," and that "it would be hard to find anywhere greater ineptitude, negligence, and carelessness in the handling of its external loans." They knew that the real purpose of the $8 million issue was "partly with a view to" repaying the National City Co. for earlier short-term advances to the state amounting to $4 million. And yet National City issued a prospectus certified to by Mr. Train declaring that the purpose of the issue was to increase "the economic productivity of the State of Minas Geraes" and stating that "prudent and safe finances had been axiomatic of successive administrations in the State of Minas Geraes."

Obviously in a city and country where sales by misleading circulars of bonds of unsound South American republics were practiced or condoned by the largest investment houses, Kreuger's prospectuses for, and sales of, bonds of Swedish match companies would pass unnoticed. And if Lee, Higginson had not handled the Kreuger issues some other house almost certainly would have. The special prosecutor, Ferdinand Pecora, examining a member of National City Co.'s foreign department before a Senate committee, asked why National City participated in the $4 million of short-term credits to the state of Minas Geraes. To keep Kuhn, Loeb and Lee, Higginson from "chiseling in" on the field of Brazilian credit, answered Mr. Train. "Chiseling in? That is not a banking term, is it?" said Mr. Pecora.

Ernst & Ernst, the American auditors of International Match, were not authorized to make a complete audit of the company and all its foreign subsidiaries. But long before Kreuger, many companies (for example, A.T.&T. and American Metal Co.) had the books of their subsidiaries audited by their own auditors; such corporations as Continental Can, American Sugar Refining, American Smelting & Refining, General Electric, I.T.&T., Socony-Vacuum Corp., ask independent auditors simply to accept unaudited statements of their subsidiaries, and reputable auditors have done so—precisely the practice followed by Ernst & Ernst with International Match subsidiaries.

Here then was a scene set for the swindler. Here was a time in which inadequate audits opened the corporate structure to corruption, a time in which unconscionable stock selling muddied the source and spring of all financing, in which acquiescence in the avoidance and even the evasion of tax laws provided a justification for secrecy and a cloak for fraud, a time in which enormous bonuses and huge loans to corporate officers broke down the inviolability of corporate funds—a time ripe for the appearance of Ivar Kreuger: swindler, dead at Numéro Cinq Avenue Victor-Emmanuel III in the March morning, in a sense signifying the Age.

May, June, July 1937

A&P: A Good Living to 90,000 Grocers
By WILDER HOBSON

The Great Atlantic & Pacific Tea Co. has these several years sold one-tenth of all the food sold at retail in the U.S.—and ten billions of cigarettes a year and much besides. If a communistic government, aided and abetted by the top-loftiest "planned economists" alive, should set out to devise the most efficient food-distribution system and should produce anything half so effective as the Great A&P, the Supreme Food Dictator would command the headlines of the world. In all Soviet Russia there is no division of production or distribution which even in the crude matter of size can compare with the Great A&P. For it 90,000 people labor with a devotion which any "system" would envy. That spick and span little red store on the corner is one of 15,500 doing a volume of business which for several years has averaged $1 billion—a volume greater than Henry Ford could boast at his peak, greater than Sears, Roebuck and Montgomery Ward and James Cash Penney combined, approximately equal to the entire automobile business of 1932.

A grocer who has so multiplied himself as to become more people's neighbor than any man before him might be expected to leave some trace of himself in the informal history of our times. And, granting that victuals are somewhat wanting in glamour, a family which has a billion-dollar grocery business might be expected to stand out with the very few other families whose names can be breathed in connection with a billion dollars. Yet you may rustle the dust of *The New York Times* and you find little except what is lettered on the directory of the Graybar Building, New York: that a man named John Hartford is president of the Great A&P. A&P executives have, indeed, been known to wager that not one of the first ten people encountered in the corridors of that very Graybar Building would be able to name A&P's president, or that "Hartford" is the name of one of the ten wealthiest families in the U.S., possessors of a vast fortune gleaned from the tills of the bright little red stores.

The Great Atlantic & Pacific Tea Co. is almost wholly owned by the Hartford family and is completely and absolutely controlled by two Hartford brothers: George L., sixty-eight; John A., sixty. They are sons of the Founder and sole trustees of 1,728,000 of the 2,086,000 common shares of the company. Since 1916, they have provided themselves and their relatives with $80 million in dividends, and have put $130 million back into the business. More recently the family trust's share of earnings has averaged over $20 million a year. The two brothers have jointly put in 100 years' work with the company. They still work—hard.

For a while the two brothers got on without electing either president. But in 1920 . . . "Well," George explains, "I thought that John would, now, make the best president." George felt quite at ease with the company's finances, staggering as they had become, and quite uneasy in the contacts with hundreds of executives, both inside and outside the company, which the company's giantism required. Whereas the well-garbed poise of younger Brother John had been sharpened through years of personal contact in A&P field work. Hence George assumed the chairmanship, retiring into a sort of holy-of-holies devoted to A&P finances, and John stepped into the president's chair.

There, at the center of their grocery, they remain today. Outsiders have learned little about them except that a portrait of their father hangs on their office wall and that both fear his memory and keep their powder dry.

Mr. John, president, is large and strong of feature, with a fine head of iron-gray hair and a striking gentleness of expression heightened by the reticence he has made almost a fetish. His grace is accentuated by what amounts to a uniform. John is a man in gray. Almost every day he wears a gray double-breasted suit, gray shirt, and a very large and floppy gray bow tie. Possibly he wears the extravagant bow tie with a sense of being informal. If so he errs for, looking as he does, tailored as he is (by the fashionable Bell), John Hartford achieves with his harmony in grays one of the most distinguished rigs in American business life.

Thus unforgettably attired, John Hartford goes about the duties of the presidency. He is the "outside" man. By force of circumstance it became his function and is now his pleasure to go outside, to be the extravert of the Hartford duet. Half the year he is traveling his vast A&P circuit, talking with division officers in Chicago or Pittsburgh or Detroit, dropping unexpectedly into some little red store and chatting with its manager, who has never seen him before. The manager is usually surprised, then nervous, but when President John Hartford departs he leaves behind a lasting impression of his grace and ease and humanity. And when he is back in New York it is President John Hartford who receives the most important visitors from "outside" in a paneled office of dim and elegant simplicity. It is John who is greatly if distantly admired in New York financial circles, who is a director of the Guaranty Trust Co. and the Girard Trust Co., Philadelphia. But he belongs to no smart Manhattan clubs. He lunches alone at twelve-thirty at the Biltmore on milk and crackers. His recreation is to ride horseback on his deeply wooded estate at Valhalla, New York. And occasionally he takes a holiday trip to Europe.

In contrast to Mr. John, the homely, plump, white-haired, older Mr. George wears rather indiscriminate and voluminous clothes and looks rather like your favorite grocer. His office across the hall from John's is bare and ordinary and George almost never leaves it during the long working hours of his long working days. Though the business is, in many senses, his meat and drink, old Mr. George has not permitted himself to enter an A&P store in years. Day after day he drives himself to work from Montclair (chauffeur sitting in the rear). He passes two or three A&P stores and eyes them with keen curiosity and inarticulate sentiment—from the street.

This chairman George Hartford may suggest a grocer, but actually he has little directly to do with groceries as anyone in the A&P organization. He is very very secluded and a very shrewd financier. Which is to say that in recent years he has been bearish. George's bearishness began with caution (he inherited every arch-conservative tendency his father ever had). It is an office byword that George has never lost a cent of surplus. As early as 1927 he sniffed disaster and refused to renew A&P leases for longer than one year. A&P now looks back on this profoundly sage ruling with the nervous delight of the man who has unwittingly stepped across a chasm—the chasm in this case being such a tragic abyss as received the United Cigar Stores with their real-estate operations. (Some years ago Charles A. Whelan of United Cigar stormed into George's office intent on buying into A&P, was shown the profit-margin figures, stormed out again, shouting: "What you fellows need is a doctor!") A&P takes most of its warehouses and 94 percent of its stores on one-year leases. Its equipment figures include practically no land. It was George who perceived two years ago that cigarette prices must come down instead of going up, and refused commitments on 15-cent cigarettes unless the manufacturers would guarantee to maintain the wholesale price until the A&P warehouses were empty of them. The counsel of George was reflected in John's utterance of 1930: "The foods known as trading items [butter, eggs, sugar, etc.] have been steadily declining in wholesale prices and, without being unduly pessimistic, I think we shall see further recessions." It was George who a year ago transferred a considerable part of A&P's bank deposits into short-term government bonds. Since the U.S. budget is still unbalanced, it is George who has seen to it that A&P's $47 million in U.S. governments are all maturities under one year.

It is when the brothers sit down together that the control of A&P becomes complete. There sits then the power which recruits hundreds of Scandinavian fishermen to sail up the Alaska coast each year for salmon canned by Chinese and Japanese in Seattle; the authority which personally buys olive oil in Spain, figs and dates in Arabia, marmalade in Scotland, more coffee from Brazil than any other corporation, etc. Strangely antithetical, strangely complementary—the two most potent brother merchants in the world.

Chain policies, on which the brothers achieve a united front, each approaches with his own bias. It greatly distresses the customer-minded John that A&P's record low margin of profit of 2.49 percent in 1929 has risen today to 2.95 (largely because the company has been unable to adjust its retail prices to the fast-falling commodity prices quickly enough to prevent making a larger margin than John favors). But cautious George flirts with the idea that an even greater margin might be advisable as an immediate safeguard. And George also flirts with the idea that the A&P might well sell more of its own and less of standard brands—while diplomatic John deplores the policy of such chains as Drug, Inc., which force their products on the public in substitution for those in demand—and suffer in loss of goodwill thereby. It might occur to George that a 10 percent wage cut throughout A&P would, presto, put an extra $10 million in the A&P profit column. But he would scarcely act on this reflection.

For George is completely at one with John in his attachment to the business which means to them, as nearly as their imagination can grasp it, a great family of 90,000 people—or rather 90,000 employees representing a total of 90,000 families.

The Hartfords' concern for the A&P family might be described in terms of employees' picnics and banquets, which are familiar jollifications in many U.S. corporations, or in terms of employees' stock-purchase plans, which are just as familiar and which have distributed some 128,000 shares of A&P common (average purchase price, $66—current market, around $144) among the personnel of 90,000. But the Hartfords' feeling for their personnel goes much deeper than picnics and stock: it reflects itself best in the fact that the basic A&P wage has remained where it was in 1928. There is very little "firing" in A&P—an A&P man is made to feel that he has a life job. In a sense, an A&P storekeeper is a man doing a business for himself on Hartford capital.

Furthermore, all but one of the divisional presidents of A&P rose from the ranks (jobs paying less than $25 a week). The company has a standing rule that new machinery replacing manpower may be bought, but that before its purchase jobs must be found for the men it will replace. Says John Hartford: "Not in years has anyone been able to hire away from us important employees no matter what financial lure was offered."

March 1933

SO BIG

Last year nearly every two-legged animal in the U.S. ate one four-legged animal. For in supplying meat to 120 million U.S. inhabitants 115 million hogs, cattle, sheep, and calves were slaughtered. The carcass weight of these animals was a trifle more than 21 billion pounds.
—From an article about Armour & Co.

June 1934

Life in American Society

The Butlers' Ball
By JAMES AGEE

Physick of the Morgan staff was not there. Some families didn't want to send their servants. But Mrs. Cornelius Vanderbilt's Anderson was, and the Winthrop Aldriches' Wetherall and the Ogden Phippses' Parr who had worked for Nancy Astor in England. In the Grand Ballroom of the Commodore, Meyer Davis's band played on and on, the grand-ballroom way a Meyer Davis band does, from ten to three-thirty. In dress, race, face, and bearing, the 3,000 guests were a mixed lot. They might have suggested a convention of tradesmen and their wives but for their conduct, which was rather more orderly. And but for a sprinkling of elderly, lean-cheeked, perfectly appointed gentlemen who spoke with good dry accents and who bore themselves with all the effortless *aplomb* of cabinet ministers. They weren't cabinet ministers, of course. Englishmen mostly, they were products of a lifelong training in bearing and manners and poise and tact: gentlemen who spoke pridefully of their life's work as a profession. They were butlers.

In England, seven years ago, Mrs. Marshall Field arranged a ball for butlers, chauffeurs, kitchenmaids, cooks, laundresses, gardeners, and tradespeople—the proceeds to go to charity. In England, where good servants and most good butlers (except Swedes) are made, and where people are used to them, the ball has become an annual custom. This winter Mrs. Field decided to organize such a party in this country. The program called it discreetly "A Dance in Aid of Bellevue Hospital Family Welfare Social Service." The press, which had whooped for a week about it, hitting a new low in condescension, dubbed it the Butler's Ball. And Butler's Ball it was and probably will be, from year to year.

Butlers were, actually, few. Perhaps because of the stinging ridicule of the press which Irish maids joined Mrs. Field in deploring. Or perhaps because butlers *are* few. Nowadays, people are beginning to do without that acme of fine service, the manservant. Though the Hamilton Twomblys still have four men in the pantry besides Berles, the Rockefeller staff is mostly women. A butler used to get $125 to $175. Today he gets $90 to $125—if he gets anything. There's no NRA for servants; the only known exception is the blanket code that Mrs. William K. Vanderbilt got up and signed for her staff.

But many of the best butlers in service were there, and enough people in all to clear around $4,500 for Bellevue. Reunions were frequent . . . "Well, if it isn't So-and-So. Well . . . " "It takes me back to the days in Huntington . . . " English butlers found it easy to get listeners for nostalgic tales of entertaining in pre-War England, where a house party meant 100 guests trailing clouds of valets and maids. Quip of the evening was, "Whose burglar are you these days?" . . . favorite pun of all butlers.

Few are the American households that preserve the English servants' hall tradition. The British ménage dines together but when dessert is served the upper servants—the *head* parlormaid, the *head* chambermaid, the personal maids and cook and butler, of course—leave the table. Together they solemnly march, carrying their plates, to the servants' hall. In order of precedence they go paired two by two. Through the evening they will play bridge. And in the morning the underservants will rise first to wake the uppers and bring them the tea that will set the executive half of the service in motion. There are not many servants' careers in this country that lead to such rewards.

Hero of the evening was Robert Hider, butler for Mrs. Field these fourteen years. It was he who helped her arrange her first servants' ball seven years ago when she was Mrs. Dudley Coats. Mrs. Field waved cheer to her Hider as he submitted to Paramount's camera, went into the ballroom where, shyly and briefly, she thanked the guests for helping Bellevue. The guests roared applause while from a box the Field staff cried "Hear! Hear!" For this short time only were employers present.

The rest was Hider's show. In charge of the ball, with a committee of handsome helpers with white badges, he was justly proud of his 3,000 guests, the big ballroom decorated with festal flags, its two dining rooms where butlers, maids, and chauffeurs bought highballs, its tier of boxes where even champagne corks popped. Hider found it a ball after his own heart. And if he had any professional opinion of the Commodore service, he kept it to himself.

March 1934

The Great American Roadside

By JAMES AGEE

The characters in our story are five: this American continent; this American people; the automobile; the Great American Road, and— the Great American Roadside. To understand the American Roadside you must see it as an inseparable part of the whole organism, the ultimate expression of the conspiracy that produced it.

You know these characters. This continent, an open palm spread frank before the sky. This curious people. The automobile you know as well as you know the slouch of the accustomed body at the wheel and the small stench of gas and hot metal. You know the sweat and the steady throes of the motor and the copious and thoughtless silence and the spreaded swell and swim of the hard highway.

This great road, you know that well. How it is scraggled and twisted along the coast of Maine, high-crowned and weak-shoul-dered in honor of long winter. How in Florida the detours are bright with the sealime of rolled shells. How the road degrades into a rigorous lattice of country dirt athwart Kansas through the smell of hot wheat (and this summer a blindness and a strangula-tion of lifted dust). How like a blacksnake in the sun it takes the ridges, the green and dim ravines which are the Cumberlands, and lolls loose into the hot Alabama valleys. How in the spectral heat of the Southwest, and the wide sweeps of sage toward the North-west, it means spare fuel strapped to the running board.

You know this roadside as well as you know the formulas of talk at the gas station, the welcome taste of a Bar B-Q sandwich in mid-afternoon, the oddly excellent feel of a weak-springed bed in a clapboard transient shack, and the early start in the cold bright lonesome air, the dustless and dewy road and the stammering

birds, and the day's first hitchhiker brushing the damp hay out of
his shirt.

All such things you know. But it may never have sharply
occurred to you, for instance, that the 900,000 miles of hard-
fleshed highway that this people has built—not just for transportation but to express something not well defined—is by very
considerable odds the greatest road the human race has ever built.
It may never have occurred to you that upon this continent and
along this road this people casually moves in numbers and by
distances which make the ancient and the grave migrations of the
Celt and the Goth look like a smooth crossing on the Hoboken
Ferry. And it may never have occurred to you that the Great
American Roadside, where this people pauses to trade, is incomparably the most hugely extensive market the human race has ever
set up to tease and tempt and take money from the human race.

For only just now are people beginning to realize that these five
characters combine in simple fact to mean a new way of life, a new
but powerfully established American institution. And that the
roadside, the most vivid part of this institution, is a young but
great industry which will gross, in this, the fifth year of the Great
Depression, something like $3 billion. Restiveness unlike any
before God and the conjunction of confused bloods, history and
the bullying of this tough continent to heel, did something to the
American people—worked up in their blood a species of restiveness unlike any that any race before has known, a restiveness
describable only in negatives. Not to eat, not for love, nor even for
money, nor for fear, nor really for adventure, nor truly out of any
known necessity is this desire to move upon even the most docile
of us. We are restive entirely for the sake of restiveness. Whatever
we may think, we move for no better reason than for the plain
unvarnished hell of it.

So God made the American restive. The American in due time
got into the automobile and found it good. The 1914 war exasper-
ated his restiveness and the Twenties made him rich and more
restive still, and he found the automobile not merely good but
better and better. It was good because continually it satisfied and at
the same time greatly sharpened his hunger for movement: which
is very probably the profoundest and most compelling of American hungers. The automobile became a hypnosis, the opium of the
American people.

After the autoist had driven round and round for a while, it became time that people should catch on to the fact that as he rides there are ten thousand little ways you can cash in on him en route. Within the past few years, the time ripened. And along the Great American Road, the Great American Roadside sprang up prodigally as morning mushrooms.

Consider the tourist cabin camp. Much has been written about it and most of it has been polking fun—at these curious little broods of frame and log and adobe shacks which dot the roadside with their Mother Goose and their Chic Sale architecture, their geranium landscaping, their squeaky beds, and their community showers. The geraniums and the architecture are inconsequential; what matters is that they offer pure functionalist shelter and that they work. Just as surely as the great Greyhound bus company grew out of the jitney, an industry is growing out of the tourist cabin.

It works, and here is how. It is six in the afternoon and you are still on the road, worn and weary from three hundred miles of driving. Past you flashes a sign DE LUXE CABINS ONE MILE. Over the next hill you catch the vista of a city, smack in your path, sprawling with its ten thousand impediments to motion—its unmarked routes, its trolley cars, its stop and go signs, its No Parking markers. Somewhere in the middle of it is a second-class commercial hotel, whose drab lobby and whose cheerless rooms you can see with your eyes closed. Beyond, around the corner, eyes still closed, you see the local Ritz with its doormen and its bellboys stretching away in one unbroken greedy grin.

All these things and more you see with your eyes closed in two seconds flat. Then you open them. And around the next bend, set back amid a grove of cool trees you see the little semicircle of cabins which the sign warned you of. You pull in by a farmhouse. The farmer's daughter appears. You say: "How much are your cabins?" She says: "Dollar a head. Drive in by No. 7." You make your inspection. If you don't like it, you drive on—to the next cabin camp.

Typically, its furniture is a double bed, a table, two kitchen chairs, a small mirror, a row of hooks. In one corner a washbasin with cold running water; in another, the half-opened door to the toilet. There is a bit of chintz curtaining over the screened windows, through which a breeze is blowing. You have just what you need for a night's rest, neither more nor less. And in the morning you will leave without ceremony, resume the motion you left off the day before without delay.

The point the satirist misses when he lampoons American folkways is that most folkways make sense. The American people have created the cabin camp because the hotel failed them in their new objective—motion with the least possible interruption. They have money to spend but not on the marble foyers of their forefathers. Their money is dedicated to motion. So they have found the cabin camp good because it gives them just exactly what they want, simply and efficiently. And they made it multiply and they called it all kinds of names from the Wee Hame to Sevenoaks Farm to Mo-Tel.

September 1934

The Havana Cruise

By JAMES AGEE

Force of habit awakened elderly Mr. and Mrs. B. early and they were strolling the long decks hand in hand a half-hour before the dining saloon opened at eight. Two heavy women in new house dresses helped each other up the stairs, their lungs laboring. They were Mrs. C. and her feeble sister. They and the B.'s nodded and smiled and said what a lovely morning it was. The sun stood bright on the clean, already warm decks, the blue water enlarged quietly without whitening, and sang along the flanks of the ship like seltzer.

Miss Cox appeared with her aunt Miss Box, a frugal and sweet-smiling spinster. Miss Box wore a simple print and a shining black straw garlanded with cloth flowers; Miss Cox was in severely informal new sports attire. Like most of the other young women, low-salaried office workers upon whom the self-sufficiency, the independence of city work and city living had narrowed their inestimable pressures of loneliness and of spiritual fear, she set a greater value of anticipation upon this cruise than she could dare tell herself. For this short leisure among new faces she had invested heavily in costume, in fear, in hope, and like her colleagues she searched among the men as for steamer smoke from an uncharted atoll.

A blond young man who resembled an airedale sufficiently intelligent to count to ten, dance fox trots, and graduate from a gentleman's university came briskly to the dining room in sharply pressed slacks and a navy blue sports shirt, read the sign, dashed away, and soon reappeared plus a checkered coat and plaid tie. The dining saloon opened. The headwaiter, a prim Arthur Treacher type, convoyed his guests to their tables with the gestures of an Eton-trained sand-hill crane in flight. His snobbishness rather flattered a number of the passengers.

Mr. and Mrs. B. studied the pretentious menu with admiration and ordered a whale of a breakfast. They may charge you aplenty, but they certainly do give you your money's worth. Mr. L. and his wife tinkered at their fruit and exchanged monosyllables as if they were forced bargains. The cool china noise and the chattering thickened in the cheerful room while, with the casualness of concealed excitement, studiously dressed and sharply anticipatory, singly and by twos and threes the shining breakfast faces assembled, looking each other over. They had come aboard in New York late the evening before, and this was their first real glimpse of each other.

All told, there were a hundred and thirty-two of them aboard the *Oriente* of the Ward Line. They were representatives of the lower to middle brackets of the American urban middle class and they were on a cruise. Roughly one in three of them was married, one in three was middle-aged. Most of the middle-aged and married were aboard for a rest; most of the others were aboard for one degree or another of a hell of a big time. The unattached women and girls, who were aboard partly for a good time and partly for the more serious, not to say desperate, purpose of finding a husband, outnumbered the unattached men about four to one. It wasn't a very expensive outing they were taking: most of them spent between $85 and $110 for passage, but $70 was enough to cover every expense, including two conducted tours of Havana. But there were bar expenses; and plenty of the passengers, particularly the younger ones, had invested pretty heavily in new clothes they could feel self-assured in; for most of them had never been on a cruise before. They were of that vast race whose freedom falls in summer and is short. Leisure, being no part of their natrual lives, was precious to them; and they were aboard this ship because they were convinced that this was going to be as pleasurable a way of spending that leisure as they could afford or imagine.

The *Oriente* is fashioned in the image of her clientele: a sound, young, pleasant, and somehow invincibly comic vessel, the seafaring analogy to a second-string summer resort, a low-priced sedan, or the newest and best hotel in a provincial city. She makes fifty voyages a year, New York—Havana—New York, carrying freight, mail, and passengers, of whom a strong preponderance are cruising. . . .

Up on the sports deck in bright sun a gay plump woman in white shied rubber rings at a numbered board and chattered at her somber female companion. The gay lady was from Washington and had friends at the Embassy in Havana. She admired Noël Coward and sat at the Captain's table. The airedale and a duplicate appeared in naughty trunks, laid towels aside from their pretty shoulders, oiled themselves, and, after a brief warm-up, began to play deck tennis furiously before the gradually assembling girls. Some of the girls wore brand-new sports clothes, others wore brand-new slacks or beach combinations. Some of them traveled in teams, most of the others teamed up as quickly as they could. They strolled against the wind, they stood at the white rail with wind in their waved hair, they swung their new shoes from primly crossed knees, they lay back with shaded eyes, their crisp white skirts tucked beneath them in the flippant air, they somewhat shyly laid their slacks back from their pale thighs, they lay supine, skull-eyed in goggles; their cruel vermilion nails caught at the sunlight. They examined each other quietly but sharply, and from behind dark white-rimmed lenses affected to read drugstore fiction and watched those beautiful bouncing blond boys' bodies and indulged the long, long thoughts of youth. The airedales were fast and skillful, and explosive with such Anglo-Saxonisms as Sorry, Tough, Nice Work, Too Bad, Nice Going. Later they were joined by a couple of other bipeds who had the same somehow suspect unself-consciousness about their torsos, and the exclamations of good sportsmanship came to resemble an endless string of firecrackers set off under a dishpan and the innocent childlike abandon of the exhibitionism acquired almost Polynesian proportions in everything except perhaps sincerity and results. To come to the quick of the ulcer, it is generously estimated that the sexual adventures of the entire cruise did not exceed two dozen in number and most nearly approached their crises not in staterooms but aboveboard; that in no case was the farthest north more extreme than a rumpling hand or teeth industriously forced open; that in 70 percent of these cases the gentleman felt it obligatory to fake or even to feel true love and the lady murmured either "please" or "please don't" or "yes I like you very much but I don't feel That Way about you," or all three; and that the man, in every case, took it bravely on the chin, sincerely adopted the attitude of a Big Brother, and went to his own bunk tired but happy.

Mr. and Mrs. L. sat quietly in the heightening sun. Mr. L. leaned far forward to let the sun fight its way through the black hair on his back; Mrs. L. incisively read *I Can Get It for You Wholesale* until the strong sun slowed her and she slept. Miss Cox, conversing with two young men, tried with her eyes to indicate that she was whichever they might prefer: good fun or an incipient good wife. Each of the men jotted her on his mental cuff as useful if worse came to worst. Miss Box read *Lost Ecstasy.* On the shady side of the ship a man in new brilliantly white sneakers sat under five fathoms of the Sunday *Times* and stuffed in the state of the world without appetite while his wife caught a beauty sleep with her nostrils inverted, her goggles cockeyed, and her mouth open. . . .

The lunch bugle sounded. A few men and fewer girls sloped in to the modernistic bar; the rest went below to dope out some more costumes they could feel secure in. The drinks were cheap, a quarter for cocktails and 30 cents for highballs, and were weak out of all proportion even to that price. Though plenty of the passengers had anticipated drinking, few of them drank much during the cruise; apparently because few others drank much. Not even the trip's topers spent more than $20 or so.

There were a number of shifts of table assignments at lunch as new acquaintances got together. It was standard, sterile, turgid, summer-hotel-type food, turkey, duck, the sort of stuffing that tastes like kitchen soap, fancy U.S. salads, and so on, and served with a pomp and circumstance that would have sufficed for the body and blood of Brillat-Savarin. The average passenger behaved a little as if this were his regular Thursday evening at the Tour d'Argent, and staggered upstairs to digest at the horse racing.

The horse racing broke up in about an hour; and the sports deck filled, and the passengers disposed themselves once again among the divisions and facilities of the morning.

Mrs. C., her sister, and a pleasant younger woman sat and passed the time of day. Mrs. C. said: "The water in the thermos bottle in our stateroom is not as cool as the water in the cooler in the corridor." The younger woman said that hers seemed to be. Mrs. C. said to her sister: "She says the water in the thermos bottle in *her* stateroom *is* as cool as the water in the cooler in the corridor." Mr. B. was saying that he and his wife both loved to see new places and try out new drinks, not really getting drunk of course, but just seeing what they tasted like. Mr. B., whose wife was below resting, struck the ash from his popular-priced cigar and said, secure and happy: "Well if I should die tonight I'd leave my wife fourteen hundred dollars, but matter of fact I hope to make that more before I'm done." . . .

The redressing for the evening ran the whole range—formal, semiformal, informal, with every variant that open insecurity or pretended sophistication could give it. There was a good deal of glancing around and checking up during dinner and quite a few made immediate revisions. After dinner *John Meade's Woman* was shown, with breaks between reels, to a packed house that received it with polite apathy. The floor was cleared of chairs, the tables filled, blue and green bulbs went on among the leaves of the dwarf tubbed trees, the weak drinks were ordered, and the band redistributed the platitudes of the afternoon among warmer colors in a warmer light.

The airedales scampered about with two pink girls who looked like George Washington. The inevitable Ship's Card, a roguish fellow of forty, did burlesque rumbas and under protection of parody achieved unusual physical contacts amid squeals of laughter. The seconds among the girls fell to the elder of the unattached men and most of them got stuck there. The third run sat and smiled and smiled until their mouths ached and their cheeks went numb, while the men passed them with suddenly unfocused eyes. The wow of the evening was a blonde who was born out of her time: her glad and perpetually surprised face was that which appears in eighteenth-century pornographic engravings wherein the chore boy tumbles the milkmaid in an explosion of hens and alfalfa. Her dress was cut with considerable extra *élan* to set off her uncommonly beautiful breasts, which in the more extreme centrifuges of the dance swung almost entirely free of ambush. She had a howling rush and a grand time. . . .

The morning opened upon the mild stare, the insane musical-comedy blue of the Gulf Stream, whereon the *Oriente* crept like a jazzy little toy. The breakfast horn laced the ship with its bluff brightness; and another day had begun.

It had precisely the same shape and rhythm. Breakfast brought the passengers together, and cast them forth upon their own resources: sports, flirting, bathing, reading, sleeping, talking, tanning. The lunch horn gave them something to do, they dressed; they ate; they played the wooden ponies. They dressed for dinner; they ate it; they played Bingo; they danced. Far out to starboard, small, frail lights walked past. They dominated the low and bone-white coast of pre-Columbian unimagined Florida, and of that dilapidated playground where wasps whine in hot voids of disheveling stucco, and Townsendites sit in squealing rockers under the slow fall of their ashes, and high-school girls are excused from civics class to snap into their one-piece bathing suits and demonstrate the teasing amenities of their hot, trite little bodies for the good of the community. The remote lights were Miami; and Miami spread, and sank into the north: and the lights thinned. The *Oriente's* faint wake, spuming with phosphorus, bent and straightened. The ship had left the shelf of the continent behind and had directed herself upon the world's deep water. Not very far ahead now, Havana lay.

The passengers saw their best of Havana before they set foot in it. The instant they landed they submitted themselves to the guidance of a spectacled brown-uniformed hog with a loud retching voice who stuffed them into a noisy flotilla of open cars and took them on two tours, called the City Tour and the Night Tour. On the City Tour they saw the Church of Our Lady of Mercy, a cigar factory, the Maine Monument, and a cemetery. On the Night Tour they saw a game of jai alai, Sloppy Joe's, the Sans Souci, and the Casino. Between tours the *Oriente* served a goose dinner for those who mistrusted the dirty foreign food.

Some of the men liked the jai alai and placed bets but a lot of the girls were bored and the general impression was it was a queer sort of a game. At Sloppy Joe's, at which no self-respecting Cuban would be caught dead, the tourists themselves seemed a little embarrassed. They huddled rather silent at the bar and few of them ordered more than one drink. Night life in one of the whoriest cities of the Western Hemisphere was represented by the

Sans Souci, meaning Care Free, and the Casino, meaning Casino. Lowing gently, the tourists stepped out of their vans. . . .

An heroic majority wrenched themselves up from four hours' sleep and spent the next morning buying cigars, perfumes, rum, and souvenirs. Back aboard, they hung at the rail and talked of Havana. Most of them were glad to be leaving it. One man raised his voice among a group and summed up: "Well, I'm telling you. When you see the Statue of Liberty you're going to say this is the country for me." The group nodded as one.

Slowly, regretted by few, Havana shrank in the lunchtime sun and faded. All afternoon the exhausted passengers slept; and awakening, came slowly to realize that somehow the best of their cruise was over. Only a few seemed to escape the blight that, as the next two days dragged on, fastened upon the passengers more and more pitilessly. Married couples, used to spending their long days apart, were wearing on each other. New acquaintances had run out of small talk and had no other and did not know how to get rid of each other. The girls knew now that none of them was going to find a husband or even any excitement to speak of.

At the last supper, with its tasseled menus, its signal flags, hats, and noisemakers, things picked up. As each latecomer entered everyone made noises, yelled Yaaay, and applauded. There was a sudden blast of music and everyone took up "Happy Birthday to You (slurring the name) dear Whosis, We're Glad to See You," and peering around to make out who it was they were glad to see. A waiter brought in a large cake flaming like a Catholic shrine and set it before an old woman, who was totally astonished. Everyone cheered and her tablemates urged her to get up. Reluctantly and with difficulty she helped her aged body half erect and sat quickly down again blushing and swallowing back tears. The lights went out and a baby spot went on and balloons fell from the balcony in a slow bouncing shower while the band played "Bubbles." . . .

It was morning. The cornetist blasted up and down the corridors. He played "The Sidewalks of New York" and "Home, Sweet Home." A Spanish steward knocked on a door, leaned in, and said, "Better wake op: see Statch."

The passenger went to his porthole. The ship was riding in silence softly past the foot of the island. The water lifted and relaxed in one slow floor of glass. The city lifted, it seemed, a mile above it, and very near; and smokeless behind the city, morning, the mutilation of honey. The city stood appareled in the sober purple and silver of supreme glory, no foal of nature, nor intention of man, but one sublime organism, singular and uncreated; and it stretched upward from its stone roots in the water as if it were lifted on a dream. Nor yet was it soft, nor immaterial. Every window, every wheatlike stone, was distinct in the eye as a razor and serenely, lost, somnambulists, the buildings turned one past another upon the bias of the ship's ghostly movement; not unlike those apostolic figures who parade with the clock's noon in Strasbourg.

September 1937

Women in Business

By ARCHIBALD MacLEISH

Before the coming of women to American business there was no office in the modern sense. The railroad and the telegraph had not yet pulled the business executives of the United States out of their factories and their shops and herded them together into the narrow streets where their bankers could nudge them at one elbow and their lawyers at the other. The elevator had not yet permitted the captains of industry and their lieutenants and corporals to pile up, one on top of the other, in the new towers which the structural engineers had taught the architects how to build. The women and the office came together. It was a conquest, one of the decisive campaigns of history. For it created a social institution which fails to arouse our excited curiosity only because we are too familiar with it to see it. It placed in unchallenged possession of that institution the American young woman.

Let no man deceive himself. The great American office is much more completely a female bailiwick than the great American home. It has, it is true, its necessary male. But so has the ant hive, which is essentially neuter, its necessary queen. The male is the name on the door, the hat on the coat rack, and the smoke in the corner room. But the male is not the office. The office is the competent woman at the other end of his buzzer, the two young ladies chanting his name into the mouthpieces of a kind of gutta-percha halter, the four girls in the glass coop pecking out his initials with pink fingernails on the keyboards of four voluble machines, the half dozen assorted skirts whisking through the filing cases of his correspondence, and the elegant miss in the reception room recognizing his friends and disposing of his antipathies with the pleased voice and the impersonal eye of a presidential consort.

The office, in other words, is woman's newest world. How is it that women were able to settle this rich and virgin territory before the pioneering male could drive his stake into a quarter section? And what kind of nation is this callipygian nation of silk knees, slender necks, narrow fingers, and ironic mouths which has established itself upon our boundaries?

To the first question there are two easy answers, both of them wrong. The economist will tell you that women have taken over the office because female labor is cheaper. His statement of fact is correct. His deduction is not. Women's wages are lower than men's for corresponding work. A male hand bookkeeper for example got in 1931 from $112 to $214 a month while a woman ditto found her monthly pay falling between the extremes of $80 and $170. But the fact that women's pay is lower, though it is the simple and brutal explanation of the prevalence of some hundreds of thousands of women in the underpaid and hopeless jobs at the bottom of the white-collar pyramid, is no explanation at all of the prevalence of women in the institution with which we are here concerned. Woolworth's, for example, was paying 45,000 girls an average wage of $11 before the NRA code because 45,000 girls were theoretically able to live at home and survive upon pay which would have starved a man. (That not all of them did live at home was no concern of Woolworth's.) In the same way and for the same reason women are to be found dominating the great paperwork factories run by the insurance companies. Anyone of sound sense who can endure the dreary monotony and dress on the meager wage can do the work. And women will endure the monotony and dress on the wage for a good bit less per month than men.

The situation in the executive office however, the kind of office which is intended when the average American uses the word, is entirely different. In the higher levels—in the case of the female secretary who gives the office its character and whose presence makes impossible the employment of male stenographers to take her orders—the difference between male and female wages is much less marked. The superior woman secretary earns up to $60 a week in normal course and may go higher. The comparable man secretary, rare and specialized worker though he is, probably earns little more. But that little more is entirely immaterial. For the employer—and this is the point which the economist forgets— would not replace the female secretary with the male if the wage advantage ran the other way.

So much for the first wrong answer. The second answer is even wronger. It is generally and prevalently believed that women enjoy certain peculiar physical qualifications for office work not pos- sessed by men. At one end is the common belief that women are naturally neater and better adapted to routine work. At the other is the more or less scientific finding that women are more deft and skillful in the manipulation of such characteristic office machines as the typewriter. Of the first belief it can only be said that there is no adequate basis for it. In native ability and predisposition men and women have not yet been differentiated by scientific standards and if women are more orderly than men the difference is due rather to training than to the fairies. One big New York law firm uses men only on its general staff partly because it considers men more amenable to organization and partly because the office manager finds men superior to women in neatness, efficiency, and devotion to detail. For the second contention that women are naturally better office-machine operators than men there is only the evi- dence of that branch of learning which calls itself psychometrics and which contends that women are possessed of a slight superi- ority in "finger dexterity." (The male will be proud and happy to know that he possesses an equally slight compensating superiority in "tweezer dexterity" —which means precisely what it says.) Without quarreling with the solemn findings of science it is enough to remark, first, that a slight superiority in finger dexterity does not account for the existence of twenty female stenographers and typists to every male, and, second, that the great court stenographers are almost all, for some unscientific reason, men notwithstanding.

The shoe, as a matter of fact, is probably on the other horse. So far is it from being true that women are physically better adapted to the office than men that the precise opposite is the case. The Public Health Service, reporting upon the ten-year record of employee absences in the Edison Electric Illuminating Co. of Boston, finds that women were absent on account of sickness almost twice as often as men—12.9 days a year against 6.9 days a year, and finds further that the common cold struck down almost twice as many women proportionately as men—seven out of ten as against four out of ten. It is worth noting in passing that the difference at least so far as concerns Edison Electric's Boston employees is not explained by female absences or account of menstruation. Only three out of ten women were found to suffer disability for that cause—and then only three-quarters of a day's disability per year per woman.

Failing science and economics, then, it is necessary to turn to human nature for an answer to the question of female domination in the world of glass partitions, telephone bells, and daylight hours. Human nature, as so frequently happens in cases of statistical failure, yields a very plausible response. And a fairly obvious response. Women, says the human naturalist, occupy the great American office simply and solely because they are women. Wages have very little to do with it. Finger dexterity has nothing to do with it. The whole point of the whole problem is merely that the modern office necessitates a daily, intimate, and continuing relation which is much more possible between a man and a number of women than between a man and a number of men. That relation, it is hardly necessary to say, is not the relation which plagues the imagination of the she-novelists who write of passion-in-industry. It is, if you will, a relation based upon sex. But it is not, in the accepted sense of that term, a sexual relation. The blond stenographer with the slick sleazy stockings and the redundant breasts is not its symbol. Its symbol is the competent, agreeable, thirty-odd-year-old, intelligently dressed woman who sits in imperturable self-respect behind the secretarial desks of half the major offices in the country.

The whole point of the whole problem, in other words, is that women occupy the office because the male employer wants them there. Women in their quality of women and by virtue of some of their most womanly traits are capable of making the office a more pleasant, peaceful, and homelike place. Why did the employer desire that kind of office? To get at that answer pure speculation is the only tool.

The upper-class home, as the upper-class home was known to the Victorians, had disappeared. The male was no longer master in his own dining room and dreadful in his own den, nor did a small herd of wives, daughters, and sisters hear his voice and tremble.

He was, on the contrary, the more or less equal mate of a more or less unpredictable woman. And he resented it.

He resented the loss of his position. He regretted the old docility, the old devotion to his personal interests. And finding himself unable to recreate the late, lost paradise in his home, he set about recreating it in his office. What he wanted in the office was not the office mistress described at least fifty-two times a year by American short-story writers. What he wanted in the office was something as much like the vanished wife of his father's generation as could be arranged—someone to balance his checkbook, buy his railroad tickets, get him seats in the fourth row, take his daughter to the dentist, listen to his side of the story, give him a courageous look when things were blackest, and generally know all, understand all.

That he succeeded in doing precisely this no man who knows America can doubt. There sit in thousands of rooms on Wall Street and La Salle Street and all the other streets upon which offices look out, thousands of women living, in the richest Victorian tradition, the lives of daytime wives. The phrase is no metaphor. Many of the best-paid secretaries in America are so literally their employers' daytime wives that their employers' death would mean painful widowhood. They hold their jobs and are valuable because they know all the affairs, all the friends, all the friends' voices, all the idiosyncrasies, all the weaknesses of one man. And that knowledge, instead of making them valuable to another employer, makes them as entirely dependent upon the one they have as he upon them. With his death they either devote a few years to his estate, as is customary with the woman secretaries to the very rich, or retire upon his bequest to them, as is common with the secretaries of men of generosity, or spend miserable months and years looking for another opportunity to begin the slow process of personal familiarization all over again with another man.

Whether or not any such speculative explanation of the male desire for a female office is sound, there can be no doubt that the desire exists and that it is the male employer who is chiefly responsible for the female secretary. Thereby hangs a tart ironic tag. Elsewhere in the industrial field the industrial conquests of women proved vain. They proved vain because the new industrial work which they found to do in the factories was merely a more monotonous and more impersonal version of the old domestic work they had formerly done at home. In the field of the office, however, the process reversed itself. In the field of the office it was not the *work* of the home which was carried over into the industrial setting, but the *setting* of the home which was carried over to the industrial work. And, more importantly, it was the employing male, not the eager female applicant, who was responsible for the result. Which is another way of saying that woman's greatest industrial conquest has been made, as her great conquests have been made from time immemorial, through the male and not despite him.

August 1935

In the Substrata

The Inertia of Misery
By ARCHIBALD MacLEISH

Dull mornings in the winter of 1932 the sheriff of Miami, Florida, used to fill a truck with homeless men and run them up to the county line. Where the sheriff of Fort Lauderdale used to meet them and load them into a second truck and run them up to *his* county line. Two counties later the sheriff of Saint Lucie's would meet them and load them into his truck and run them up to *his* county line. In the end the sheriff of Brevard County would *not* meet them. And whence they would trickle back down the roads to Miami. To repeat. It was a system. And it worked. The only trouble was that it worked too well. It kept the transients transient and it even increased the transient population in the process. But it got to be pretty expensive, if you sat down and figured it all out— trucks and gas and time and a little coffee. That was last winter.

Next winter there will be no trucks, not because the transients will have disappeared from Miami; if anything, there will be more blistered Fords with North Dakota licenses and more heel-worn shoes with Boston trademarks rubbed out next winter than there were last. But because the sheriff of Miami, like the President of the U.S., will next winter think of transients and unemployed miners and jobless mill workers in completely different terms.

The difference will be made by the Emergency Relief Act. The Act itself with its $300 million for direct relief loans to the states is neither an adequate nor an impressive piece of legislation. But its passage constitutes an open acknowledgement of governmental responsibility for the welfare of the victims of industrial unemployment. And its ultimate effect must be the substitution of an ordered relief program for the wasteful and uneconomic methods employed during the first three years of the depression.

The methods were never seriously capable of success. They were diffuse, unrelated, and unplanned. The theory was that private charitable organizations and semi-public welfare groups, established to care for the old and the sick and the indigent, were capable of caring for the casualties of a worldwide economic disaster. And the theory in application meant that social agencies manned for the service of a few hundred families, and city shelters set up to house and feed a handful of homeless men, were compelled by the brutal necessisities of hunger to care for hundreds of thousands of families and whole armies of the displaced and the jobless. The result was the picture of heterogeneous groups struggling under the earnest and untrained leadership of the local men of affairs against an inertia of misery and suffering and want they are powerless to overcome.

September 1932

On the Dole: 17 Million
By ERIC HODGINS

It is difficult to identify the villain. Some people will insist that the villain is the machine, whose constantly improving technology operates constantly to throw new groups of unemployed upon the market. Others will argue that the villain was the onset of war, which forced us to expand our capital plants beyond the necessities of normal peace-time consumption. Others will insist that if

Mr. Roosevelt could only "reassure business," five million men would be back at work within half a year. Others will insist that the villain is capital which, by going on strike to maintain an impossible wage scale for itself, is depriving industry of the opportunity to produce goods. And some will still blame it all on poor, luckless Mr. Hoover—whose principal crime was that he was there when it happened. Choose your own villain.

No one yet knows the true extent of unemployment, but the most widely accepted estimate placed the figure at 10.7 million for July. Since the average U.S. worker accounts for the support of two and one-half persons, the present unemployment figure means, roughly, that there are 27 million people for whom private industry is no longer providing subsistence. Twenty-seven million people are 21 percent of the country's population. The actual relief load now being borne by federal, state, or local governments is 17 million; there are still 10 million odd who have no jobs but who have not *yet* been forced to apply for relief.

It is not wholly just to blame industry for the present state of affairs. Industry as at present conceived in this country exists to create *goods*. It does not exist to create *jobs*. The most economical creation of goods carries with it the proviso that they must be turned out by the minimum number of factory hands. Industry's goal, thus seen, is increasing *dis*employment. Yet society's ambition remains comfort and security for all. Between these two extremes there is a great gulf, and it is within this gulf that the largest number of the almost 11 million unemployed are at present submerged. The productive processes of our present economy have gone on to one triumph after another; the distributive process has simply gone to pieces.

October 1934

The Permanent Social Burden
By JOHN CHAMBERLAIN

The victims of the Depression divide into two categories that require differing social treatment. There are those who are not permanently destroyed by time and change as potential gainful

Men lived in jungles like this, moving from one city where there were no jobs to another city where there were no jobs.

Concrete pipes served as homes for jobless men in Oakland, California.

workers. And there are those who are so destroyed. These latter make up what could be called the permanent social burden. From now on government in the U.S. will have to take care of anyone who falls into this classification.

By 1942 Social Security will begin to take care of the percentage of the social burden that is disabled by age. Since our population is growing older, this will tend to become an increasingly large category. Men and women who have never worked, who have disabling physical and psychical characteristics will have to be cared for by asylums, hospitals, and as part of the public assistance plan of Social Security. This has nothing to do with the unemployed who still remain potential gainful workers. Since they are the victims of the business cycle the ultimate good medicine for their plight is not unemployment relief: it is general economic policy designed to increase production to a point that will give all of them jobs.

If it be granted that U.S. citizens won't stand for a mere dole, government can continue to do the emergency job of caring for business-cycle, victims. It is our guess that such agencies as the Works Progress Administration have come to stay. Americans are pragmatists; they put their trust in what has worked. And since WPA has worked, even if expensively, it will almost certainly be a light to guide statesman and politician alike in the future. Whether you like it or not, the past depression has set up benchmarks that will still be followed long after Harry Hopkins and President Roosevelt have gone to their reward.

October 1937

A Ferment of the Times

By RUSSELL DAVENPORT

Last August a group of despondent men with sweat pouring from their faces met in Washington, D.C., for the purpose of performing a major operation. When they were finished almost half of the venerable American Federation of Labor was cast off to wander at large upon the land as the Committee for Industrial Organization under the leadership of John Llewellyn Lewis.

At the head of the table, in shirtsleeves, sat William Green, ex-coal miner, Odd Fellow, Elk, Baptist. Around him sat the assembled might of the old-line, conservative craft unions—twelve of the A. F. of L.'s fifteen Vice Presidents.

These nabobs of American labor did not refer to their performance as an operation. They called it a trial.

The C. I. O. is an informal committee consisting of the presidents of thirteen autonomous labor unions. John L. Lewis, of the United Mine Workers, is their chairman. The thirteen have pledged $500,000 for their drive for vertical industrial organization, which the A. F. of L., organized around craft unions, opposes. The C. I. O. is a crusade—to organize workers in industries that have never been able to get into the A. F. of L. on a satisfactory basis, to wit: the steel industry, steel fabricating, automobiles, electrical (radios, electrical equipment, etc.), boots and shoes, rubber, gas and byproduct coke, cement, aluminum, gas filling stations, lumber and sawmill industry, and wholesale meat packing—all almost entirely unorganized. In these twelve strategical industries there are nearly 3,500,000 unorganized men.

The C. I. O. has saved its first $500,000 pile of ammunition entirely for the steel industry, on the theory that if that citadel can be captured the whole industrial line can be turned. Steel has become the Verdun of the American labor movement. Up and down the Monongahela, where the houses cling to the hills like migrant birds; into the rolling valleys of Youngstown; down the ample curves of the Ohio; along the flat shores of Lake Michigan in the shadow of great cranes and Hulett unloaders, the C. I. O.'s voice is raised against the entrenched hostility of steel. Offices have been opened in towns that never saw a union office before. Signs have been carried in streets where no union ever before dared to raise its head. And practically every day meetings are held in that vast territory, openly or furtively, in parks, in convention halls, in cockeyed shacks on the edges of towns, or even on isolated farms leased for the occasion.

The instrument of attack is the Steel Workers' Organizing Committee, whose headquarters is no shanty. S.W.O.C. has set itself up on the thirty-sixth floor of the big Grant Building in Pittsburgh—which is said to contain more steel companies than any building in the U.S.

Its activity in steel is not fortuitous. It grows out of the soil where rank-and-file leaders tried unsuccessfully and by themselves to force a national steel strike in 1934. Moreover, the ferment of the steel soil is not unique, but rather typical of the ferment in all of American industry. And this ferment itself is typical of the times. After every great depression society awakes to forces from beneath. And in these periods labor organizing has been a genuine expression of forces bigger than the leaders themselves.

October 1936

Pitiless John L. Lewis
By JOHN K. JESSUP

John L. Lewis has two shaggy red eyebrows either one of which a French gendarme would be proud to wear on his lip. His rusty-iron hair rises as abruptly as a hedge from his shaved neck and luxuriates all over his head like the feathers of a Houdan rooster. His face, the color of rock, is as innocent of any sign of self-mistrust as if it were really constructed of some artificial substitute for flesh. At fifty-six he is girthy but solid, and he can twist his huge frame from the waist, to look suddenly behind him, with the speed of a cat. He takes no exercise and he has not brandished a pick for twenty-five years but he was strong enough to fell huge William Hutcheson, head of the carpenters, at the A. F. of L. convention last fall, and he not so long ago heaved a delegate from the cigar counter of the English Hotel in Indianapolis into the street. Even at rest he gives a feeling of exhaustless strength.

Even more than his strong arm and quick, uncluttered brain, his tongue is perhaps John Lewis's most potent weapon. In him the native eloquence of the Welsh has flowered in all its spell-weaving pomposity. He can be both ungrammatical and absurd. Even in private conversation he is sometimes the platform orator, now an oboe, now the drums and brass; and in such a conversation you may recognize whole sentences that he has used before in a public address.

Perhaps Donald Richberg (who was former director of the National Industrial Recovery Board, successor to the NRA) evoked the most picturesque abuse. "Mr. Richberg, springing from the loins of labor...secretly conspired with the leaders of the auto-mobile industry to deceive the president and bludgeon labor. Like medieval ruffians they lay in wait during the day and emerged after nightfall to perpetrate their deeds.... One can imagine the giggling falsetto cackle of Mr. Richberg when the strain was over.... For Mr. Richberg, who knows of these things of which I speak, I express my personal contempt."

John L. Lewis is probably the most purposeful man who ever emerged from the miners' life. And there is no more indurating cradle.

The running of any union is no job for a squeamish man, but the running of the United Mine Workers, especially as it had to be run from 1919 to 1933, is surely one of the least dainty jobs in the whole range of respectable vocations. It is not simply that miners are hard-bitten, heterogeneous, articulate, sensitive, and accustomed to handling dynamite. It is that they have been forced to compete with one another for a steadily diminishing quantity of work. The mines developed a terrific overcapacity during the war. By 1923 their capacity (bituminous only) was nearly 1 billion tons; their production has never exceeded 580 million tons. Yet a coal mine, once opened, can rarely be removed from competition by a mere bankruptcy. The only flexible part of the supply is labor, which is over 60 percent of the mine cost of coal. Against the steady incursion of oil, gas, and the better utilization of each ton of coal, the 2,000 bituminous operators of North America (to say nothing of the many thousand in-and-out operators of "snowbirds" and "gopher holes") have been no more capable of collusive resistance than so many pushcart peddlers. They have clamored in a chronic buyer's market; their impulses are centrifugal; and those of their labor are hence largely the same.

But the post-war spurt of tonnage from the low-wage South soon showed itself to be something far more ominous than plain regional competition. U.S. Steel had bought 100,000 acres of coal lands in West Virginia and Kentucky in 1917 alone. The Mellons bought another 125,000 acres. The largest digger in that dark and bloody ground was (and is) U.S. Coal & Coke, a U.S. Steel subsidiary. The virulent anti-unionism of the South, in short, has its roots in the big northern consumers of coal. As long as Big Steel is free to tack up a sign at a single pit head announcing a wage cut, the United Mine Workers of America is in danger of becoming a mere "rear guard of labor's retreat to cooliedom."

Thus John L. Lewis has been forced by the realities of American industry to broaden his labor front. He has learned that if any segment of American labor allows itself to be treated as a commodity, the rest of labor suffers. That is why he wants to organize all labor and why he must try to organize it on vertical lines. The issue is not unlike slavery. Whether you think the planter or the abolitionist is the tyrant depends on where you sit, and whether you think a monlithic industrial union like Lewis's or a monolithic anti-unionism like Steel's and Detroit's is the tyrant depends on the same thing. But one has to drive the other out.

Lewis is not writing any labor party platform yet. He is simply trying to organize America's mass-employing industries for his own cogent reasons; if a labor party flowers from that, he is for it. It could hardly govern more mistakenly, he says, than the bankers have. But that is about as far as his visions of the future go. He is a business unionist.

It was the miners who were the nucleus of the British Labour party; in spite of its strong Socialist wing, that party has yet to govern England. In America, the last man who came close to getting labor into politics was the Socialist Eugene V. Debs, whose career shows some similarities to Lewis's and one difference: Lewis has never been in jail. The emotional Debs may or may not have burned with a purer flame for the cause of industrial democracy than John L. Lewis. But you cannot reform society from Atlanta. To make an industrial union or a group of them you need not a set of social objectives so much as a flexible tongue, a ready opportunism, and a pitiless hand.

October 1936

Washington

SEC, the New Shrine

By WILLIAM P. HARRIS and H. CLARKE

At 1778 Pennsylvania Avenue, N.W., Washington, D.C., there is a shabby building that the Interstate Commerce Commission once called home. Today over its functional façade a black stripe bears a cheap gilt legend: Securities and Exchange Commission. The building is a place of monastic cubbyholes. Glass partitions cut long, dim corridors through it, screening the cells where men think and think. On scattered corners of the upper floors the commissioners sit, distinguishable to outsiders only by the names and titles painted on the doors. Eventually you get to Room 1102. This is the SEC's main hearing hall, a large, poorly lighted auditorium whose walls have echoed the plaints of the most potent U.S. financial voices. The SEC is one of the New Deal's principal agencies of reform.

It has three major and three minor statutes to administer. These laws have been given it by indulgent Congresses over the past six years. In that time the SEC's budget has grown from $1.5 million to $5.4 million, its staff from 700 to 1,600, and it has ten district offices reaching into the far corners of the country.

To the plenipotentiaries of U.S. business and finance the SEC is a symbol of paralysis. They agree that some financial reform is desirable, but they challenge nearly all the legislative tools set up to effect it. They chafe under the requirements of the Securities Act of 1933, which demands disclosure of facts relevant to the issue of new securities; they curse the Securities Exchange Act of 1934, which set up the Commission itself, gave it police powers over the exchanges and authority to demand disclosure of facts on outstanding securities.

It is said that the SEC and its laws have shifted the center of U.S. finance from 23 Wall Street, which houses Mr. J. P. Morgan and his associates, to 1778 Pennsylvania Avenue, N.W. Mr. Morgan's address is a temple—and so is the SEC's shabby building. They are temples in which repose the deepest feelings of a community. Twenty-three Wall is the chief memorial of a business era that came to an end ten years ago, and the SEC is a shrine to the outraged feelings of the voters of 1932, though few of them know it. Back in 1932 those feelings had not been intellectualized.

In the depth of the Depression few citizens of the U.S. had reasoned that big combinations of capital make for big swings in industrial activity. Few of them pondered deeply on the foreign-exchange crisis, the Federal Reserve System, or the subtle mechanics of inflation. All that most of them knew was that something had gone terribly wrong with money and with the value of those things they had always thought to be the equivalent of money. If a $1,000 bond was not almost as good as $1,000 in currency or in the bank, then why call it a $1,000 bond? If a man could not treat the market value of his brokerage account as if it were a bank account, then what did they mean by calling those things "securities"? The citizens probably did not figure out that the field of highly negotiable securities was a part of the credit area; that the credit area was an extension of the actual currency area; that the whole area might loosely be called monetary and therefore might be brought under the constitutional power of Congress to regulate the value of the dollar. But when Franklin Roosevelt spoke of chasing the moneychangers from the temple, he found the measure of their unanalyzed feelings. The people then realized that the place where money was being handled was indeed the temple—which was a dramatic way of saying that all of these forms of money were the concern of public policy. And look at who the handlers were. The sacks of gold dust no longer thudded on the bars of Virginia City, the plantations were no longer traded for a stack of chips on the green baize table of a river steamboat. The last wide-open frontier was the canyon of Wall Street. There were the men with the sporty vests, the roadsters, the chorus girls, and the flamboyant habits. It did not much matter that the Street had its solid citizens too, and that these men held the balance of power. It was obvious that this area of the sacred domain of "money" was dangerously and irresponsibly run. It was inevitable that it should be regulated by the government—i.e., the SEC which administers most of the new laws through which the government now curbs the once unbridled individualism of finance.

The laws themselves were inevitable; and no responsible man on Wall Street wants to see them wiped wholly off the books. The positive results for the Street have been very real. But the group of men who wrote the laws are still in power. They, with intellectuals in other government agencies, are sometimes referred to as the "Third New Deal," and it is they who have given the SEC its glowing and controversial corona. This group is just beginning to bring into action the most drastic of its laws; and it is apparently planning to push still further the governmental salient in the domain of finance.

June 1940

The War

A.D. 1939
By FRANCIS SILL WICKWARE

On the afternoon of Friday, September 1, a crowd of out-of-town visitors began to pour into New York to see the World's Fair over the Labor Day weekend, and a crowd of New Yorkers began to pour out. The New York Central had 140 extra trains coupled up for the weekend, and the Pennsylvania had over 110. On the streets of New York parked taxicabs were hemmed by throngs listening tensely to the radio bulletins, which were flashing across the networks at brief intervals, twenty-four hours a day, and making the newspaper headlines stale before they were printed. Gdynia was blockaded, Nazi bombs dropped on Warsaw, and while the British Cabinet considered this aggression that it was pledged to resist, the last mobilization steps were taken and a mass exodus started from London.

Saturday was a day of unbearable suspense. Under the hot, calm sky over Long Island Sound the sailing was listless; on boat decks and on beaches people clustered around the little portable radios that had become so popular that summer, combing the dials for the voices of Mr. Kaltenborn and Mr. Swing. Scarcely a program was completed without a sharp interruption for "latest news bulletins." It was a confusion of bombs and shelling and mobilization and fortified lines and blackouts and mass aerial attacks. . . .

And then it came—Neville Chamberlain at a microphone in London saying, "I have to tell you that this country is at war with Germany."

The first business day after the Labor Day weekend gave the New York Stock Exchange its busiest session in nearly two years— 5,932,000 shares. The day's first sale was in New York Dock preferred, up ⅞ at the opening, and thereafter gains of from ⅝ to 3¾ points were recorded in the initial sales of New York Central, General Electric, General Motors, Chrysler, Standard of New Jersey, and International Nickel. Owing to a dearth of sell orders it took until eleven o'clock to open up a market in steel stocks, and then the specialists came to the rescue and the first quote came across the tape. Big Steel was up 8⅝ followed by Bethlehem at 78, up 9¾, and Republic at 26, up 6¾. As reported, "Governors and technical experts of the Exchange hung on the fringes of the 'Steel Crowd.' Nearby stood William McC. Martin Jr., youthful president, smilingly going through the first wild market since his assumption of authority."

The bond market was an equally melodramatic place that day, with the volume of trading over $59,000,000, the heaviest in history. In the commodity markets initial opening bids lifted many prices the maximum permitted, leaving millions of dollars in orders unfilled and brokers with nothing to do.

By the middle of the month the composite index of ninety stocks had risen more than 12 percent, with sharp gains by the traditional "war babies"—steel, sugar, aircraft, and railroad equipment—also by the low-priced rail and coal-mining stocks. Particularly encouraging was the ten-point rise in agricultural prices, which was well sustained all fall, and a bumper crop of nine to ten billion farm dollars was predicted for 1940. Finally, the market upturn was accompanied by a wave of heavy industrial buying—the September advance in new orders received by manufacturers was 61 percent above August, the swiftest one-month advance in ten years.

The real news was made not by the stock market but by business itself. The biggest gains were being registered in the heavy industries. Steel was in the forefront—October production in tons was the highest for any month on record. With carloadings up to the best October level since 1930, railroads not only had their repair shops working at capacity to refurbish decrepit rolling stock, but generated the biggest volume of new equipment orders that had been seen since 1936 or earlier.

And so it went. Cotton consumption by textile mills reached a near record of some 700,000 bales in October. The aircraft industry received $200 million in new orders in the first ten war weeks, releasing an estimated $25-million plant-expansion program to bring the industry's annual capacity up to over $500 million in 1940. The U.S. Maritime Commission (which had just launched the *America*, largest passenger ship ever built in the U.S.) promptly upped it rehabilitation and shipbuilding program with a request for bids on thirty-three new cargo or passenger-cargo ships to be constructed at a cost of some $66 million. With air-travel volume setting another record on top of a long series of records, American Airlines announced an order for fifteen new Douglas DC-3's, with United, T.W.A., and others also planning fleet expansions to care for the increased traffic expected to clear through the new $40 million LaGuardia Field. The chemical industry gave promise of near-record earnings for the fourth quarter, and International Agricultural planned a $2,500,000 potash plant for fertilizers, also aiming to become the first important U.S. producer of potassium sulfate, an essential tobacco chemical.

The nine months' net profits of 320 leading companies by 1940 (compiled by National City Bank) stood at $589,500,000 compared with $296,400,000 in cold 1938. The only industries in the entire list that declined in the face of the advance were petroleum, mining and quarrying, baking, and beverages, although Coca-Cola had the best third quarter in its history. . . .

Smaller than the business gains but still substantial were rises in factory employment and payrolls, in department-store sales, and in national income. There was more money all around and— thanks to the forward sweep of technology—the physical world in 1939 was a pleasanter, more convient, and more exciting place in which to spend it. To spend it on a new automobile meant getting (in Packard) an actual refrigeration system in some models; seats (in Nash) that converted into a big enough bed; a new kind of transmission (in Oldsmobile) that eliminated the clutch pedal; new, safer, sealed-beam headlights in most models.

The average American wife waited more anxiously than ever for nylon stockings to appear on the counters of her favorite store after reading that girls at the du Pont exhibit at the Fair had gone all summer without a run in their special pre-release nylons. She counted on equipping her kitchen with super-Pyrex when Corning announced a glass that could be heated cherry red and dropped into ice water without cracking. Even better was news that the Sterilamp (developed first as a meat preservative) was a specific for tough beef.

The physical well-being of Americans was further protected by medical technology. In case of pneumonia the sulfanilamide derivative sulfapyridine would give a citizen a better chance for survival than he could have had before. If cancerous, he might undergo the slow-freezing process and be kept in a hibernation coma for five days, with mechanical refrigeration taking the place of the old (early 1939) ice-packing method. If undersexed, the male sex hormone was isolated and available for him. If a surgical case, he and his medicos were safer in the operating room than they used to be, since the new explosion-proof operating lamp ended the danger of ether, ethylene, and other gas blasts.

Materially richer, with more things and more knowledge at his disposal, the average American was better off spiritually and politically than he had been for some time. He hated war, and a war was going on, yet in the U.S. this did not seem to signal a Wellsian end of civilization that he had dimly expected. What it might eventually do to Europe and the world no one could guess, but temporarily its effect on the U.S. seemed on the whole more good than bad.

January 1940

The Forties

"We must be the great arsenal of democracy," the President proclaims. The picture now is of everyone suddenly at work. Government money that went into New Deal projects flows into the construction of military bases and industries making the tools of war. There are new and different landscapes, portraits of new heroes. Money is not the problem, only production. The great arsenal, created almost overnight, pours out its good to overwhelm enemies on two fronts thousands of miles apart. Is it fair to say that Capitalism wins the war? It is the deciding factor, at least, with its genius for making things and its know-how with science and technology. The war ends, leaving a heritage of tools which may be used for the construction of peace if men are wise enough to see it. One artifact portends a second industrial revolution. Meanwhile, the loose money around and the surge of consumer demands create the biggest boom in Capitalism's history.

The Martial Years

The Earth Movers Mobilize
By CHARLES J. V. MURPHY

A group of Westerners assembled one morning in February, 1931, at the Engineers Club in San Francisco. They were all contractors, attended by their engineers, lawyers, and financial men. Two were aging Mormons who had graded the roadbed for the Western Pacific when it went through Utah. Two others mixed railroad work with general contracting. One specialized in sewers and tunnels, one was a bridge builder, one a building contractor, and one a sand, gravel, and paving man. They had come together to do collectively what they could not do individually. The outcome of the meeting was a loose confederation of builders and earth movers called Six Companies, Inc.

In the next five years, Six Companies built Boulder Dam, at that time, the biggest dam on the face of the earth, went on to build the Bonneville dam and powerhouse on the Columbia River, took over and completed Grand Coulee, and sank the great piers for the Bay Bridge between San Francisco and Oakland.

When the war put an end to most of the New Deal's dam-building and irrigation and power projects, the Six Companies got into war construction. Now they are building Liberty ships, small aircraft carriers, tankers, troop ships (C-4's), tank landing ships, and destroyer escorts. They have a piece of the Alaska Military Highway. On islands of the Pacific they have built underground storage tanks of unprecedented depth and complexity, barracks, and gun emplacements. They are in the mysterious and portentous Army undertaking in the subarctic known as "The Canol Project" (Canadian Oil), a 400-mile pipeline through the wild mountainous country between Fort Norman, on the Mackenzie River, and Whitehorse in the Yukon.

They live dramatic and varied lives. Some 850 Morrison-Knudsen workers at Wake Island were either killed or have died or are Japanese prisoners. Sudden death is never a stranger to contractors. At Boulder Dam they lost 110 men in five years. Let's look at them in those prewar year.

It was the two Mormons, W. H. and E. O. Wattis, brothers, ranchers, and sometimes contractors, both in their seventies, and founders of Utah Construction Co., who first got the group together in San Francisco. The Wattis brothers were obsessed with the idea that they could put together a group of companies that could build Boulder Dam.

The great purpose behind Boulder Dam was to stop the wild and costly floods that were forever inundating the Imperial Valley, and to provide drinking water for the coastal cities of southern California, and power and irrigation for southern California, Nevada, and Arizona.

Frank Crowe, of the Six's Morrison-Knudsen, speaks of Boulder with awe. "The Colorado is a wild river. One day it rose forty feet in forty minutes. It became a wall of yellow mud that kept rising until I though it was going to wash us right out of the canyon. . . ."

For five long years the mud, the remorseless current, the swift floods were Frank Crowe's responsibility. "We had 5,000 men jammed in a 4,000-foot canyon," he says. "The problem, which was a problem in materials flow, was to set up the right sequence of jobs so they wouldn't kill each other off." Henry J. Kaiser, the sand and gravel man in the consortium, worked out the method for handling the aggregates. "We never lost an hour on account of not having materials," Crowe says. Boulder was built in five years— two years and two months ahead of schedule.

But the new Secretary of the Interior, Harold L. Ickes, threw the Six Companies into consternation by charging them with 70,000 violations of the eight-hour-day law and fining them $350,000. The government contract bound the contractors not to resort to overtime except in emergencies; this was a Depression device for spreading the work. Crowe and the others, on the theory that "the dam was a continuous emergency," had not taken the overtime clause too literally.

Ickes's charges were splashed over the nation's newspapers. Kaiser hired a publicity man to whip up a booklet entitled "So Boulder Dam Was Built," a dramatic record of never-ending crises; thousands of copies were air-mailed to Congressmen and high government officials. Kaiser went on the air to describe the immense obstacles that had been overcome. In the negotiations that followed the fine was reduced to $100,000.

Boulder was more than a monument to the Six Companies; it was a gold mine. The profits, after taxes, were $10,400,000, prorated according to the capital contributions.

The time was the mid-1930's. The New Deal was trying to spend its way back to prosperity via a vast program of public works—not one but a whole series of Boulder Dams. There were the great projects of Bonneville and Grand Coulee on the Columbia River, and Shasta on the Sacramento.

The Columbia is swift and deep, its normal flow equal to the Colorado at flood. Some contractors had serious doubts that foundations for a dam could be safely anchored. But Kaiser argued that the river could be licked, that the job would enable them to hold together the wonderful organization they had assembled; that they would make a lot of money fast. He had his way.

Bonneville was a triumph. "They said it couldn't be done," Kaiser exclaims with a theatrical roll to his voice, "but my kids went ahead and did it." Bonneville was completed in four years—one year ahead of schedule. The Six Companies' net profit on this $16.5 million job was about $3 million.

They won some and lost some. They lost Shasta and the first phase of Grand Coulee but got in on the second phase. They finished Grand Coulee in 1942, broke the world's record for concrete poured in a single job, and netted $7.2 million before taxes for the group.

Kaiser, for one, caught the scent of an important truth. It was that you could operate on government money.

One of his big schemes now was to take on the powerful West Coast cement combine and pry loose some of its profitable business. Cement represented a major part of his costs. He took an option on a big limestone deposit near San Jose. And he also had a promise from the Southern Pacific on a freight rate. That was about all he did have. He had a name, Permanente Corporation, but he had no cement plant and knew nothing about running one. But he figured correctly that Ickes, who was against the kind of identical bids that the West Coast combine was in the habit of submitting, would have to back him.

Kaiser's men started building a plant in June; the first cement was produced on Christmas day of that year. It has become the world's biggest cement plant, with a capacity of five million barrels

Harry W. Morrison

Stephen H. Bechtel

DRAWINGS BY RICHARD LINDNER

Henry J. Kaiser, Sr. and Jr.

John A. McCone

Felix Kahn

Ralph M. Parsons

a year. The limestone and the clay quarries are in the brown hills a quarter of a mile from the great kilns. A mile-and-a-half-long gravity conveyer-belt system, braked by generators that supply electric current to the huge shovels that dig out the limestone, testifies to the ingenuity of the man who prides himself as a mover of materials.

The immediate consequence was an 11 percent reduction in the price of cement. But this was a small matter compared with what the plant was to mean, not only on the West Coast but in the islands of the Pacific. The year was 1939.

The whole of the Six Companies consortium, like much of U.S. industry, was at war. Two of the partners, Steve Bechtel and John McCone, had had a study made of the shipbuilding industry. Bechtel concluded "that shipbuilding was a real possibility for our kind of operations." In September, 1939, the Maritime Commission called for bids on five C-1 cargo ships under the so-called long-range program. The Six Companies hastily formed the Seattle-Tacoma Shipbuilding Corp. with Todd Seattle Dry Docks on a fifty-fifty basis. Their $9-million bid was successful. The new partners divided the task. The Six Companies was to build the shipyard, and Todd was to run it.

In 1940, a representative from Britain's Consolidated Steel Corp., Ltd., came to Washington in connection with a $14-million British order for sixty freighters. The deal provided that thirty ships be built on the East Coast and thirty on the West. To handle the East Coast operation, the Six Companies added the Bath Iron Works as a partner, forming the Todd-Bath Iron Shipbuilding Corp. around a seven-basin yard to be built in South Portland, Maine. For the West Coast operation they set up the Todd-California Shipbuilding Corp. around a seven-way yard to be built at Richmond, on San Francisco Bay. The British paid for the yards and agreed to pay a fee of $160,000 per ship.

The British turned to the Six Companies because they had nowhere else to go. All the established yards were too small to handle the order, or too heavily burdened with naval, Maritime Commission, or private business. The British had many misgivings. A member of the British mission, visiting the Richmond site two months after the contract was signed, remembers seeing "a vast sea of mud" and wondering what his people had bought.

A month later Admiral Vickery, head of the Maritime Commission, launched the emergency Liberty-ship program and the same need forced him in his turn to deal with these ambitious newcomers who were ready to promise him the world. In January they were given contracts to build three additional yards (in Portland, Los Angeles, and Houston), and these were soon followed by orders for a total of eighty-seven new ships, plus a second twelve-way yard alongside Richmond No. 1.

The first ship built for the British took 196 days, from keel-laying to delivery. Today an Oregon yard, run by Edgar Kaiser, has cut the time to twenty-seven days. There are now 243,600 men and women working in all the group's yards, turning out a ship every 10.3 hours.

The Liberty ship was a simple standardized design that the Maritime Commission felt could be entrusted to the green yards. But the Six Companies refused to stay in this rut. "Give us the design," Henry Kaiser dinned into Admiral Vickery's ears. "We'll build the ships." Today, in addition to the Liberties, they are producing troop carriers (C-4's), 16,600 deadweight-ton tankers (T-2's), auxiliary aircraft carriers, and escort vessels (frigates), and commanding about 25 percent of the Maritime Commission's program.

The war also took the Six Companies for the first time into a complex industrial venture. In the summer of 1940, after Roosevelt had announced the 50,000 plane program to a nation starved for light metals, Kaiser saw the potentialities of magnesium. Dow, with an electrolytic process, was accounting for all U.S. magnesium, but other processes were available. Kaiser decided the most promising of them was the "carbothermic reduction" technique developed by an Austrian named Fritz Hansgirg. The inventor had recently arrived in San Francisco from Korea, where he had built a small magnesium plant for the Japanese two years before. The only one in the U.S. who knew enough about his process to be able to design a plant, he was put to work designing one. Having no plans—the Japanese had kept those he used in Korea—he had to work from memory.

Kaiser decided to build the installation in lovely Santa Clara Valley, alongside the Permanente cement plant—the natural gas used for heating purposes in making the cement could be economically used as a cooling agent in the magnesium process—and before steel was up, he was saying that the plant would produce twice as much magnesium as the whole industry had produced before the war.

But the process being new, Kaiser's men continually ran into bugs. Since it takes furnaces ten days to cool off, two weeks were lost every time they had to be shut down for repairs. Several men were burned or gassed to death as a result of haste and carelessness. Three were killed when a small explosion blew out a rubber-hose connection and caused the fantastically inflammable magnesium to burst into a consuming flame.

Kaiser and his men admit that they have not lived up to their original schedule. But all in all, they are proud of what they have done. Costs are still not competitive but they insist, despite the skepticism of some of the Six Companies partners themselves, that they will perform the near-miracle of reducing costs by more than 50 percent by next year. They point out that the Hansgirg process is potentially the cheapest on the basis of raw-material cost, and they are developing byproducts that alone, they think, will reduce costs (by 2 or 3 cents a pound); the plant is going at 67 percent of capacity. When it is running at full capacity, costs should drop more.

At the magnificent plant in Permanente Canyon, the charming, the purposeful, and the big are merged in a breathtaking pattern—enormous hammerhead cranes, row upon row upon row of retorts, humming conveyor belts, flower beds, fountains, cool white concrete buildings. Everything is arranged according to a gravitational logic—buildings and processes descend the hill in a seemingly effortless way.

While Kaiser was sweating and fighting his way through an untried metallurgical process, other Six Companies boys were sticking to the good old tried process of contracting. W. A. Bechtel Co.—through an affiliated company, Bechtel-McCone-Parsons—was spreading itself all over the world—designing and building refineries in the Persian Gulf, at Curaçao, and in the sub-Arctic. It was building and running a huge airplane-modification center at Birmingham, Alabama. It is perhaps the most difficult technical job, after magnesium, in the whole Six Companies portfolio. To the center comes a good part of the bomber output of Willow Run and other plants for changes to meet new tactical or special geographic conditions—modifications that are either too specialized to be dealt with on the assembly line or too new for the line to catch up with save at the cost of extensive retooling.

The Canol adventure, under Bechtel sponsorship, is a construction job. A big oil field has been opened up less than 100 miles below the Arctic Circle; a 600-mile pipeline is being driven across the wild mountainous country to Whitehorse; and at Whitehorse, which is on the Alaska Military Highway, a refinery is being constructed to produce gasoline for trucks and planes. There have been broad hints that drilling (by Imperial Oil Ltd. of Canada) has revealed a structure that may become one of the most important oil fields of the continent. It should end the costly hauling of gasoline from California to Alaskan bases for the bombers that soon will be striking at Japan.

The Six's MacDonald & Kahn stayed at home and built cantonments, dams, and airfields. Pacific Bridge went out to Pearl Harbor to install graving docks for the Navy; and after the Japs struck, the Navy impressed Pacific Bridge's superb talents as an underwater specialist for the raising of the sunken ships. From its old railroad building crews Utah Construction Co. has recruited men to go to Samoa to work on airfields, and sent others north to work on the Alaska Military Highway.

When Kaiser invited the partners to join him in steel, they did not warm up to it. He had to go into steel by himself.

The West Coast never has had an integrated steel industry, i.e., one making its own pig iron. West Coast steel mills have always had to rely on eastern or Rocky Mountain plants for all their pig iron and most of their steel ingots, and have never come near meeting the West Coast demand for finished steel.

By the spring of 1941, steel was becoming scarce. Kaiser was having trouble getting it for his ships. He made a formal proposal to OPM, asking $150 million for an integrated steel plant. Drawn up in a hurry, the proposal was vague in spots and mentioned five different possible locations. But for four months, he all but submerged official Washington under telegrams and memos, and finally his proposal went through.

He put up his integrated steel mill at Fontana, California, in the San Bernardino Valley area about fifty miles out of Los Angeles. No undertaking of his has been surrounded by so much outside pessimism. Fontana will have to be equipped to make tin plate, wire, pipe, and lighter steels before it can compete in the postwar Western market. The iron mine at Kelso is good for only six or eight years, and there are no proved big mines nearby. Coal comes from Utah, 807 miles away. More important, Kaiser had to borrow $106 million from RFC and needs $5 million more for working capital. If his shipyards work at capacity, he may be in good shape, but if the war ends suddenly he may be faced with the necessity of selling securities to the public (which the Six Companies had avoided like the plague) or letting RFC foreclose.

Neither Kaiser nor his men seem very worried. "What have we go to lose in Fontana?" asks Henry's son, Edgar. "Only the dollars we otherwise would pay in taxes."

August, September, October 1943

Henry Kaiser, an American Hero

By GILBERT BURCK

Henry Kaiser, four years ago a more or less unknown western contractor, is today the nation's most portentous industrial phenomenon. Simply on the basis of press mentions and the frequency of his conferences with government officials, he is indisputably the No. 1 businessman of the hour. More important, he has received a popular acclaim that few if any industrialists ever have. Part of this is the result of his spectacular ability to get things done.

The man who both gets things done and aims to do bigger things in the future has always been an American hero. His personal mail on some days runs to several thousand letters—much of it from citizens convinced that he holds the key to the nation's salvation and their own.

He is not very heroic looking. He has jowls like those of a venerable Great Dane, he has a paunch, and he waddles like a duck. In his more somber moments, when his mouth is clamped in a straight line, he has the look of a country preacher preparing to warn his flock against the temptations of the flesh. When he lets himself out, however, he radiates geniality, and makes the humblest hand feel at ease. The only men who know how portentous he really is are those who must listen to his endless outpourings of ideas and carry out his countless orders.

Kaiser was born in 1882 in Canajoharie, New York. His German-born father was a custom shoemaker. The only boy of the four Kaiser children, Henry cared nothing for making shoes. Always building things, he kept the house littered with tools and materials. When he was fourteen he got a job as a delivery boy in a Utica department store. Four or five years later he hired himself out to a photographer in the nearby resort town of Lake Placid. "At the end of the first year," he says, "I had a half interest in the business. At the end of three years I owned it in full."

He set up shop in the resort town of Daytona Beach, Florida, and made enough money to put up two small buildings there. As business increased, he added a store in Palm Beach and a counter in a St. Augustine store where he printed and finished other people's photographs, and made a specialty of postcard landscape scenes.

He had married one of his Lake Placid customers, a Miss Bessie Fosburgh, whose lumberman father was well-to-do. Kaiser, however, neither waited for nor expected any of Mr. Fosburgh's money. He sold his photographic business. After some cogitation, he picked the hardware business and went to Spokane, Washington, and went to work with the Hawkeye Sand & Gravel Co., buying a little stock, arranging to pay for more out of his earnings as a salesman. He was twenty-six when a Chicago construction firm named J. F. Hill landed a contract in the city of Spokane, and Kaiser called on the company to sell his line of aggregates. He left with a job to build and manage their sand-and-gravel plant. Hill sent Kaiser to Vancouver in 1913 to put up another sand-and-gravel plant where Kaiser saw a chance to get into the construction business on his own. With money borrowed from a Vancouver bank, he bought some secondhand wheelbarrows, concrete mixers, and a couple of teams. With these he successfully bid a $250,000 paving contract in Nanaimo. And out of this came the Henry J. Kaiser Co.

His friends have always worried that he will work himself to death. Even in his private life, he cannot relax or cease to compete. At Lake Tahoe, where he now spends the summer, his speedboats are among the fastest on the lake. Nothing is too trifling for his attention or too good to be left alone. He buys most of Mrs. Kaiser's clothes; if the Kiasers give a dinner party it is he who decides the courses and the seating list. He is constantly rebuilding and redecorating their home in Oakland, California.

He reacts emotionally with the same intensity that he works. His younger son. Junior, explaining a decidedly emotional brochure describing the Fontana steel mill, said: "Father likes a bit of hearts and flowers in our literature." This side of Kaiser's character was revealed at its most intimate during the blowing in of Big Bess, the first blast furnace at Fontana, named after his wife. Most public affairs staged by Kaiser's organization are graced by a professional quartet called the "Oregon Sentinels," who wear the gray uniform of the shipyard mounted police. At the climax of the ceremonies, facing hundreds of new workers, Kaiser motioned the Sentinels behind him. While they softly hummed his favorite song *Let Me Call You Sweetheart*, he launched into an impassioned oration on the subject of love. "The greatest thrill," he said, "is to know that I love not only mother but each and every one of you."

But when hard pressed or thwarted he is intensely unsentimental. Among his intimates his rages and threats are as famous as his appetite. The cords swell in his neck; his round body shakes all over, the words are flung out with trip-hammer speed. Men who have been bawled out over the telephone say they could hear him pounding the table a continent's span away. Aroused, often over something relatively insignificant, he can be violent, taunting, goading, brushing aside all argument. He has been seen in several episodes of lapel seizing and shoulder spinning, one involving a three-star general, another a federal investigator.

There may have been an element of bluff in these displays. Some years ago Kaiser addressed a big meeting of the Associated General Contractors, whose members perversely resolved to take a course opposite to the one he wanted. "Henry ranted and stormed," a friend said. "He looked as if he would drop dead of apoplexy any minute. There was a recess and I met him five minutes later in the hall. Henry was cool as a cucumber. 'How am I doin'?' he wanted to know."

He sometimes seems almost carried along by the terrific momentum he has generated. "Henry doesn't want any more money," says Harry Morrison. "He just wants to do things."

An example was his venture into cargo planes in July, 1942. Angry at Admiral Vickery for diverting material from him to another shipbuilder, Kaiser got together with Palmer Hoyt, then publisher of the Portland *Oregonian* and agitator for an aircraft industry in Portland, and whipped up a radio speech announcing he was going to build cargo planes in his shipyards. He said that if nine shipyards were converted to building huge flying boats like

Glenn Martin's Mars, they could be produced at the rate of 5,000 a year in ten months. His men were astonished when they listened to the broadcast. They had never heard Kaiser even mention the cargo-plane idea. But before they could reach him, the U.P., A.P., several American and even foreign papers were asking for more details.

Kaiser had to go through with it. Within a couple days he was journeying across country to talk before the National Press Club, writing and rewriting his speech. It was a whopping success. The country was deeply stirred. Meantime, Kaiser was looking around for a plane to build. He considered the huge Mars and the very much smaller Curtiss Commando. The Navy discouraged him on the Mars, and he hunted around for something bigger than the Commando. But he couldn't find what he wanted, and the aircraft industry wasn't very cooperative. Kaiser jumped in and tied up Howard Hughes. He and Hughes are now making three huge prototype Duramold cargo planes in the Hughes plant in Culver City, California.

But Kaiser now seems more interested in a revolutionary flying wing than he does in Hughes, and Hughes seems more interested in a military plane than in Kaiser. Although they have got $18 million in government money, nobody has any idea when production will begin.

For the last six months Kaiser has not been so concerned about the details of his war plants. Aware that industry and labor have let much go by default, he is not ashamed to consider himself as at least a joint savior of the free-enterprise system. Last December he made a speech before the National Association of Manufacturers. "We are not summoned," he warned them, "either to show the way to a decent standard of living ... or to surrender, perhaps for the last time, to the compulsions and directions of the dictator state. . . ." He urged them to adopt a "plan to end all plans; a plan which would restore the confidence of the people in industrial leadership." He described the country's needs, then dared the auto industry to design and announce its 1945 models for delivery six months after war's end, dared general contractors and makers of road machinery to plan a new highway system, dared real-estate men to organize housing companies.

He himself is setting an example. Day and night he thinks and talks postwar planning. He often refers to what he calls World War III, or the social and economic upheaval that must be avoided after

World War II. Kaiser in pursuit of a postwar abstraction is as relentless as Kaiser in pursuit of a thousand tons of steel plate. One of his Six Companies associates tells of leaping dripping from a morning shower in San Francisco to take an urgent telephone call from Kaiser in Washington. "Henry talked for an hour and a half. His main point was that he wasn't worried so much about this war as he was about the next one because there was no Brotherhood of Man. It made no difference to him that I stood there all the time with just a towel around my middle."

Kaiser has set up a Development and Engineering Division consisting of some fifty engineers and inventors, who, in addition to their war work, run down any postwar lead that occurs to Kaiser as likely. He already is well along on several projects. He gets very indignant when he sees a 3,000-pound car running around carrying a 150-pound man; and hopes to make the new lightweight jeep he is working on the basis of his lightweight postwar automobile. He is working up a plan for overhauling the railroads.

He has already tried and tested what he thinks could be a nationwide plan for medical care. The idea, which is ecstatically presented in a little book *Kaiser Wakes the Doctors* by Paul De Kruif, is simply one of putting medical care, like hospitalization, on an insurance basis. Back in 1933, when the Six Companies was building Parker Dam, the chief medical officer, Dr. Sidney Garfield, had tried the plan and made it work handsomely. At Grand Coulee and other projects, Kaiser set up a prepaid health plan costing 50 cents a week per man, and amortized the investment out of income.

Kaiser's gusto, the catholicity of his postwar ideas, has begun to worry his young men. They sometimes wonder how long he will go on collecting more enterprises, never pausing to figure how they will finally fit together. "We keep telling him," one of them says wistfully, "that we ought to take stock to see whether we're just a big bubble that's going to go pfiff. But he won't listen."

August 1943

Mysterious Union Carbide
By LAWRENCE P. LESSING

A bare 100 yards east of Fifth Avenue and Forty-second Street in New York, one of the most thronged crossroads of the world, stands a building that hundreds of thousands pass daily and almost no one ever sees. The building stands inconspicuously above these rushing eyes, a pilastered brick structure out of the unglamorous earlier years of the century, with a heavy clock jutting from its corner and a heavy, scrolled shield above, inscribed: Union Carbide and Carbon Building. You might easily mistake it for a bank or trust company. Union Carbide & Carbon Corp. occupies an almost similar mute relationship to the U.S. economy—a $365-million chemical skyscraper anchored deep in the vitals of the nation's life. Yet there is possibly no other great U.S. corporation about which more people know less.

To be sure, any reasonably informed citizen might marshal a few resounding generalities. Union Carbide is among the top twenty of the mightiest corporations in the land and one of the bluest chips in investment markets. Few self-respecting portfolios are without a block of its 9,278,000 outstanding common shares. In physical size Carbide lies somewhere between Du Pont and Allied Chemical, the chemical mammoths, and in the front line of technical efficiency and earning power. But beyond saying that Carbide makes money regularly, the average man's information soon peters out.

The average citizen, therefore, is never apt to see Carbide in anything but a roseate haze. Yet Carbide is one of the great underpinnings of industry. And this fact cannot be too heavily underlined at this time. For though Carbide has less in the way of direct "defense orders" than many other chemical companies, no other company is more indirectly basic to the industrial mobilization that is modern war. Carbide is one of the greatest assemblies of potential bottlenecks there is, and it is currently bending and groaning to its enormous production job with everything it has.

Steelmakers know Carbide as the major supplier of alloys for alloy steels and giant graphite electrodes for the furnaces in which to make them. Metalworkers of all kinds know Carbide as a major supplier of oxygen and acetylene gas and oxyacetylene apparatus for welding, cutting, and cleaning metals. Chemical manufacturers know Carbide as a basic source for a line of organic compounds of stunning versatility. Electrical and radio people know Carbide as a major element in carbon brushes for motors and generators and dry batteries for all uses. . . . Yet even the industrialists concerned are somewhat like the fabled blind men groping over an elephant. It is a fantastic beast, they can avow. But no one among them has ever seen the animal whole.

The reasons for this are to be found partly in the nature of the business and partly in the nature of the management, which is composed largely of engineers with a passion for anonymity. Outsiders who have been permitted even so much as a glimpse of the central mysteries are few indeed. Stories are abundant of the distinguished visitors being taken up on a West Virginia hillside and "shown over" the great South Charleston chemical works from a distance of a mile or more. Nor are the faces and names of Carbide's officers any better known than the faces of its factories. Even a major figure in the industry confesses to having met Jesse Jay Ricks, president of Union Carbide & Carbon Corp., only once and fleetingly.

"But you know," says President Ricks, "there are a great many times when we haven't got it in the neck just because we haven't had our necks out." However, most of the reticence arises from the peculiar nature of the business.

It ranges through hundreds of seemingly unrelated products, many of which the popular mind doesn't even associate with the chemical industry. It extends all the way from metals of great atomic weight, through water-white liquids, to gases that can be neither seen, smelled, nor tasted. Carbide is as much in physics as in chemistry, in that broad zone known as physical chemistry. And its processes pivot upon the physical extremes of man-made heat and cold—heat centered in its electric-arc furnaces at 6,650° Fahrenheit, and cold in the fractional distillation of liquid air down in the subsubarctic region of $-325°$ Fahrenheit. And by these two poles Carbide has steered its course for nearly a quarter of a century with a singular sense of direction.

Between these physical extremes Carbide operates against a backdrop peculiarly its own, at once medieval and futuristic, in a kind of Wagnerian drama of the elements. Its electric furnaces thunder and crackle and flame like the crucibles of some monstrous alchemist. Its carbons are molded and baked in great black plants in troglodytic gloom. And its oxygen and chemical units soar in aluminum-painted fancy—converter columns, tanks, stills, and bulbous piping—like some cold city of another planet. Carbide geography is equally spectacular, following the natural wonders, especially waterpower. For next to Aluminum Co. of America, Carbide is probably the biggest corporate user of electric power in the country. Hence its plants cluster around Niagara Falls and the Soo (Sault Ste. Marie), rise up beside the precipitous mountain streams of Norway, expand out to the new Bonneville Dam, and extend along the Kanawha River valley in West Virginia, where coal and hydroelectric power combine. Or they follow basic industries—oxygen and acetylene plants spotted like service stations wherever steel and metalworking flourish. Or they follow raw materials—natural gas in West Virginia or petroleum gases piped next door from oil refineries in Indiana and Texas. Carbide owns and operates a big tungsten mine in the high Sierras, vanadium mines in Colorado, and other mines and quarries elsewhere. And it draws rare ores and other materials from China, Rhodesia, New Caledonia, the Gold Coast, South America, and most of the world.

In World War I Union Carbide represented a quarter of a century of developments in the control of intense heat and cold, in carbides and acetylene gas—and many financial mergers. As War I began, ordnance and munition needs shot the demands for ferroalloys in steelmaking to staggering levels. Shipbuilding, railroading, tanks, guns, and all the metal fury of war pushed the oxyacetylene business into gaseous expansion. Engineers from one of Carbide's acquisitions, Linde Air Products Co., which had been organized in 1907 by a group of Clevelanders to exploit in the U.S. the German Linde process for the fractional distillation of liquid air, curled up for a few hours, sleep a night on drafting-room tables, and one construction engineer's hair turned swiftly and prematurely snow white. Linde went into the war with seven plants and came out with thirty-two.

Now Carbide is again rushing to national defense. Sweaty, metal-masked workmen stand braced with long poles before its furnace beds, pushing them to the limit and uneconomically beyond, full around the clock. Carbide is producing more ferroalloy tonnage, more calcium carbide, more oxygen, more electrodes, and more chemicals than ever before in its history.

June 1941

The Tranquil Engineers of G. E.
By GILBERT BURCK

When you walk into the executive headquarters of General Electric at Schenectady, you might think you were entering the old literature-and-arts building of some midwestern university rather than the nerve center of one of the world's biggest and most complex war-production machines. The red brick of the forty-year-old structure glows with neatness and modesty, and the wooden floors of its narrow halls creak discreetly. Inside the plain, unadorned offices, quiet as a schoolroom, solemn executives sit conversing moderately, dictating judiciously, thinking carefully. Promptly at 12:30 P.M., as if classes were adjourned, they wash up and file down the halls to the office lunchroom. They behave as calmly as if they knew precisely what they had to do every day for twelve months ahead.

Yet they have reason for acting frenzied. General Electric is not only making more different war products than any other American company but is also undergoing more radical changes in less than two years than it has in any twenty previous years. By the end of 1942, G.E. will have tripled what it used to regard as its "normal" volume. Beyond that, it is completely altering the composition of its volume. Last year, for example, it made some $100 million worth of household appliances; by the end of 1942 practically all of them will be replaced by lethal appliances. All the turbosuperchargers it produced in 1939, on the other hand, were made in a single room and were worth less than $100,000; by the end of 1942 they will require several whole buildings and be worth hundreds of times more (the precise amount being a military secret). In 1936 annual production of marine turbine and gear sets amounted to less than $1 million; by the end of 1942 it will exceed $300 million—more than G.E.'s total billings in any year from 1931 through 1936.

One reason G.E. displays so tranquil a self-reliance before so gigantic an assignment is that it has habitually taken things in stride. It began in 1892 as a merger of an electrical company owned by a Lynn shoe manufacturer named Charles A. Coffin and another company organized by J. P. Morgan. Under Coffin's management it skirted the 1907 depression. Under the dual leadership of Owen D. Young and Gerard Swope, who succeeded Coffin, G.E. earned a reputation for being a model corporation, glorified its name, and increased its sales by taking on consumers' goods, for which it competed with more dignity than ferocity. Its profits have been consistently large, its dividends consecutively generous, and its stock a perennial blue chip.

But there is more behind the company's quiet assumption of competence than all this refulgence. G.E. is run by engineers, men who (whether they are actually graduate engineers or not) approach problems in an analytical, orderly fashion and try to account for things with mathematical precision. They are highly rational, sometimes humorless, and completely poised. Tolerating no prima donnas, not even among the scientists and inventors the company has publicized so widely, G.E. engineers have merged their erratic tendencies, if any, into the corporate personality. Their minds work with the accuracy and uniformity of slide rules, and they take the durability of G.E. as much for granted as they do the binomial theorem.

It was only natural for these engineer-managers to regard the war almost as if it were primarily another phase in the company's history. Whenever any phase of the company's history becomes important enough to demand the time of several top men, G.E. habitually chooses a management committee to attend to it. By the spring of 1940 war orders were beginning to be important and promised to become rapidly more important. So President Charles E. Wilson sat down and dictated a memo announcing the appointment of a four-man Defense Advisory Committee (now called the War Projects Committee) to integrate and expedite all the company's war orders.

The group meets daily—and even days on end—if necessary. Its special problems have been to accelerate the acquisition of more factories, more men, more supplies, more and different research and engineering, and the change of consumer-goods facilities to war products.

When the subject of the postwar world comes up, G.E.'s engineers haul out a sheaf of blueprints on which the new world is worked out to three decimal points, and in which its own position is as clearly defined as the details of one of its turbines.

This project, begun a year ago, was assigned to Vice President David C. Prince, in charge of the Planning Committee. He broke down an estimated postwar income of $110 billion. He figured that output for food, housing, etc., would rise from $55.2 billion (in 1940) to $64 billion, consumers' durable goods would rise from $8.3 billion to $13 billion. He estimated that if G.E. gets 25 percent of the electrical market, as it has in the past, it will gross $722 million. Charlie Wilson says, banging his hamlike fist, G.E. is a billion-dollar company and is going to stay one.

March 1942

Shot, Shell and Bombs

By EDWARD MORROW

"The basis of the tactics of the U.S. Army may be said to be a belief in the almighty power of materialistic fighting strength. . . . U.S. forces, who place all faith in firepower, are weak in hand-to-hand combat." —Japanese field commanders reporting to Imperial Army Headquarters.

"[Eisenhower's] unfavorable experience in four Aachen offensives has not dissuaded the Allied commander from employing matériel superiority in old-style operations . . . but even the greatest matériel superiority will eventually be exhausted." —Max Krull on D.N.P.

The German and Japanese commentators were both wrong and right. It was wrong to assume that American soldiers had no stomach for close combat; the contrary was shown at Salerno, in the Battle of the Bulge, at Tarawa and Iwo Jima, and on Okinawa. But they were right in saying that U.S. military men rely heavily on matériel, on tremendous artillery preparation and air bombardment. That is settled American military policy: if tons of explosives will save the life of a single American soldier, tons will be used. They have been used. In the first two days at Cassino, for example, U.S. guns fired 11,000 tons of shells. In tactical bombings, U.S. planes smothered German positions with explosives, while the shattered Luftwaffe could reply but weakly. In Pacific actions, where battleships have thrown 14- and 16-inch shells at the Japanese islands day after day, the disparity has been fantastic.

American generals could expend ammunition in this seemingly profligate manner because they had it. They had it because American munitions production surpassed prewar estimates not only of the enemy but of American military men as well. This production came from one of the most remarkable plants ever created—a $3-billion industry for manufacturing explosives and loading them into shells and bombs; a plant built in three years, scattered across the country, and covering two-thirds as much ground as the state of Rhode Island; a plant manned by 225,000 workers, more than half of them women, who had to be taught everything, and managed for the government by companies (e.g., Quaker Oats and Coca-Cola) likewise innocent of any explosives experience; a plant kept at high effciency through competition but without a profit motive; a plant that introduced mass-production methods into one of the most conservative crafts in the world; a plant operated in spite of a sea of troubles.

The measure of the job done can perhaps best be expressed thus: in 1944 and so far in 1945, the U.S. has produced each month almost as much ammunition as in the entire nineteen months of its participation in World War I.

The figures numb the mind: The U.S. has made more than five billion pounds of TNT. . . . Taking July, 1941, well after the start of the "defense" period, as 100, production has risen 5,900 percent. . . . Up to the end of 1944, 15 million tons of ground-artillery ammunition and aerial bombs had been manufactured . . . and so on.

Fuse-assembly lines, which started by producing 400 fuses an hour, now produce 2,500 an hour.

From January, 1943, to the spring of 1945, the productivity of labor in loading plants went up about 150 percent. But for these gains ammunition production would have required more than half a million persons and twice as much land.

Costs came down as effciency went up. TNT, which cost 50 cents a pound in the last war and 17 cents a pound before this war, now costs about 6¼ cents a pound. Composition B, a combination of RDX and TNT, cost 30 cents a pound in 1943 and 11 cents a pound in 1945. The cost of loading a 500-pound bomb, which was $18.97 in January, 1943, had been cut to $4.07 early this year.

This tidal wave of destructive production is all the more amazing because it was the achievement of a nation that for a generation had been bent on ignoring the possibility of conflict and forgetting the arts of war. After World War I, U.S. ammunition plants were dismantled—even the plans from which they had been built were lost. During one year of the Coolidge Administration, the entire

Ordnance Department had an appropriation of $7,750,000, of which about one-seventh could be used for ammunition experiment and manufacture. The Nye Committee and the "Merchants of Death" uproar of 1934 made munitions a highly undesirable business. Such war planning as the Ordnance Department did was almost surreptitious: officers and civilian employees were assigned to the design of munitions plants and inspection of possible sites as "holdover jobs" —that is, jobs to be done when there was nothing else to do.

September 1945

The Pacific Sweep

By RALPH DELAHAYE PAINE, JR.

Okinawa, the greatest and most ferocious battle yet fought in the Pacific, marks, as well as any single event ever can, the close of one phase of the war against Japan and the opening of another. What dawned on April 1 over the gnarled pines and ancient tombs behind the Hagushi beachhead, where Admiral Turner's amphibious forces landed, was the Battle of Japan. The theater had shifted from atolls and tropic jungle and limitless ocean expanses to the fragile towns and terraced fields of Asia itself. Okinawa is an island—but it is Asia.

Okinawa and the associated operations represent the biggest amphibious assault of the Pacific, and that assault precipitated the greatest sea-air battle of all time. But above all, Okinawa was the end of the great Pacific sweep, the magnificent westward advance that thrust our fleet and our bases across the central and western Pacific to the waters of the East China Sea. From Tarawa to Okinawa was less then seventeen months. The achievement is unique.

The great land campaigns of western Europe and Russia, enormous though their scale has been, can be related to the past. Von Moltke can be applied to the Battle of France; Hitler can be read in connection with Napoleon. But for parallels for the central and western Pacific the books will be searched in vain. Past naval battles and campaigns—Salamis, Lepanto, Trafalgar, Jutland—are dwarfed beyond valid comparison. New measures of naval power have been established rendering traditional standards obsolete. Technology, geography, and the times in which we live were so compounded as to release the American genius upon a unique problem, one that in all probability will arise only once upon this earth.

The solution on the sea and under it, in the air and on the particles of land involved, was peculiarly American. The weapons, the strategy and tactics, the spirit and pace of the actions brand it indelibly made in the U.S.A.

The three-dimensional war of the Pacific is so technical, and its parts so complexly interrelated, that it is impossible to isolate any one determining factor of success—unless it be that vague if very real thing, the American genius. There were three outstanding lines of development upon which that genius was lavished: the development first of carrier warfare, second of logistical support at distances and under conditions enforced by Pacific geography, and third of amphibious warfare. Not the least of these was logistical support.

As decisive battles approached, the Navy was defending a shifting sea frontier of 7,500 miles, extending in a giant arc from the Aleutians down through Midway, the Hawaiian Islands, and such atoll outposts as Johnston, Palmyra, and Canton islands, down through Samoa, the Fijis, the New Hebrides, and New Caledonia, down onto New Zealand and finally Australia at the southern and southwestern extremes.

The rhythm of the supply line is never perfect, the demands never constant, and the major bases like Pearl and Guam serve as great catch basins when supplies are accumulating and as immense reservoirs during a major operation when expenditures are high. Moreover they stock a range and variety of supplies and spares that would merely clutter up the smaller bases.

Guam is something new in Pacific logistics. From the Marshalls on, the Navy has fought typically from anchorages like Majuro, Manus, Eniwetok, and Ulithi—places that have become as familiar—if not so alluring—to the U.S. sailor as Brooklyn, Bremerton, or San Diego. The fleet is now so large that it is difficult to find anchoranges big enough to hold even the forces operating in one area. A fleet anchorage like Ulithi in the western Carolines bears little resemblance to the orthodox ideas of a naval base. The natives have been herded together on one of the low coral islands.

More than half a million tons of
supplies were landed in the first
ten days after the Okinawa invasion.
In a few months Seabees and Army
Engineers transformed the island
into the finest advance base
in the Pacific.

U.S. COAST GUARD PHOTO

Another is reserved for recreation for the ships when they come in—beaches for swimming, and dry land on which to picnic and drink beer. Ashore on the other islands are the characteristic airstrips, the Quonsets, tents, and barracks, the offices among the palms, the boat landings, and a few temporary docks.

Virtually all normal facilities of a naval base are afloat in ships, barges, and floating drydock, in stores ships, tankers, provision ships, repair ships, water-distilling ships, floating warehouses, aviation supply ships, refrigeration ships, ammunition ships, jeep carriers. The salvaged hull of the old battleship *Oregon* that rounded the Horn in 1898 is a floating storehouse. Except for the shelter afforded by the surrounding reefs, the entire operations could be carried on as efficiently at sea.

From the depots on the West Coast through to the advanced bases the movement of supplies is still within the limits of traditional logistics—enormously complicated in detail but a problem amenable to accumulated experience in procurement, accounting, inventory control, warehousing, materials-handling techniques, and shipping. Available shipping has been the determining factor in all planning. There has never been enough shipping but the stringency has made for efficient use of it—indeed for efficient operation all along the line.

The paperwork required as material passes along the line is fantastic, but paper—paper by the thousands of tons—is the only tool adequate to keep track of it. The basic papers are the allowance lists, the lists prepared from experience showing down to the last bolt, bulb, and chocolate bar the expected consumption of a given unit for a given period. Sudden changes in tactics, unpredictable losses, unforeseen combat conditions always upset supply routine. Demands for smoke oil for screening against suicide planes put a terrific strain on the oil industry. Urgent calls brought forth a flood of belly tanks that, as soon as operating ranges decreased and planes found less and less need to drop them, backed up on bases and depots as far as Oakland. But allowance lists are constantly modified in the light of experience and reshaped to fit each individual operation. And from these lists the mainland supply depots and annexes always have a fairly accurate picture of what will be needed forward. The supply units forward try to maintain stocks at a given level—sixty or ninety or one hundred and twenty days—and requisition accordingly.

Many emergencies are met by air supply. Air freight can handle anything up to cruiser propellers; on one occasion a five-ton hub was put on one plane, the three-ton blades in others, and flown from Pearl to Manus. Air evacuation of wounded has become routine. More than 15,000 were taken out of Okinawa in the first two months after the Yontan field was serviceable for transports.

For the Okinawa and related operations the planning started last September. Some idea of the complexity can be gleaned from one phase of the problem: getting ships and men at the right point at the right time. Exclusive of small landing craft, some 1,400 ships took part at Okinawa. Ships travel at different speeds. LST's cannot make much more than eight or nine knots; LSD's eleven or twelve; attack transports, fifteen. Units moved from all areas of the Pacific. The northern attack group at Okinawa trained and staged and rehearsed in the Guadalcanal area. The southern attack group left from Leyte. The floating reserve staged from the Marianas and from Espíritu Santo in the New Hebrides. General Buckner's Tenth Army headquarters and service units embarked at Pearl Harbor, and certain garrison elements staged from the West Coast. All had to have surface screens and air cover. Some units had to be serviced on the way out; some had to be combat-loaded in forward anchorages. All had to arrive at a pinpoint on the charts at a precise moment after steaming anywhere from 1,200 to 8,000 miles. And they did.

Whether the Japanese will surrender before their country is devastated from the air is not a question any American can answer. Americans who will devote hundreds of millions of dollars of equipment to effect the air-sea rescue of one lone pilot adrift in the sea can never penetrate the mind of a people who produced the Kamikaze. The burden the Navy has carried so brilliantly in the Pacific will inevitably be shared more and more with the Army and its Air Forces. But the Navy has performed its historic duty: the Navy got them there.

July 1945

Science

Basic Science: A Way to Peace
By LAWRENCE P. LESSING

The figures fall a little flatly on the page. About $10 billion of U.S. funds for scientific research and development in four years of war. About $500 million spent by the Office of Scientific Research and Development (OSRD) in mobilizing the basic sciences and scientists. Some 15,000 scientists—aerodynamicists to zoologists—engaged in some 2,500 research contracts with nearly 500 institutions. The grand total itself, with research costs all mixed up in government contracts and the services, is only an estimate. But $10 billion may serve to symbolize the most intensive and extensive use of science by government in any equal period of history. A record of OSRD's activities is now in the process of filling eighty to ninety fat official volumes, which may well take a decade of peacetime industry to digest. And shining malevolently in OSRD's crown is atomic power, that great new force for good or evil. . . .

This much may be put down as basic: given the will, talent, and funds, there is almost no physical problem within bounds that will not yield to applied science. The tools are at hand or can be invented. The only major problem is to decide what is best to be done.

The consensus of all parties is that the main drive of U.S. science now must be to explore and expand basic science. The battle has been over the means to that end. A bill setting up a National Science Foundation was a compromise, with the imperatives of national defense carrying the major point. The Air Forces and other branches are plugging for big programs of their own, and the Navy has already launched an Office of Research and Inventions to spend some $40 million a year on what it calls "basic research" — though no military bureau is ever able to keep to really basic research in its overcharged desire for applied results. U.S. industry is doubling and tripling its research facilities and expenditures—all applied research—and the competition for scientists, already short in the universities, is one of the most crucial of the day. Without a top U.S. science policy, a restraining hand, and quick repairs on the universities' deficits of teachers and graduate students, this can only further wreck the basic sciences.

Basic research is most peculiar. It does not depend on money, though it needs money. It cannot arise from planning, though it needs planning. It lodges in the erratic and creative recesses of man's brain. No definite results guaranteed.

The sharpest distinction is expressed in one scientist's observation that for $50 million he would take on the job of building a rocket to carry an expedition to the moon, because all the technical details are known and lying about. But he would quote no figure on developing a theory of nuclear-energy levels or why the drawing of wire alters its electrical resistance according to no known laws. These last two are basic research, and will not come out of money alone. The right man with a slide rule and a bit of wire might get an answer for 50 cents; $20 million might go to 200 men, with no answer forthcoming. There are thousands of subjects like these—the destiny of spiral nebulae, the properties of newly discovered subatomic particles called mesons, problems of combustion, basic problems in meteorology—in which the discovery of new laws would have resounding implications. The problem is how to arrive at them.

Science, like happiness and other great creative objectives of life, rarely responds to direct assault. The most wasteful way to do research is to pour $16 million into infantile-paralysis research alone, or $25 million into cancer alone; for, just as penicillin was discovered wholly by chance in investigating staphylococci, the real answers may lie anywhere in unrelated fields. Yet, in spite of waste, the attempt must be made. The new foundation proposes an infinitely broader fertilization of the whole field of science—and may be equally wasteful. Basic science is extremely risky. If you're not out on a limb, it isn't basic research.

Dr. Leo Szilard, asked to explain the great European flowering of science, said, "Leisure." It was not a sin in Europe to be at leisure or doing "nothing" in the practical sense. In the U.S. the needs of a growing nation were forever pulling science out of the laboratories into industry, or out of pure research into administration, with all the major honors and rewards for the practical doers. To counteract this, Szilard suggests that the new foundation set whatever strict talent standards it wishes, then give to worthy young scientists $12,000 a year for life to pursue whatever interests them, with government matching $5,000 for every $1,000 they spend on research. Fantastic as this may sound to practical minds, there is no doubt that some such social techniques will have to be explored by the new foundation if it is to serve its ends.

Those ends are now deeply and inextricably bound up in building the peace. Science is not going to crush anybody, if we put it to use for the proper ends and draw science into our councils. It is going to crush everybody if we don't. There is the old moral issue reappearing in new and vital form. The proper ends of science now are peace and the works of peace, freedom and the works of freedom. Sometime, in spite of everything we can do— and everything must be done that reason and good counsel turn up—we may be at war again. And then a free science will be ready to our hand, stronger than ever, strong with the strength of many million men. But now it is peace.

June 1946

Mechanical Brains

By LOUIS N. RIDENOUR

An army publicity release announcing the ENIAC, an automatic computing machine of unprecedented speed and capabilities, was made available to morning newspapers of Saturday, February 16, 1946. Reporters who went to Philadelphia for the first publc showing of the ENIAC (Electronic Numerical Integrator and Computer) saw a roomful of electronic equipment that could solve the complex ballistic problem of a shell's flight in less time than it takes the actual shell to hurtle from gun to target. Some papers did not run the story; most cut it considerably. Editors, obviously, were not convinced that the portents of a new era were at hand.

Since then, however, the belief has been growing that the computers of which the ENIAC is merely the forerunner will have profound effects not only upon science and engineering, but upon business and government as well. Indeed, the belief is growing that these new machines, because of their similarity to the human brain and their potential ability to fit into complicated control mechanisms, are the beginning of a second industrial revolution.

As an example of the vistas opening up, consider the Air Force's Project SCOOP, or Scientific Computation of Optimum Programs. SCOOP is an extension of an economic research project developed by Professor Wassily Leontief at Harvard. Its idea is that the industries of the country interact with one another in a measurable and predictable way. Thus the production of shoes, for example, has a determinable influence on the cattle business, and on the business in thread, nails, chemicals, and transportation. Leontief hopes to set up equations that will express all these complicated interrelationships. Once this is done, he hopes by means of the new machines to predict the impact on the nation's economy of any program proposed by the Air Force. If he is right, it may be possible to determine whether the building of heavy bombers in wartime does more damage to the enemy economy or ours; this was a matter of some disagreement during the recent war. In any event, the great new computers promise to promote many basic studies of economic behavior.

All together, various agencies of the federal government, led by Army Ordnance, which pioneered in the field and sponsored the ENIAC, are spending several million a year on computer development. . . . Firms with vested interests in business machinery or electronics are furiously busy behind the scenes. One major university, Illinois, is building a machine on its own; several others are working on government contracts. Even the highly abstract Institute for Advanced Study at Princeton, which has never before concerned itself with equipment or experiments, has undertaken the design and building of one of the most ambitious machines yet attempted.

Much of this work is a gamble, in the sense that what is being attempted has never been done before. Today's computer engineers may sometimes wonder whether history will remember them as it does Charles Babbage, who was Lucasian Professor of Mathematics at Cambridge a century ago. Babbage was the first to envisage a computing machine of the modern type. He obtained large sums of British government money for its construction, and he died without completing it. The mechanical engineering of his day simply was not equal to the task of building his "analytical engine," which was to work by means of intricate wheels and levers. In the intervening century small computing machines of the familiar desk type came into wide use; but not until the late war did anything resembling Babbage's dream appear.

The modern high-speed automatic digital computer has the following major parts:

An **arithmetical organ** to perform the individual additions, multiplications, or other operations called for by the problem. It is made up of complicated vacuum-tube circuits, and is a close electronic parallel of the desk computer.

A **memory organ** to receive, store, transmit, and erase (as required) not only the numbers that are involved in the problem as initial information or as intermediate results, but also *orders,* which are instructions to the machine to perform some specific individual operation. This organ is presently the least satisfactory part of machines being designed.

A **control organ** to keep track of the calculation, determine which individual operation should be performed next, and cause its execution. This takes the place of the human computer's brain. It is a complicated electronic device that channels numbers and orders from the memory into the arithmetical organ, oversees the operations performed on them, and returns the results to the memory for retention and future use.

An **input-output organ** to enable the machine to communicate with its human masters. This permits the machine to be supplied initially with data and instructions appropriate to the problem, usually by typing out numbers and orders on a suitably modified Teletypewriter. It also enables the machine to display final results (or, on request, intermediate results) by the same means.

When a mathematical problem is to be presented to such a machine, it must be programed: that is, broken down into the individual steps to be performed one after another. The numerical information entering the problem must also be supplied to the machine. The input organ reads the program of orders and numbers into the machine's memory at the start of computation, and the work thereafter is done entirely within the machine. . . .

Inevitably, machines of such abilities invite comparison with the human brain. People have loosely called them "thinking machines." This designation is rejected by many of today's scientists, who believe that today's machines do not pretend to originate anything, or to think, precisely because we do not yet know how to order them to perform this service.

It is true that the elementary organization of modern computers has many parallels with what we know of the organization of the human brain. The computing machines we are now building, however, are enormously simpler than the brain, and therefore enormously limited by comparison. The brain has 10 billion neurons for responding to stimuli; the ENIAC has only some 18,000 of the all-or-none electronic circuits that serve it in place of neurons. Presumably, the limitations of today's machines as reasoning devices arise entirely because of the gross simplicity of the best machines we now can build.

It must not be inferred that the advantage is all on the side of the brain. Computing machines, even those of the present day, are incomparably superior to the brain in speed of operation. Their electronic circuits have a time of complete action, from stimulus to response, lasting less than a millionth of a second. In comparison, the "synaptic delay," which separates the arrival of impulses on a neuron and the propagation of impulses in response, is nearly a thousandth of a second. A human computer with a desk calculator can multiply together two numbers, each having ten decimal digits, in about fifteen seconds; a modern machine will do the same problem in less than half a thousandth of a second.

This speed has important consequences. First, it is clear why the machine must operate entirely automatically. It is so fast that it cannot stop and wait for pitifully slow human reflexes to instruct it on each individual operation; hence it must have a control organ whose speed matches that of its computations. Second, the machine's great speed defines its use and its very reason for being. Since it can perform calculations 10,000 times faster than human computers, such a machine is clearly not needed merely to expedite calculations of the orthodox sort. Instead, it will enable scientists to make systematic attacks on new or unformulated problems in fields where expensive experiments go on in lieu of computing, or no work has as yet been done.

The high-speed computing machine is the experimental laboratory of the applied mathematician. Faced with a new problem, he can run off on the machine a number of special cases of its numerical solution. From a study of the results, he can begin to make guesses about the general method of handling the new problem. Many mathematicians believe that they can thus solve problems now without solution, using something less than the deep physical insight that was necessary for such great advances as Maxwell's electromagnetic theory of light, or Einstein's relativity.

Many scientific problems can be formulated mathematically on the basis of what we know today, but not solved. The whole theory of non-linear differential equations is in a primitive state, though these equations are fundamental to our understanding of such important phenomena as the passage of a shock wave (from an explosion, say, or from the leading wing edge of a supersonic airplane) through a compressible fluid such as air. Aerodynamics has been notorious in its recourse to experimental trials in lieu of the analytical treatment of problems. To drive the fans of the wind tunnels planned for the Air Force's great Air Engineering Development Center would take something like the entire power output of Boulder Dam. Dr. John von Neumann of the Institute for Advanced Studies at Princeton estimates that some three-quarters of such expensive and difficult work would be unnecessary, given adequate computing facilities.

The capability of the digital computer is summed up in von Neumann's remark that it is "the totality of all simple gadgets." This means that a computer can do anything that any machine can be built to do. Its applications in business are immediate and clear. It can handle the accounting, payroll, billing, and tax computation of any company, no matter how complicated the rules.

More than this, the machine can play an important role in management. Operating a business consists mainly in making decisions that will affect its future position. Such decisions are made on the basis of an executive's assessment of the meaning of the pattern of internal and external relationships: with employees and with society at large. The trends of change in such relationships are also important. A century or so ago, an executive's brain could store and process all the relevant information, and deduce significant trends. Today the job of information storage and processing is far too big for one or even several brains.

The date at which the revolutionary new computers will be available to business is problematical. So far, only five machines are finished and operating: an early relay-type computer, built by Bell Telephone Laboratories; two more advanced relay types, called Mark I and II, built by Professor Howard Aiken of Harvard; the ENIAC, now at Aberdeen Proving Ground; and the Selective Sequence Electronic Calculator, a blend of electronic and punched-card techniques, built by I.B.M. and unveiled last year. None of these machines is so ambitious as the ones now in development.

Most of the advanced work is, as usual, being done in universities. Aiken of Harvard will soon complete a Mark III machine. The University of Pennsylvania, which built the ENIAC, is completing for Army Ordnance a more advanced successor called the EDVAC. The Institute for Advanced Study is expected to have a model of its advanced machine going sometime this year. A group at M.I.T. is working on a machine of extremely high speed, whose completion is some years away.

Granted that our new ability to perform complicated computations rapidly will have a profound impact on science, including social science, and on large-scale management in business and government: are other results to be expected? Norbert Wiener, an M.I.T. mathematician whose interest in the social influence of technological change is keener than most scientists', thinks so. In his recent book, *Cybernetics*, he suggests that we are on the eve of the second industrial revolution.

In the first industrial revolution, machines replaced animals (including man) in doing physical work. Despite the obvious superiority of machines to men in mechanical work, however, man has so far excelled and dominated the machine by the use of his sense organs and his judgment. In the work of making a large excavation, for example, no possible standard of living, however low, will enable a man with a hand shovel to compete with a power shovel on a purely economic basis.

The shovel operator's presence at the controls defines the state of our technology. We have not yet progressed far enough to complete the control organization of the machine—its sense organs and nervous system—save by inserting a man, whose remarkable adaptability enables him to serve those higher functions that our engineering has not yet satisfactorily mechanized.

Thus, while the first industrial revolution involved the substitution of machinery for man's musculature, the second will replace by inanimate devices man's senses, nervous system, and brain. It cannot be doubted that this is desirable from the standpoint of "doing the job." Though certain men at certain times perform superlatively in controlling machines, the overall performance of a satisfactory automatic control system is likely to be preferable, since a machine cannot be frightened, distracted, bored, or unionized as readily as a human operator can.

In our society "doing the job" is ordinarily reckoned as the leading consideration, so that men will presumably be replaced by the new machines as rapidly as our technology permits. The present activities of some labor organizations seem calculated to encourage this trend. Rising wages put a premium on high productivity per worker, and thus on fewer workers. Any acts of capricious irresponsibility or malicious obstructionism on the part of labor unions (and some union activities must have this aspect to employers) put a premium on as complete an elimination of the human worker as possible.

The subsidiary social effects of "doing the job" are usually unforeseen and often undesirable. Wiener speaks of a possible future society in which the white-collar worker, the machine operator, the man who uses his endowments in any routine sort of way, will be as unable to compete with the machine as the human beast of burden with the motor truck. Some time ago, he writes, he discussed with labor leaders the possible social consequences of such a development. The picture of Professor Wiener—who is unusual among professors in looking exactly like one—debating these abstract considerations with hardboiled labor leaders is extraordinarily appealing. Undeniably, however, the social consequences of machines that can perform the functions of the human brain are incalculable, and may be disastrous.

Devices of mechanical sensing and control extend far beyond the digital computers. They include all sorts of gauges, servo-mechanisms, and the like. But the digital computer is likely to be embodied in every complicated control mechanism as its brain, the inanimate substitute for the cerebral cortex that is the most complicated and most adaptable part of man's nervous system. The automatic digital computer is currently the highest expression of man's mechanization of mental function. As such, it is the most profoundly significant symbol of the second industrial revolution, which is on the way.

April 1949

Peace

The Capitalist Takes a Holiday

By JOHN McDONALD

Salmon fishing is the greatest of freshwater sports. When a solid thirty pounds of aquatic game, capable of hurling himself over a fifteen-foot waterfall, casually plucks a gay one-inch trifle some distance from your light rod, the jolt of astonishment to both you and the fish concentrates in one moment of unstable equilibrium its quintessential sensation. For such a moment you may have traveled a thousand train-miles to eastern Canada or Newfoundland, five or twenty-five jeep-miles from the railroad station, and a terminal stretch by canoe or on foot; and then with your not inexhaustible arm you may have laid out countless casts of the fly along the runs and pools of a wilderness river, in the company of clouds of waspish black flies, for a number of despairing days and dreamful nights.

The events subsequent to the strike matter too, as gold in the sack matters to the prospector. The equilibrium is broken with an explosive rush and a long, scudding leap, and the salmon is running downstream with his ally the current, your screaming reel warm, its line melting into the river. He might go right on and bang off if you let him. But you go after him, leaving your canoe if you were in one, following along the shore and pulling back against him from the side. He is vulnerable to side strain and bears over toward your side of the river; in large, powerful water he may come around in a vast eddy and right back at you. But most likely you will just get him, in a state of sullen rage, into quieter water downstream. You will then groan with anxious pleasure at the pull, dropping the tip of your rod to slacken the tension, or holding it steady, in accordance with your tactics, as he takes long runs into high sweeping leaps. There is no feel in fishing quite like the wild run of a salmon. Gradually you work your way below him, at which his contrariety sends him plowing back upstream, with the current against his strength and so in your favor. Outwitted in mobile maneuvers, he stops, jigs and jerks the line with mulelike kicks of such vigor as to make it unbelievable that the fly will hold—and often it does not, resulting in the awful sensation of a loose line washing away and your heart sinking to your boot. But if you are skillful, have him well hooked, and can keep him from settling into a long bottom sulk, you should have him in thirty minutes or much less; if he succeeds in sulking you may tug it out for a couple of hours, and you may be a quarter of a mile from where the struggle began before you draw him exhausted inshore and he lies over on his side to be tailed, netted, or gaffed onto land and quickly knocked out. The silver sunbeams shining in the green, wet grass inspire hope enough to carry you, if necessary, through the rest of the season and the whole of the next.

May 1946

The Boom

By SIDNEY OLSON

There is a rich queerness to the U.S. scene in this summer of 1946. Everything is bright and sharply visible, but the sum of it doesn't seem to make much sense. Like a surrealist landscape, it is brilliant, gaudy, carefully drawn, and yet somehow nightmarish, distorted, and spotted with irrelevancies. This is the postwar, this is the dream era, this is what everyone waited through the blackouts for; now the lights have come on but the spectacle is so vast and confusing that it is hard to understand. The U.S. is a great collection of contradictions, ironies, excesses, and shortages. Hand in hand go the grossest vulgarities and the profoundest soul-searchings. A revival of religious feeling heaves up in the middle of the age of doubt. People spend more—and save more—than ever before.

The Great American Boom is on, and there is no measuring it; the old yardsticks won't do. The people and their money behave queerly, and very humanly, which is to say contrary to the economic graphs. Most economists were caught short by the staggering retail-buying boom last fall, when the sale of consumers' goods was limited only by the number of people who could get into stores and the durability of salesclerks. Government economists not only failed to foresee a shortage of labor but predicted great unemployment during the reconversion period. Their charts are not charts of the U.S. people; the U.S. people are not always predictable.

So the Boom is on, the biggest in American economic history. Almost all the curves are up. The market is bull—or was when this went to press. There is a powerful, a consuming demand for everything that one can eat, wear, enjoy, read, dye, repair, paint, drink, see, ride, taste, and rest in. The nylon line is the symbol of 1946—at any given time of day, all over the U.S., thousands of women are patiently shuffling into hosiery stores.

Throughout the nation there is at large a vast force of spending money, surging violently about the economy, like an Olympian bull in an old curiosity shop, battering its way in and out of stores and through the banks and into the stock market and off to the black market and on into the amusement industry. Everything that is made is bought up as fast as it appears. There seems to be no bottom to the demand, no bottom to the American purse. Toulouse-Lautrecs at $30,000, mink coats at $15,000, men's wrist watches at $1,000—all sell just about as fast as egg beaters, table radios, and pork chops.

The Boom now under way is an abnormality, a thing far beyond such a peaceful thing as "prosperity." It is the sudden release of an unprecedented amount of money into a market unprecedentedly bare of goods.

The country is short of lumber, coal, steel, tin, lead, antimony, textile piece goods, shellac, glass, lead pipe, paint, copper, mercury scrap, platinum scrap, men's suits, children's clothing, film, cameras, towels, automobiles, trucks, tractors, bourbon, Scotch, pianos, radios, washing machines, telephones . . . the list of shortages is endless, almost; the demand is fantastic; everyone seems to have money, no one seems to go broke.

"An optimist, in the atomic age, is a person who thinks the future is uncertain." —Lindsay and Crouse *(State of the Union).*

June 1946

The Fifties

It is the Chemical Century. There is another phe-
nomenon to be noticed. The management of companies by
their founders and proprietors is now being shifted to
corporate bureaucracies, i.e., echelons of men trained in
appropriate techniques. The development, which has been
going on gradually over the years, is now very evident; a
group portrait of the managers at Du Pont (which is
preeminent in the Chemical Century) shows how the
technique works. In the development of these manage-
ment techniques corporations begin a self-conscious ex-
amination of themselves, of their own attitudes and
mores. Fortunately for Capitalism, there are still some
traditional entrepreneurial types around, and their por-
traits hang among the corporate bureaucracies, and
among the bureaucracies of government, which are also
multiplying and exerting a sometimes stultifying force.

In one corner of the gallery six prophets look down on
the scene and hazard their guesses at what the world is
going to look like in 1980.

The Chemical Century
By LAWRENCE LESSING

Chemicals must now be considered the premier industry of the U.S. Its rise has been recent, precipitous, and largely unnoticed. For most of the first half of the century the title was held by the automobile industry, which is now leveling off on a high plateau of maturity. For the rest of the century the title is likely to be sharply contested by that loose federation of industries pivoting upon the electrical-electronic-nucleonic sciences, which also has had an enormous growth whose ends cannot yet be foreseen. But as of now, the chemical industry cannot be matched by any other in dynamics, growth, earnings, and potential for the future.

From being only a small inorganic chemical industry at the turn of the century, far outstripped by Germany's organic industry through World War I, U.S. chemicals must now be reckoned among the great industrial forces of our times. By World War II it had grown so strong that it was ready to beat the Germans at their own game.

The industry's role then was largely to supply the managerial talent to build and run some $3 billion in government war plants. The peak of that program was the creation of a $1-billion synthetic-rubber industry out of almost nothing in two years flat. The industry also supplied much of the indispensable talent for building or operating another $1 billion or so of atomic-energy plants.

Beyond that, the industry opened its own plant valves wide and in four years poured into the war economy some $20 billion in basic chemicals, intermediates, dyes, solvents, drugs, resins, plastics, coatings, fibers, filaments, and the hundreds of other chemical products that now permeate all industrial life. When the war ended, the industry simply turned back most of the specialized plants to government, and flipped its chemical stream back to peacetime channels.

By 1948, with new capacity flooding in, the stupendous ten-year record (based on twenty-three companies) stood at: a 111 percent rise in total assets to about $3.3 billion; a 234 percent jump in net sales; and a 125 percent increase in net profits. The industry is now at the stage of consolidating and digesting one of the most rapid expansions of physical plant in history.

Such statistics cannot frame the whole bulging picture. They refer only to those primary producers that, in the main, supply basic chemicals and intermediates to industry. These include some fifty companies, led by Du Pont, which is still the giant.

But the chemical industry is larger than any of its largest statistics. It now feeds all sixty-eight industrial divisions of the U.S. Department of Commerce. If all its basic and process-industry ramifications were rolled into one, they would account for at least 20 percent of the total national product. Chemistry, in fact, is a great, yeasty force at the center of the economy, creating new industries and re-creating old ones, and working changes on all sides.

March 1950

Du Pont, a New Phenomenon
By LAWRENCE LESSING

E. I. du Pont de Nemours & Co., founded in 1802, is a new phenomenon, not yet clearly defined or accounted for by the old or new economics. Du Pont is Big Business. It is one of that handful of great corporate growths—neither monopoly nor the pure competitive ideal of nineteenth-century liberalism—that find themselves in uneasy conflict with the crosscurrents of the age. That such bigness meets some vital need of the people and the times is bluntly and brutally proved in war. When the huge, complex Hanford plutonium works had to be created in a hurry for the atomic-bomb program, only a company of the size and skill of Du Pont could have rushed it through from design to production. When the stepped-up program for the new hydrogen bomb called for another tremendous plant last July, it was again Du Pont that was called in. Yet it is typical of the disjointedness of the times that even while Du Pont was being enlisted in the greatest of all projects to prevent the next war or, failing that, to win it, Du Pont was in the midst of a heavy antitrust attack from another branch of the government seeking to penalize it for bigness.

Neither Du Pont nor any other intelligent Big Business, however, can pin its justification on war. Du Pont's contributions to peace have been more considerable than any of its contributions to war, and its bigness resides inherently in the greatness of the country and the technology it serves.

Du Pont is in the rank of great corporations that by their mastery of organization, mass-production technology, and growth have lifted themselves to a new level of competitive enterprise more stable and orderly than any heretofore. These new corporate growths seem to move to a new set of laws. They pursue, for instance, the reverse of immediate maximum profits at minimum risk. Words such as "monopolistic competition" or "oligopoly" — revealing a healthy distrust of private concentrations of power— raise emotions that only obscure the effort toward clear definition. The companies themselves have not been blameless in giving cause for attack, but a clear definition and recognition of this new level of enterprise have become imperative.

The background from which the modern E. I. du Pont de Nemours & Co. sprang, a background roughly paralleling the industrial history of the U.S., may be swiftly laid down.

Black powder built it, and up to 1915 Du Pont was almost wholly an explosives manufacturer. In 1912 a historic antitrust decision split the company into three parts, and this jolt, plus the obvious need for a U.S. chemical industry shown in World War I, set Du Pont to diversifying into chemistry. In fifteen years it acquired some fifteen smaller companies and half a dozen major processes to give itself background and market bases upon which to build. Most of these acquisitions linked logically into its explosives raw materials, nitric acid, nitrocellulose, and cellulose. The development of coal-tar dyes to beat the German blockade, plus the high-pressure synthesis of ammonia from coke and air, put Du Pont on the ground floor of modern chemical development.

On this foundation, with acquisitions tapering off early in the Thirties, Du Pont built its present towering structure. It may be said that Du Pont was lucky to have entered the chemical field when it did, and that it has ridden its luck ever since, for in the chemical business one thing leads swiftly to another. But other companies started from equal or better positions. Something besides luck accounts for Du Pont, and that something is management.

Shortly before ten every Wednesday morning, nine men stroll into Room 9064 of the big, air-conditioned Du Pont Building in Wilmington, Delaware, take places at a large oval table, and, with time out for lunch, usually remain in session all day. This is Du Pont's Executive Committee, composed of the president as chairman and eight vice presidents, and it is the head of the business. The president has no power not derived from this committee, and on it he has only one vote. The vice presidents have no authority on their own, and they are not vice-presidents-in-charge-of anything. Their collective function is to think; their chief field of action is policymaking.

This radical form of committee management was initiated in Irénée Du Pont's term as president in 1921 to meet the needs of Du Pont's swiftly diversifying business. In its human nuances, linkages, philosophy, and controls it explains more clearly than any other factor how Du Pont works.

The new form owes a great deal, including most of its original management, to the hard school of explosives. Basically, though not functionally, it is a military form of organization, in which a sharp separation is made between staff and line. The Executive Committee is the general staff, along with a powerful, interlinked, nine-man Finance Committee, which holds the purse strings. Ten separate industrial operating departments form the field or line commands, each as big as many an important corporation, each headed by a general manager charged with an investment and maximum authority to run the business. Attached to staff and line are fourteen auxiliary departments carrying on such company-wide functions as purchasing, traffic, engineering, and long-range research.

No chart, however, can show the shrewdness with which this structure is adapted to human nature and the peculiarities of Du Pont. Traditionally the president of Du Pont has been a Du Pont by birth, and there is no denying the continuing power this prolific family exercises, as founders and major stockholders, upon the destinies of the company. The brothers Pierre, eighty, Irénée, seventy-three, and Lammot, sixty-nine, all past presidents, are family patriarchs, with Pierre still on the Finance Committee and Lammot chairman of the Bonus and Salary Committee. Ten members of the family are on the board, and a half-dozen younger Du Ponts are down the line. Management in 1921, however, recognized that this highly technical business would require many talents at the top and would quickly be sunk if one man tried to know everything. Irénée also underlined a Du Pont policy by retiring at forty-nine, giving as his reason, "I'm slowing up." (Du

Pont's present president is forty-five-year-old Crawford Greenewalt, who married Irénée's daughter, Margaretta; he graduated
from Massachusetts Institute of Technology and was chief technical coordinator of the Hanford plutonium project.)

Many an industrialist and economist is still skeptical that Du
Pont's committee management can work, and look for a hidden
power behind the organization chart. There is none. The organization works for Du Pont because it is molded to a new set of realities
and is strictly observed. The "Ex Committee," enjoined as individuals from any day-to-day decisions in the business, is removed
from the battle to deliberate and coordinate overall strategy, a job in
which nine heads are better than one. The general managers,
given personal authority, snap out the daily decisions that run the
business, a task that no committee could do. Below, around, and
between the general managers many ad hoc committees may
operate, for the problems are complex, but the general manager is
the boss. The Ex Committee must take positive action in broad
areas without destroying this initiative below.

Every Friday, when carefully staggered monthly departmental
reports and other reports of a wide nature flow in, the group
buckles down to a long weekend of reading and readying itself for
its Wednesday meeting. In addition to these reports, a typical
agenda may include two or three large appropriation requests, a
look into a new product coming up, or discussion of a new market
or field of research. Decisions are usually unanimous, but five-to-
four splits occur. There is no question that the president as
chairman wields great powers of prestige and leadership over this
assembly, and as chief executive officer of the company he has
certain defined powers, but he can be, and sometimes is, voted
down. It is a democratic give-and-take. Teamwork is carefully
nurtured throughout the corporation. It begins far down the line at
the plant-foreman level, and rises by steadily reviewed stages of
authority and compensation through thirteen levels of responsibility. Labor relations pivot upon the foremen, who are trained in
it. With a pension system dating from 1904, disability and other
benefits, high wages in a high-wage industry, and inculcated fair
play, Du Pont has kept notably free of major trouble, even through
the postwar uneasiness.

Likely managerial timber is spotted in its early thirties, usually
after about ten years' service and at the assistant-director-of-a-
division level, and it is closely followed by age groups. Periodically,

a "skimmer" chart is run on each department, plotting salaries by ages. If too many top-bracket salaries bunch up at the aging end of the curve, the department head is asked quietly but pointedly: "Where are your good young men?" Picked young men are deliberately moved about, across functional lines (from research to production or sales and vice versa), across departmental lines (from stable to expanding divisions), to develop rounded executives and get a steady transfer of ideas.

Venture and technology have shaped Du Pont, as they have shaped the whole upsurging chemical industry. It is axiomatic to the Ex Committee that Du Pont must be on new ground regularly and periodically. It is axiomatic to them that if anything has been done in the same way with the same equipment for twenty-five years it's suspect. The chemical industry exists on change, on continually improving older products and regularly introducing new ones. Nearly 55 percent of Du Pont's present assets are accounted for by "pulling itself up by its chemical bootstraps," creating markets where none existed before.

This has led the committee to define Du Pont's function as the tackling of those big chemical jobs in which its large capital, technical, and managerial resources can make a distinctive contribution. This narrows down to tackling the hardest jobs, which only a few companies have the resources and diversity to carry through with any speed or success. That is Du Pont's working rationalization of bigness.

This rationale cannot be squared with the black and white picture of competition painted in the nineteenth century, based on the early immutable commodities of the industrial revolution, a major source of antitrust confusion. This is the way twentieth-century chemical industry works. It is competition on multiple levels of meaning and value.

At the top level it is competition among about a half-dozen companies of superior resources and another half-dozen of medium size to develop new products.

At the middle level, as more producers come in to cash in on the successful new product or its equivalent (alternatives are usually prolific in chemistry), more intense price competition comes into play. On this level Du Pont puts little effort into maintaining any fixed percentage of market, for returns are diminishing and its resources are more gainfully employed in developing still newer products.

At the bottom level are such old, universal products as sulfuric acid and ethyl alcohol, widely produced, basic to the industry, and priced to the bone.

The whole complex is brought to focus on the oval table on the ninth floor of a Wednesday morning. A new venture comes before the Ex Committee. It may have started in the research of the Chemical Department as a new chemical that an industrial department saw a use for and began to pay research costs on, while it investigated for itself, made small amounts, and began testing the market. Up to this point the departments move as they will within their budgets and within capital-expenditure limitations up to $50,000 on a single project, or up to $100,000 if a single vice president can be persuaded to initial the voucher.

Only at this point, if the department thought it had something, would the Ex Committee begin to hear about it. When the department is ready to propose a large semi-works or commercial plant, it sends a project report to the committee for decision, spelling out its reasons, sales forecasts, cost data, and expected return. The committee weighs it against the policies, strategy, and budget of Du Pont as a whole.

The cord by which this whole operation is controlled, from the industrial departments up to the Ex Committee and Finance Committee, is return on investment. Du Pont is one of the few to follow this controversial practice, elevating it above net return on sales. There is a general Du Pont rule that no project will be considered that returns below a given percentage, but there are four subdivisions of this rule. The first covers "necessity" projects, such as laboratories, recreation facilities, safety equipment, which have no direct return; the second applies to laborsaving projects with relatively low returns but important in promoting labor-cost savings; the third applies to new products, on which a lower return will be accepted in expectation of potential growth and to get into the market; and the fourth covers additional capacity for old products, on which the highest return is required, because the older a product the more dangerous it is to keep putting money in it. To average around 10 percent on the whole, individual percentages must swing from nothing to well above 10 percent on a range of some 1,200 different product classifications, and the hands that guide this extraordinary act of equilibrium must be steady.

To aid them there is a chart system of analysis that, in its workings, is uniquely Du Pont. On the fourth Wednesday of each month the Ex Committee has a session in the Chart Room, in which, hanging from a network of overhead trolleys, are 350 big charts carrying a running account of the industrial departments' businesses and of Du Pont as a whole. A group of departments is reviewed at a time so that each averages about four reviews a year. The charts are whipped before the committee, unusual points explained. The whole session normally takes about two hours. The chart system, of course, heads up everywhere to return on investment, which is turnover multiplied by earnings-as-percent-of-sales. If the return in any department varies any significant amount from the required figure, the general manager is on hand to explain, and the trouble is traced back to its source through the chart system. If return is too low, it may be from a bad inventory situation or other sources. If it is too high, it may be from too high prices, which fail to develop turnover and broader markets, and something will be done about it. For this business, like all the great mass-production businesses native to this soil, is based upon the cardinal principle of selling more for less.

How big Du Pont may grow is not entirely within its own volition. "Two billion a year? Sure," says Crawford Greenewalt. "Five billion? That might be more difficult to manage." This is the young chemical industry talking, barely of age and still growing. If Du Pont doubles again in size in the next decade, others in the industry will do even better. It is an extremely big kettle, the chemical industry. [Du Pont's sales in 1978: $10,584,200,000.]

But there is some indefinable point even in chemistry where great size begins to tell on efficiency, where a business becomes too big for any small group of people to manage. Leading up to that point, however, Du Pont and the enterprise system it notably represents can grow only by taking chances in the market and allowing market to determine ultimate size. As soon as Du Pont gets so big that it becomes slow on its feet, competition will cut it back down to size. If the U.S. is aiming at some other mystical system of values, such as the non-materialism of the East or the regimentation of totalitarianism, this is not the course. But if material well-being is the buttress of essential human values and much else, this is the system that has produced the goods in an abundance and power seen nowhere else.

Orlon: A Case History

One day last July a golden, new, synthetic fiber named Orlon began spinning out of a new Du Pont plant at Camden, South

Carolina. Even before the plant was completed, with a capacity of seven million pounds a year, ground was being broken for a second plant across the road to add another 30 million pounds by 1952. Altogether, about $60 million had been committed to these new plants, and the research, development, and pilot plants that went before them, at a time when only a few thousand pounds of experimental yarn had reached the trade and few people had so much as seen a thread of Orlon.

In man's search for covering, centuries of selection and artifice had narrowed dozens of natural fibers down to the four basic and most useful: cotton, wool, silk, and flax. When chemical science late in the last century came to attempt manufacturing fibers of its own, these were the objectives, but the chemist could only begin slowly and crudely to imitate them. First came Chardonnet's "artificial silk" in the 1880's, forerunner of rayon. In 1920, Du Pont bought U.S. rights to the viscose process from France's Comptoir des Textiles Artificiels and set up Du Pont Fibersilk Co. in a plant at Buffalo, New York. Du Pont's intimate knowledge of cellulose chemistry through smokeless powder contributed heavily to the next ten years of tremendous rayon development. At the time rayon was developed chemistry had barely penetrated the molecular structure of matter, and both viscose and acetate were simply exterior chemical modifications of natural cellulose, more properly semi-synthetics. By the mid-Twenties, however, chemists had begun to get a grip on the structure of big molecules or super-polymers, and Du Pont determined to get inside this structure in the hope of reproducing, not exact chemical counterparts, but the long, chainlike molecules of natural fibers. This fundamental exploration led to nylon, the first completely synthetic organic fiber, equal and superior to silk in strength and elasticity, but not quite in luxurious feel.

Nylon swelled the already considerable volume of Du Pont's Rayon Department, and became a separate division.

At the end of the war Du Pont was faced with the decision whether to pump capital into building more capacity to maintain relative position in the established fibers, or to risk it on new fibers that might bring greater diversity, balance, and health to itself and the whole textile industry. Du Pont being Du Pont, it wasn't a hard decision to make.

Orlon, the new fiber Du Pont decided to produce, was turned up in 1941 when Rayon's pioneering-research section, experimenting with acrylonitrile to increase the wet strength of rayon, decided that it ought to polymerize into a good fiber itself. Du Pont's Chemical Department had done fundamental work on the polymerization of acrylonitrile, now proceeded to work toward a practical fiber. By that time the war was at full tide and the development had to wait. A small pilot plant turned out some of the fiber for submarine battery separators and radar domes, where its acid-resistant and electrical properties were unique, but costs were out of reach. Dr. G. P. Hoff, onetime nylon research director and now manager of the Acetate Division, which handles Orlon, was asked to evaluate the new fiber, then called Fiber A, and he pronounced it good—"but we don't have a process." "Well, get a process!" said the Rayon Department's manager.

There was no practical solvent then to dissolve the hard, intractable, ivory-white polymer of acrylonitrile to wet-spin it like viscose or dry-spin it like acetate. A suggestion from one of Rayon's university consultants set in motion a search through the Chemical Department's past experimental work, which turned up a family of solvents that gave good fiber qualities, but they were some of those rare chemicals for which a whole process had to be worked out. Unlike nylon, the new acrylic fiber couldn't be drawn at room temperature (stretched three to eight times original length to orient the molecules into long, parallel chains for final strength). A tricky piece of equipment had to be devised to draw a continuous thread of Orlon at elevated temperatures, and this alone took three years.

But once the earliest process solutions were in sight, Orlon moved with greater speed. When only 100 pounds of improved fiber were in hand from the pilot plant in 1946, the Rayon Department was sure, from its fiber experience, that it had something. By then teams were working over production processes while other teams were exploring all the fiber's characteristics and economics. When a few thousand pounds had been coaxed from a new semi-works plant late in 1947, Du Pont was ready to plunge on a full-scale plant. By then a market-research team had carried some of the yarn into customers' mills for test, and chalked out the first markets, while all the other teams kept swinging at improving processes, dyeing, and so forth. As soon as the dyeing problem was cracked by modifying the fiber slightly or dyeing under pressure, the second plant was ordered, quadrupling the capacity of the first.

Orlon is so far the nearest thing to wool. Reproducing the air spaces between fibers that give wool bulk and warmth, Orlon staple is 25 percent bulkier and hence warmer than wool of equal weight. Wool is highly vulnerable because most of the best grades are imported and world production has been declining while population has been growing. Already Orlon, though still high priced, can compete with the best suitings, and Du Pont's aim is to get it down to mass-market levels.

The force of all this is to supply textiles with a range of new properties that must eventually reorient the whole field. Other new fibers are bound to appear, adding still newer properties. The only important fiber so far untouched by all this is cotton, and to break into this low-price market would require some chemical phenomenon not yet in sight. But this does not mean Du Pont won't try. What impels Du Pont is well explained by one of Rayon's executives: "The technology of our business is not an isolated phase of our activity. It flows in an endless stream through the complex network of the organization; it carries away worn-out tissues; it nourishes new cells; it carries with it the means of combating sickness in our operations; it is essential to the mechanism of the brain, so that all our thinking is influenced by it. While the stream flows we are healthy and growing—when it stops we are dead."

October 1950

The Organization Man

The Transients
By William H. Whyte, Jr.

For a quick twinge of superiority there is nothing quite like driving past one of the new Levittown-like suburbs. To visitors from older communities, the sight of rank after rank of little boxes stretching off to infinity, one hardly distinguishable from the other, is weird. Appalling—if this is progress, God help us . . . 1984!

The onlooker had better wipe the sympathy off his face. What he has seen is a revolution, not the home of little cogs and drones. What he has seen is the dormitory of the next managerial class.

The most important single group in these communities is what has been variously called business bureaucrats, industrial civil servants, technicians of society—the junior executives, research workers, young corporation lawyers, engineers, salesmen. The bond they share is that they are (1) between twenty-five and thirty-five, (2) organization men, and (3) all on the move. It is significant enough that there are now so many of them that whole towns have to be built to hold them; more significant, it is these unostentatious, salaried nomads who will be running our business society twenty years from now.

Even if part of the American Dream is still true, one big chunk of it is dead, finished, kaput. For the future will be determined not by the independent entrepreneur or the "rugged individualist" whom our folklore so venerates; the future will be determined by Organization Man.

After the war, one thing looked sure. Americans had had their bellyful of moving; now, everybody agreed, they were going to settle down and stop this damned traipsing around. Here is the way things worked out:

Americans are moving more than ever before: Never have long-distance movers had it so good; according to figures provided by the five leading firms, moving is now at a rate even higher than in wartime. And compared with prewar, the five firms are all moving at least three times as many families, and one is moving ten times as many. Furthermore, not only are more families moving, those who move move more frequently; one out of every seven of its customers, Allied Van Lines reports, will *within a year* pick up stakes and move again to a new state, and seven out of ten will be "repeaters" within the next five years.

The more education, the more mobility: If a man goes to college now, the chances are almost even that he won't work in his home state. Of men who complete college, 46 percent move. Of those who worked their way through in a college outside their home state, about 70 percent don't go back. And for all college men, incidentally, the higher the grades, the more likely they are to go to work outside their home states.

Organization people move the most: To judge from studies by direct-mail experts, the greatest amount of address changing occurs among managerial people. Similarly, records of long-distance movers show that the greatest single group among their customers, upwards of 40 percent, consists of corporation people being transferred from one post to another.

The impact of this transiency on U.S. society is incalculable. The small town, for example, has long exported some of its youth; but what was once a stream has become a flood. It is no longer a case of the special boy who had to get out of town to cross the tracks or find an outlet for his energies; now as many as three-quarters of the town's young college men may be in the same position.

And they will never go back. Once the cord is broken, a return carries overtones of failure. "I'm fed up with New York," says one executive, "but if I went back to Taylorston I know damned well they'd think my tail was between my legs." The point is that he probably would think so too; one of the great tacit bonds the transients share is a feeling, justifiable or not, that by moving they acquire an intellectual sophistication that will forever widen the gap between them and their home towns. "Dave and I thought often about going back to East Wells," a successful young executive's wife explains. "It is a beautiful old New England town and we both had such happy times there. But all the people who had anything on the ball seem to have left. There are a few who took over their fathers' businesses, but the rest—well, I hate to sound so snobbish, but dammit, I *do* feel superior to them."

But the most important reason they can't go home is that they won't find it there if they do. In the rapid growth of the metropolitan areas, once self-contained market towns have been transformed into suburbs, and more important yet, the plant expansion of U.S. industry has turned others into industrial towns. In many towns, as a result, the migration of the young people has been offset by such an influx of newcomers that those who have stayed put are in the position of being abroad at home.

For some towns the tensions have been near explosive. Even though the influx swells local coffers, the townspeople, in somewhat the way natives view the "summer people," view with apprehension the people moving into the developments nearby, and the fact that many of the "new people" have no intention of staying long doesn't make them easier to take. And the townspeople's attitude is reciprocated enough so that the developments going up around the town often form a ring of animosity; citizens of the older communities know something has hit them, and though they're not exactly sure just what it is, they sense, correctly, that those "horrid developments" despoiling the old so-and-so place are the symbol of it.

The shift to organization power that has brought so much of this about has been in the making a long time. As sociologist Max Weber long ago noted, before the turn of the century the trend to a "bureaucratic" organization of society was already in high motion. Since then the trend has been steadily accentuated, until today most college men almost automatically see their future in terms of the salaried life of an organization.

The reasons are obvious enough. While there is an undue assumption by many young men that entrepreneurship equals insecurity, if the young man has no independent income or capital what is he to do? The big organization wants him; wants more of him, in fact, than are available. Its recruiters go to him before he graduates from college, and they promise good starting salaries (currently: $275 to $335 a month), good extra training, and a secure future. To join up seems both the line of least resistance and the logical course.

Clearly, the big organization is now the prime vehicle for a career, and in more institutions than the corporations. Even in the professions the emphasis has switched to the organization; of the professional men who graduated in the last decade, only about one in five is working for himself; the bulk are to be found in group clinics, law factories, AEC labs, corporation staff departments.

In the wake of this shift to the big organization is the moving van. Certainly the recruit does not join up because he *wants* to move a lot, and it is often in spite of it. But moving, he knows, has become part of the bargain, and unsettling as transfer might be, even more unsettling are the implications of not being asked to transfer. "We never plan to transfer," as one company president explains, a bit dryly, "and we never make a man move. Of course, he kills his career if he doesn't. But we never *make* him do it." The fact is well understood; it is with a smile that the recruit moves— and keeps on moving, year after year; until, perhaps, that distant day when he is summoned back to Rome.

It is not just more moves per man. Even companies reporting no increase in the number of times each individual moves report an increase in the sheer number of men being moved. G.E. has compared a cross section of its forty-five-year-old executives with one of its thirty-five-year-olds; in the ten years after they had become twenty-five, 42 percent of the older group had moved at least once; during the same age period, 58 percent of the younger had moved.

Corporations never planned it quite that way. Decentralization and expansion, rather than deliberate personnel policy, have created the necessity of filling vacancies out in the empire. Now, some companies are coming to believe that periodic transfer is a positive good in itself; and even where no immediate functional reason exists, it might often be important to move the man anyway. What better way, they ask, to produce the well-rounded executive?

Instead of leaving transfer to be determined haphazardly by different departments, some companies, like G.E., have made such decisions part of a systematic managerial program. By thus making a man's "permanent" assignment (i.e., one lasting at least three years) part of a deliberate rotation policy, the man is given "more choices in life to make," and the company, as a result, is given a pool of seasoned talent. Other companies agree; by deliberately exposing a man to a succession of environments, they best obtain that necessity of the large organization—the man who can fit in anywhere. "The training," as an I.B.M. executive succinctly puts it, "makes our men interchangeable."

May 1953

Dot and Charlie Adams Land in Park Forest
By WILLIAM H. WHYTE, JR.

Park Forest, Illinois, is virtually a sampling of today's junior management—the twenty-five- to thirty-five-year-old junior executive with a wife, a salary between $6,000 and $7,000, one child, and another on the way.

Park Forest is not a venture in utopia but a shrewd business operation designed to meet some new social facts of life. Though there was a great floating population of young veterans after the war, there was little available housing suitable for young people with (1) children, (2) expectations of transfer, (3) a taste for good living, (4) not much money. Why not, figured a group of businessmen, build a whole new community for these people? The group incorporated as American Community Builders, brought in former Federal Public Housing Commissioner Philip Klutznick as president, and bought up 2,400 acres in the cornland thirty miles south of Chicago.

The final plan was to build clusters of rental garden apartments (rent for two-bedroom duplex: $92) around a central shopping center, and then, as time went on, build ranch-type houses for sale ($11,995) on the periphery of the area. These would be merchandised at bargain rates. The real money would come from the waterworks and the company's cut (ranging up to 10 percent) of every dollar spent in the shopping center. In effect, a city was being built to provide a market—a constantly rotating, non-satiable market of 30,000 people, many of whom would ever be poised at that stage when families just begin to lay up possessions.

When the doors to Park Forest were thrown open in 1948 the rental courts were islands in a sea of mud, but the young people came streaming out from Chicago. The first wave of colonists was heavy with academic and professional people—the place, it appeared, had an extraordinary affinity for Ph.D's. Since Chicago is one of the great business training grounds of the U.S., however, another kind of affinity has proved even stronger: poised at the nexus of America's junior-executive migration, Park Forest quickly became a haven for the corporations' young transients.

For most of its renters, Park Forest is a sort of way station, a phase in life, and beyond a certain point continued residence can carry overtones of failure. Some people "flunk out" of Park Forest because they are not making the grade; far more leave precisely because they *have* made the grade. However glowingly they speak of the no-keeping-up-with-the-Joneses and the other attractions of Park Forest, transients say frankly that they expect eventually to graduate to someplace like Winnetka, the Main Line, or Westchester County. Anyway, they explain, the decision is out of their hands; someday soon the boss may call John in for a little chat and they will be moving on.

Are the Park Foresters a rootless people? If by roots we mean the complex of geographical and family ties that has historically knitted Americans to local society, these young transients are almost entirely rootless. But they are not plagued by instability or loneliness. They have found what they have been looking for. They have found it in each other; through a sort of national cooperative, they have developed a *new* kind of roots.

DAN WEINER

The 5:57 from the Loop disgorges junior executives who have become suburbanites.

Let's take, for example, a couple we shall call Dot and Charlie
Adams. Charlie, a corporation trainee, is uprooted from the
Newark office, arrives at Apartment 8, Court M-12. It's a hell of a
day, the kids are crying, Dot is half sick with exhaustion, and the
movers won't be finished till late.

But soon, because M-12 is a "happy" court, the neighbors will
come over to introduce themselves. In an almost inordinate display
of decency, some will help them unpack, and around suppertime
two of the girls will come over with a hot casserole and another
with a percolator full of hot coffee. Within a few days the children
will have found playmates, Dot will be kaffeeklatsching and
sunbathing with the girls like an old-timer, and Charlie, who finds
that Ed Robey in Apartment 5 went through officers' training
school with him, will be enrolled in the Court Poker Club. The
Adamses are, in a word, *in.*

Their relationships with others in the court, they find, transcend
mere neighborliness. Except for the monastic orders and the family
itself, there is probably no other social institution in the U.S. in
which there is such a communal sharing of property as in Park
Forest. Except for the $200 or $300 put aside for the next baby, few
of the transients have as yet been able to accumulate much capital
or earthly possessions, and so they share to make the best of it.
One lawn mower (with each man doing his allotted stint) may do
for the whole court. For the wives there is a baby-sitting "bank"
(i.e., when one wife baby-sits for another she is credited with the
time, and when she wishes to draw on it one of the wives who has
a debit to repay will sit for her). To hoard possessions is frowned
upon; books, silverware, and tea services are constantly rotated,
and the children feel free to use each other's bicycles and toys
without bothering to ask. "We laughed at first at how the Marxist
society had finally arrived," one executive says, "but I think the
real analogy is to the pioneers."

But the court social life, important as it is in rooting the transient,
is only part of the acclimation. Before long Charlie Adams may feel
the urge to shoot out a few extra roots here and there, and, having
normal joining instincts, may think a mild involvement in some
community-wide organization just the thing. Tentatively, he makes
a few inquiries—nothing strenuous, understand, awfully busy
with company work; just want to help out a little. Instantaneously,
or no longer at least than it takes one person to telephone another,
the news is abroad. Charlie will never be quite the same again.

He has plunged into a hotbed of Participation. With sixty-six adult organizations and a population turnover that makes each one of them insatiable for new members, Park Forest probably swallows up more civic energy per hundred people than any other community in the country. As elsewhere, of course, the apathetic outnumber the active—but not by so much.

"Actually, neither Fred nor I are joiners, like some of these silly characters around here," one wife explains, "but it's gotten so now I practically have to make an appointment to see him Saturdays."

Park Forest's incessant civic activity is particularly relevant to business. For the young executive it provides a leadership training it would take him years to get otherwise. They feel that community work may also improve their promotion chances. A check with employers indicates that they are right. Excepting those men who seize on community activity as a compensation for career frustrations, the average young man who is civically active would appear to have a statistically better chance to get ahead than his less active brothers.

Do places like Park Forest spoil one? We noted earlier that most of the people who move to package communities move out of a simple economic necessity; we must also note, however, that *after* exposure to such an environment some people find a warmth and support in it that makes other environments seem unduly cold—it is somewhat unsettling, for example, to hear the way some residents of the new suburbs occasionally refer to "the outside." Not too surprisingly, alumni of package communities often go considerably out of their way to seek out a similar community when the next move comes up.

June 1953

The Wife Problem

By WILLIAM H. WHYTE, JR.

The American corporation is approaching a very large question. Should the wife belong to it? In one sense, the question is not a new one; for generations business has been aware that executives' wives play a great if imponderable role. What is new, however, is that "the wife problem" is now becoming in many cases a matter of regular company policy.

Increasingly, corporations are interviewing the wife before hiring an executive, and some are not uninterested in fiancées. About half of the companies on which *Fortune* has data have made wife-screening regular practice. Roughly 20 percent of its otherwise acceptable trainee applicants, one large company estimates, are turned down because of their wives.

If the prospective executive lives elsewhere, companies frequently suggest strongly that he bring his wife along for the interviews. This can be a harrowing experience for the wife. If the company is a close-knit one, she may undergo what amounts to a community interview in depth. This is particularly the case when the present management group has been long entrenched; since an unwise choice, they feel, can upset the delicate social balance achieved over the years, self-protection demands that everyone be given a chance to look over the couple.

"I've seen a lot of trouble along this line," recalls one management consultant. "Up comes a chief engineer for an interview. He makes a swell impression and is hired. Thirty days later he appears and when the company introduces him around, his wife is the wrong kind of person. I have seen whole organizations get stirred up by this and the company says never again—next time we see the wife first. I know a company that has had to bring in two men in the last two years. They brought the man and his wife to town for the weekend and had all the top people meet them socially to get a line on them. In both instances the men were passed up because of their wives." The company is still looking.

Some companies have supplemented the screening with more objective investigations. One life-insurance company, for example, investigates the wife's credit ratings and, in addition, checks around to determine how popular or unpopular she has been in her community. Similarly, some organizations take pains to find out whether or not the wife has independent capital of her own; if it is sizable, they believe, it tends to mitigate the man's economic drive.

The initial screening is only the beginning of the corporation's interest. At the Container Corp. of America, it is the duty of all vice presidents to get acquainted with their subordinates' wives, and on their travels they are expected to meet the wives of executives in the field. Thus, when a man's name comes up for promotion the company has the answers to these questions: What is the health of the family? What is their attitude toward parenthood? How does the wife run her home? Does she dress with taste?

Management consultants would like to see even more of same. "In our consulting work on personnel and management problems," says one consultant, "we always recommend to our clients that personnel records of executives include data on the wife. It is a personality appraisal. Does she complement him? Is she a helpmate or a millstone? A nagger? Understanding? Does she resent his traveling? Does she criticize him publicly? Is she loud? Is she a lady? The immediate superior of the man in question fills this out over a period of meetings with the wife."

As in the primary interview, companies generally find all this out in a social sort of way. In the case of an impending promotion one company has the wife seen individually by three different people at carefully arranged casual dinners or luncheons. Somewhat similarly, companies occasionally stage parties to appraise wives; seeing them under fire, executives explain, makes for a good short cut.

The effect of all this surveillance on the husband's career is substantial. In the home office of an insurance company, to cite one not untypical example, the president is now sidetracking one of his top men in favor of a less able one; the former's wife "has absolutely no sense of public relations." In another company a very promising executive's career is being similarly checked; his wife, the boss explains, is "negative in her attitude toward the company. She feels that business is her husband's life and no part of hers."

The little woman who gets tipsy in front of the boss is not quite the joke her celebration in cartoon and anecdote would indicate; indeed, it is almost frightening to find out to what degree executive futures have been irretrievably influenced by that fourth martini. And it need happen only once; recently the president of a large utility felt it necessary to revise his former estimate of two executives. At the last company dinner their wives drank too many glasses of champagne. "They disported themselves," he says, regretfully, "with utter lack of propriety."

Important as the screening process may be, most executives realize that it is, at best, only a negative measure. For even with the most cooperative wives there can be much misunderstanding over such topics as travel and long hours. Therefore it is the company's duty, they argue, to *sell* the wife on the corporation's point of view.

The result is an increasing use of such media as films, brochures, and special mailings to drive home, in effect, the idea that the corporation isn't stealing her husband from her, and even if it were, it would work out for the best anyway. "We may make what seem to her to be untoward demands on the husband," says F. K. Doscher of the Lily-Tulip Cup Corp., "but he benefits in the long run. If we do all the things we do for a man, why should we endanger our stake in him by failing to try and influence a constructive attitude at home that will abet it?"

For his part, Doscher plans to send wives bimonthly booklets on the industry plus a personal letter. "Now if she reads the booklet," he explains, "she can't help but get excited about the business—at a bridge party, if a doctor's wife tells of some medical discoveries, the Lily-Tulip wife can tell about how her husband's industry has donated 25 million paper cups and food containers for civilian defense. She needn't feel her husband is just a businessman grubbing away making money, but that he is doing something worthwhile too."

Says one bank president: "The days of the strictly home wife are gone. She has become indispensable to our entire scheme of business."

Among U.S. corporations, easily the most conspicuous and successful example of integration has been Thomas J. Watson's International Business Machines Corp. "Our wives," Watson explains, "are all part of the business. We started with just a few hundred people in 1914 and decided that no matter how large we grew we would carry it on in the family spirit. We always refer to our people as the 'I.B.M. Family' and we mean the wives and children as well as the men."

As a result, the company can correctly claim that it makes available "complete social satisfactions." For $1 a year I.B.M. people enjoy a country club with swimming pool, bowling, eighteen-hole golf course, softball, tennis, picnics, and parties of all kinds. Even the children are integrated. At the age of three they may be enrolled in a special children's club, and at eight go on to become junior members of the big club. "Successes here," says one official, "are guys who eat and sleep the company. If a man's first interest is his wife and family, more power to him—but we don't want him." "We've got quite an equity in the man," another explains, "and it's only prudence to protect it by bringing the wife into the picture."

In fairness to the wife, it follows, she must be recompensed somehow for the amount of time the company demands from her husband. Companies recognize the fact and are consequently more and more providing social facilities—from ladies' nights to special clubs—to increase the sense of identification.

There is, of course, another side to the picture. Some companies not only look on the wife—to borrow one executive's explanation—as none of their damn business, but take active steps to see that she *doesn't* get close to them. A sampling of executive views—Oil company: "We are just as happy if we never see her at all." Tool company: "If wives get too close to management, they always get too status-minded. That means trouble." Motor company: "Wives' activities are their own business. What do some of these companies want for their $10,000? Slavery too?"

November 1951

The Top Floor

For God's Sake Won't You Learn to Use English!
By WILLIAM H. WHYTE, JR.

In company after company, executives have been setting up "writing clinics," staging correspondence-improvement courses, holding school in conference and public-speaking techniques, and, at the very least, peppering subordinates with "For God's sake won't you people learn to use English around here" memos. Meanwhile, a look at the anatomy of this language that is to be redesigned.

First, the written variety—and that infamous jargon, which, for want of a better term, we'll call businessese. In sounding out a hundred executives on the subject, *Fortune* found that their views coincided remarkably, particularly so in the matter of pet peeves (principally: "please be advised," "in reference to yours of...," "we wish to draw attention," "to acknowledge your letter"). The phrases of businessese are everywhere so uniform, in fact, that stenographers have a full set of shorthand symbols for them. After all, everybody knows the symbols, and, furthermore, wouldn't a lot of people be offended by the terseness of more concise wording? There is something to this theory. Since businessese generally is twice as wordy as plain English, however, the theory is rather expensive to uphold. By the use of regular English the cost of the average letter—commonly estimated at 75 cents to $1—can be cut by about 20 cents. For a firm emitting a million letters a year, this could mean an annual saving of $200,000. Probably it would be even greater; roughly 15 percent of the letters currently being written wouldn't be necessary at all if the preceding correspondence had been in regular English in the first place.

Where do the terms of businessese come from? Most, of course, are hand-me-downs from former generations of businessmen, but many are the fruit of cross-fertilization with other jargons. A businessman who castigates government bureaucrats, for example, is at the same time apt to be activating, expediting, implementing, effectuating, optimizing, minimizing, and maximizing—and at all levels and echelons within the framework of broad policy areas. Similarly, though he is amused by the long-hairs and the social scientists, the businessman is beginning to speak knowingly of projective techniques, social dynamics, depth interviewing, and sometime soon, if he keeps up at this rate, he will probably appropriate that hallmark of the sound sociological paper, "insightful." Businessese, in fact, has very nearly become the great common meeting ground of the jargons.

Why do people who in private talk so pungently often write so pompously? Above all is the simple matter of status. Theorem: the less established the status of a person, the more his dependence on jargon. Examine the man who has just graduated to a secretary and your are likely to have a man intoxicated with the rhythm of businessese.

Not only does businessese confer status, it protects it as well, by its magnificent usefulness for buck passing and hedging. "All you have to remember," one executive says, "is the one basis which characterizes all such intracommunication: let the language be ambiguous enough that if the text be successfully carried out, all credit may be claimed; but if the text be unsuccessfully carried out, a technical alibi can be set up out of the text itself."

For this purpose there is a regular subglossary of businessese. Most notable terms: "in the process of," "under consideration," "in the not-too-distant future." People who have to submit periodic reports to their superiors are particularly dependent on such terms—salesmen, for example, would have a hard time if they couldn't report of some prospects that they were "very impressed." ("I am allergic to that word," says one sales manager. "It results in so few orders.")

The full application of businessese to hedging occurs when more than two heads are put to work on a problem. As the members of top management sit around the table, a relatively simple policy statement is introduced for discussion. This is kicked around a bit, as the saying goes, for though it certainly is a fine statement, couldn't agree with it more, there are just a few little angles and suggestions that maybe ought to be noted. Thereupon each executive adds his qualification, until finally the original statement has been at once pointed up, toned down, given more dignity, made more forceful, altered to anticipate possible objections, concretized, amended, and resolved. There is nothing, as so many people say, quite like what you get when everybody on the team works together.

There is another category of business English—that brand to be heard at the banquet table and the convention.

It might best be called *reverse* gobbledegook, for in almost every outward respect it is the opposite of written jargon. Where written jargon is multisyllabic, the other is filled with short terse words. It is English that is on the beam, English with its feet on the ground; in short, *shirt-sleeve* English.

The Composite Business Speech herewith:

"It is a pleasure and a privilege to be here with you today. These great annual meetings are always an inspiration to me. After that glowing introduction by our toastmaster I must confess, however, that I'd like to turn the tables and tell a little story on Chuck. When I say it's about the nineteenth hole those of you who were at the Atlanta conference last year will know what I mean. But I won't tell it. Chuck Forbes is too good a friend of mine and, seriously, we all realize what a tower of strength his yeoman service has been to the association in these trying times.

"Yes, gentlemen, trying times. So you'll pardon me if I cast aside the glib reverberation of glittering generalities and the soothing syrup of sugar-coated platitudes and put it to you the only way I can: straight English.

"We're losing the battle!

"From every corner the people are being weaned from the doctrines of the Founding Fathers. They are being detoured from the high-speed highways of progress by the utopian highwaymen.

"Now, the man in the street is a pretty savvy fellow. Don't sell him short. Joe Doakes may be fooled for a while, but in the end he wants no part of the mumbo jumbo the global saboteurs are trying to sell him. After all, he is an American.

"But he has to be told.

"And we're not telling him!

"Now let me say that I do not wish to turn the clock back. None of us do. All forward-looking businessmen see themselves as partners in a team in which the worker is a full-fledged member. I regard our employees as our greatest business asset, and I am sure, mindful as I am of the towering potentials of purposeful energy in this group of clear-sighted leaders, that, in the final anaylsis, it is the rock foundation of your policies too.

"But the team can't put the ball across for a first down just by wishing it. The guards and the tackles can't do their job if the quarterback doesn't let them in on the play. And we, the quarterbacks, are muffing the ball.

"How are we to go over for a touchdown? My friends, this is the $64 question. I don't know the answers. I am just a plain-spoken businessman. I have no secret crystal ball. But I do know one thing: before we round the curve into the homestretch we have a job to do. It will not be easy. I offer no panaceas or nostrums. Instead, I would like to suggest that the real key to our problem lies in the application of the three E's.

"What are the three E's?

"Enterprise! Endeavor! Effort!

"Each and every one of us must appoint himself a salesman—yes, a missionary, if you will—and get out and do some real grass-roots selling. And when we hit the dirt, let's not forget the customers—the greatest asset any business has.

"Let's not fool ourselves: the surface, as our chairman has so wisely said, has hardly been scratched. The program is still in its infancy. So let me give it to you straight from the shoulder. The full implementation, gentlemen, depends on *us*.

"So let's get on the beam! Let's get down to earth. In good plain talk the man in the street can understand, let's remind Joe Doakes that the best helping hand he will ever find is the one at the end of his own shirt sleeve.

"We have the know-how.

"With sights set high, let's go over the top!"

November 1950

The Superiority of Business Manners
By ROBERT SHEEHAN

Business manners have been improving so much that now they appear to be superior to the manners encountered in ordinary social intercourse—say, at cocktail parties and dinners, in restaurants, Parent-Teacher Association meetings, clubs, and common carriers. Even in the supposedly genteel academic world, it is not unusual for opposing theorists to attack each other in the most personal kind of way, and in the arts, of course, the studied slur and the vituperative feud are a way of life for some practitioners. Some areas of business are still pretty rough and tumble too, and at a private cocktail party there is nothing to restrain the businessman from being as big a boor as the next fellow. But not in the office; sheer ritual forbids it. For all one knows, some of the rituals observed in business intercourse today may have no more substance than that convention of the Middle Ages, Courtly Love, in which the knights and their ladies were as much interested in the gallantries and swoonings of the courtship as in the actual pleasures of the bedchamber.

Take, for example, the method of receiving visitors that many a corporation president practices today. No longer does he merely rise from his chair, shake hands, indicate your chair, and proceed crisply with the business at hand. Instead, he sweeps out from behind his desk and greets you warmly at the threshold of his office. More often than not, he deserts his desk entirely, and pilots you to a nook on the opposite side of the room. As you loll back on a couch, he draws up a chair and begins to talk to you from across a coffee table, and not necessarily, for the moment, about the business at hand.

This is all very charming, but is it practical? For a businessman to tread such stately measures throughout the working day, often suffering fools gladly the while, takes time, and time is expensive. But most executives are quick to rationalize their behavior in terms of self-interest and ultimate profits. "An ingratiating manner," says a top management consultant, "often tips the scales in a business transaction, and an exhibition of rudeness can be absolutely fatal." He cites a scandalous case in point.

Not so long ago, a rather unprepossessing shareholder of a middling-sized West Coast company presented himself to the president and politely suggested that his holdings might entitle him to a place on the board. "We do not have the time," the president replied, "to educate an outsider in this business." As it turned out, however, the shareholder had the time, and the money, to acquire effective control of the company, and his first order of business, understandably, was to force out the president.

Actually, it is the topmost officers who are usually most meticulous about their manners, and most prodigal with their time for the sake of the amenities. Nearly 40 percent of some 150 company presidents interviewed for this report claimed they answer their own telephones without any screening whatsoever. People who call from the other end of the line might well be astonished at this claim, but in any event presidents can give good reasons why the practice *should* be followed. The president of a large midwestern insurance company who does answer his phone (and also dials his own numbers) says, "I find that 95 percent of the calls coming in are ones I want to take. Why screen out the 5 percent of nuisance calls at the risk of irritating the other 95 percent?"

It was the president of an aircraft company who put the problem most vividly. "Suppose," he says, "I lose ten or fifteen minutes a day taking fruitless calls. But then Captain Eddie Rickenbacker urgently phones me long distance from a pay station to hell-and-gone somewhere. Do I want him juggled around from secretary to secretary, or quizzed on who he is and what he wants?" Somehow, the picture of Eddie Rickenbacker sweating it out in a phone booth, his face aglower under those fierce eyebrows, seems to clinch the case for accepting the unscreened call.

The majority of executives, however, still feel the need for screening if for no other reason than to divert calls that properly should go to other people in the organization. But they want the screening process to be as subtle and painless as possible. For a secretary to ask, "Who's calling?" or "What did you wish to speak to him about?" is now considered a criminal offense. "May I tell him who's calling?" is just about the limit of allowable inquisitiveness.

Some executives, nevertheless, still foolishly hide behind the skirts of their secretaries, a breach of business etiquette on a par with the table ostrich who explores his teeth under cover of his napkin. The genuinely perfect secretary, of course, is one who never permits a breath of suspicion that *she* is deciding whether or not the caller shall be connected with her boss. A secretary's words can kill. It is amusing to learn, for instance, that the phrase "He's in conference" is now regarded as utterly cornball, and in fact offensive, though the equally elusive "He's in a meeting" is permissible. But the best practice of all, it is agreed, is for the secretary to give the caller a precise idea of what the executive is doing, e.g., "He's holding a budget session with the divisional vice presidents right now. May he call you when he's free?" Such candor is disarming and preserves the caller's self-esteem. Of course, it's important that the executive *does* call back when he's free, else the fraudulence of the whole routine is exposed, and the sting of the rebuff is compounded.

But the supreme telephone insult, virtually all executives agree, is to place a call through your secretary, and make the party at the other end of the line hold the connection until you're ready to come on. Says an otherwise uncholeric executive, "When I answer my phone, and a female voice says, 'Please hold on a minute, Mr. Zilch is calling,' I promptly hang up."

Should an executive accept telephone calls while visitors are present? On the one hand, it is embarrassing to a visitor, and an imposition on his time, to be required to sit and gawk while the host-executive takes call after call, some of them of an obviously confidential nature. On the other hand, it may be practically essential for the executive to answer some of the calls. Some executives merely offer a brief "Beg pardon," and brazen it out. A better practice is for the executive to anticipate, if possible, such calls as are critical. At the outset of the interview, he can then say to his visitor, "I am expecting an important call, which with your permission, etc." If the call does come, some executives prefer to excuse themselves and take the call in an anteroom. If done gracefully, it is more comforting to the visitor, who doesn't then have to go through a foolish pantomime to prove he's no eavesdropper. If feasible, of course, the best behavior is to quench all calls. But here again some subtlety is in order. The overt command to "Hold all calls, Miss Bettersby" may be flattering to the visitor, but more likely it makes him edgy and apprehensive. Said one executive, "I'm damned if I know just what to do in some situations."

The severest test of business manners is occasioned by the appearance of unscheduled visitors. Is it not, to begin with, a breach of etiquette to present oneself in the office of an important executive without an appointment? Maybe so, but the practice is widespread, and executives are remarkably tolerant in their reactions. As one bank president said, "A customer is never an interruption of my work; he is the purpose of it."

At any rate, "accessibility," or at least the appearance of it, is a fetish among top officers today. Therefore, all over the U.S., as you read this, thousands of executives and their unscheduled callers are executing a business ballet that might be called "the Fast Shuffle." After identifying himself to the lobby receptionist, the visitor is escorted to the executive's anteroom, where he is received by a personable secretary. The secretary jots name and purpose of visit on a piece of paper and dissolves through a door to the inner office. In a moment the executive emerges and gives the visitor the big hello. After that, one of several gambits may be followed. The executive apologizes for his crowded schedule, and may invite his visitor to return later in the day, next day, or next week. Sometimes it is suggested that another officer of the company is really better qualified to handle the mission. In that case the executive may summon a subaltern, linger long enough to introduce him to the visitor, and wish them both Godspeed and success.

What happens when a host-executive is so extravagantly charming that a visitor simply will not get up and leave of his own accord? At this point most executives stop playing games and take the simple, short route out of the dilemma. "I have one of those *rising voice* techniques," one executive pridefully explains, "and I use it to make a summarizing or concluding statement." Others insinuate such good-bye-please phrases as "Next time you're in town, we'll pursue it further," or "When we're not so pressed for time, let's etc., etc." Executives of a more conspiratorial nature press a hidden button, which brings in a secretary with a little note, at which the executive frowns and says, "Tell him I'll be with him in a few minutes."

As a last resort, most executives find that the "rise and remain standing" technique is effective, though a construction-company president reports that he also puts on his hat just to make sure. And one of those retired Army generals who took over a command in private enterprise used to clap his hands together smartly and cry, "Well now, does that answer all your questions?" Finally, there is an executive in Texas who, when visitors overstay, is said to take an electric razor out of his drawer and begin to shave.

When one turns from the treatment of outsiders to the broad field of intramural office manners, one finds there are a few interesting and relatively new points of protocol that bear reporting.

Office manners are both more considerate and more democratic than they used to be. The boss must make the same show of accessibility to his employees as he does to his customers, and to this end there has been established the shibboleth of the "open door."

As a symbol, the open door may score a point, but that it actually aids communication or raises the general level of manners is rather dubious. Do the employees really come streaming through that open door? "Thank God, no," is probably what most bosses would say in the moment of truth.

Sometimes the symbol is completely hollow. There is an insurance-company president, for example, who is particularly proud of his open door. But the fact is that the executive offices are in haughty isolation on a floor on which 99 percent of the help would fear to be caught dead. About once a month a female personnel officer takes new employees on an indoctrination tour through those hallowed chambers. As she approaches the president's office, she turns, with finger to her lips, and whispers, "Shhh. If we're real quiet, I think Mr. X's door is open a crack, and perhaps we'll be able to see him at work!"

More to the point is the manner in which the boss approaches or summons his subordinates, and here there has been a creditable advance in democracy and gentility. The cryptic command, submitted through a secretary, is less and less in favor. And ditto with buzzer systems. The preferred method is to telephone the subordinate in person, invite, not order, him to drop by, and explain at least in general terms the reason for the conference. Better still, when the geography of the office permits, is for the ranking officer on occasion to trot down to the subordinate's quarters.

This, in turn, poses a little etiquette problem for the junior executive. Should he rise when a senior officer enters his office? Certainly he shouldn't "snap to" and suck in his gut. But despite some company presidents' protestations that the gesture is quite unnecessary, an ambitious junior probably does himself no harm by coming to his feet. A revealing comment comes from a hearty New England executive. "When they give me that routine," he said, "I simply tell them, 'Relax.'" But then he adds, "I suppose it's only the courtesy paid an older man by a young man, and perhaps the young executive who doesn't possess that kind of everyday, natural manners isn't apt to have other desirable business qualities."

When it comes to the use of first names in business, however, the old standards have been rudely shattered, though no conscious discourtesy has been involved in the process. An executive who gets around said this is now a first-name country, and the practice extends throughout most business with the occasional exception of the president and the chairman of the board.

Of 150 businesses queried, 85 percent could be said to operate on a first-name basis, and the list seems to cut across all regions and all types of businesses and industries. The usage, of course, varies in degree. There's a Texas oil company where the president admonishes the veriest newcomer to "call me Harry." There is a West Coast utility which says that "equals and near equals deal with each other on a first-name basis. The newest or youngest is immediately called by his first name, and if he feels comfortable about it, replies similarly." There's one curious instance where the president is called "Jim" by all employees except the top executives, who cling to "Mr."

But now for a strong word of caution. The 15 percent that stick to "Mr." feel strongly about it. A mortage-company official bit off his answer to the question in one sentence: "I don't call people in business by their first names." A life-insurance president said, "That fast jump to the first name—I don't know if it irritates, but it gives you pause, makes you wonder if he has the balanced judgment you're looking for."

So for newcomers and juniors, the consensus of advice is, obviously, to wait for the veterans and seniors to offer the first name, and then, playing it by ear, find the moment when a first-name response comes naturally and comfortably. The sensitive junior will not, of course, overlook the danger in waiting *too* long;

in a first-name country, a forty-year-old who persists in calling his fifty-five-year-old boss "Mr." might seem to be implying that the poor old fellow is about through.

If the burden of this reportage on the manners of the modern American businessman seems too good to be true, readers are entitled to take a small discount. Obviously, in answering a query on good manners, most men muster their own best manners and temper their views with charity. Nevertheless, the consensus was remarkable, and such dissent as was expressed was not from the finding that good manners prevail, but was concerned with the danger of overdoing the thing.

Said a utility-company president of a neighboring oil company notable for its politesse, "For my money, bosses are too bloody servile. They act like an overanxious shopgirl trying to make a sale." And there was the Chicago banker who said, "I'm afraid most of us conform too much. We run the chance that we'll all be mice, and there'll be no rats to lead us."

January 1957

How to Fire an Executive

By PERRIN STRYKER

Few executives will dispute the statement that of all their chores the most unpleasant is the job of firing a fellow executive.

They are not only reluctant to face up to it, they are loath even to talk about it. On this subject there has been no pooling of ideas and publishing of experiences as is to be found on other management problems. This is regrettable, since the firing of executives is a peculiarly varied, complicated, and continuous operation of management.

A large part of every executive's life is a continuous effort to escape being fired. Some of a manager's tactics against the threat may be positive and forthright, such as doing an outstanding job. Or he may employ such defensive tactics as acquiring confidential and critical information about the company—or marrying the boss's daughter. But an executive's surest defense against the threat of firing is to make friends—with the boss, of course, but also with his colleagues and subordinates. And the more skillful he is at this, the harder it is for management to fire him.

In earlier days top management would fire managers nearly as fast as it fired rank-and-file employees. John L. Handy, who heads an executive-recruiting firm in New York City, recalls that back in the early Twenties, when he was in the rubber business, top management at Goodrich fired executives wholesale when rubber prices fell. "The saying was that men twenty years with the company just got their service pins and a kick in the pants."

Abrupt firing tactics are still practiced, especially by owner-managers. One executive tells of watching a woman who heads a cosmetics firm go to work on a colleague who had come into her office to resign. She walked over to him and said, "Don't you know that no one ever resigns from this firm? You're fired!" She then slapped his face, shoved him out into the hall and into the elevator, and tossed after him the hat and coat he had dropped during the onslaught.

But in the great majority of cases today the firing is a slow process. As Handy puts it, "Most managements are now the worst old softies you ever saw. They act as if getting rid of an executive was like kicking a child." One reason for this, of course, is that executives nowadays have become heavily imbued with the doctrines of human and public relations.

No pattern of firing tactics seems characteristic of any one company or industry. Only one tactic seems universal: an executive is practically always fired verbally. Writing is too blunt an instrument for an operation that usually lacerates an executive's most delicate equipment, namely, his ego. And there are dangers. One president who put a terse dismissal notice in a vice president's desk was outmatched by a brilliant countertactic: the vice president never let him know he had received his missive, and the embarrassed president did not send another. The vice president thereafter did his job so well that he eventually became executive vice president.

Usually the president will make the firing a gradual process. The approach may be extremely tentative, as when he takes a manager to lunch and plants a seed of doubt in his mind by asking. "Are you really happy in your job with us?" In one case the approach during a luncheon talk was so diplomatic that the manager didn't realize he'd been fired until he related the conversation to his wife, who broke the news to him.

In more roundabout tactics, as one executive put it, "the situation just deteriorates." Another executive was more specific: "Put them on ice and they'll leave. Give them little to do for three months, and they'll bring the matter up." Here are some other ways of freezing a man out of his job:

1. *The "unavailable" treatment.* An executive can simply keep postponing a meeting requested by a disfavored subordinate. Or the latter may write a memorandum on some subject and then be told repeatedly that the boss "hasn't got around to reading it." If the executive finally succeeds in getting into the boss's office, the boss may hear him out and then curtly advise him, "Don't bother me with that. I haven't the time."

2. *The gradual freeze-out.* This treatment may be started by slowly reducing an executive's authority, or by ridiculing his suggestions in front of others. The treatment may be extended, as in this case cited by an executive-recruiter: One top executive in a steel company was given a three-month leave in Florida; while he was gone the company asked the recruiter to search for a replacement, and when the man returned he was given a different office and asked to make a special study of a subject that was outside his own field. Later he was appointed a "consultant" to the company, but given nothing to work on. At last, the man resigned.

3. *The bypass.* The variations of this treatment range from omitting an executive's name from important memoranda and excluding him from conferences, to taking assignments away from him. Sometimes top management may discover a personal habit that an executive will not break, and use it to break him. The production chief of one company—it also happened to be in the cosmetics industry—insisted on devoting his Sundays to his wife and children. Accordingly, the president and general manager began scheduling meetings on Sundays. When the production executive continued to refuse to attend them, the general manager told him he had to let him go because of his lack of interest in the firm.

Another variation of the bypass is to withhold essential facts from an executive. One advertising-agency partner, for example, got some information about a client's product directly from the client and deliberately concealed it from the executive handling the account. Later, in a meeting with the client and the account executive, the partner referred to this information and questioned his subordinate about it, openly embarrassing him. The executive, long nettled by other tactics, shortly resigned.

Sometimes a bypass tactic will backfire. One personnel consultant recalls a case where, during the three-month illness of an executive vice president, the president established close working ties with the general manager and eventually told him, "It doesn't matter if old Bill comes back; you go ahead and report to me directly anyway." This, however, shortly made the general manager's relations with the executive vice president so uncomfortable that the general manager resigned.

There seems to be no end to the variety of freeze treatments that have been applied to unwanted executives. A company reorganization program is especially full of possibilities. The president can eliminate the man's job completely, or consolidate two departments, demoting one department head to assist the other. Or he can first confuse the man by assigning him to a new job, without specifying what his responsibilities and authorities are—and then criticize him sharply whenever he assumes either. As one purged executive put it. "You can be a round peg in a round hole, and somebody can make the hole square."

Some bypass techniques may be twisted around so that they appear to be "opportunities." A president may reassign a sales executive to a top job in manufacturing, suspecting that the man will fail to make the grade. This maneuver, according to one management consultant, may be adopted when a man of limited talents reaches a top executive level after years of promotion and the company wants to avoid looking foolish by charging him with incompetence after so many years of service.

Occasionally, a boss may resort to downright trickery. Thus one clothing manufacturer, suspecting that his sales manager was on the prowl for a better job, placed a blind newspaper ad for a man who could offer exactly the kind of experience the sales manager possessed. The victim took the bait, answered the ad by letter, and was swiftly fired for his disloyalty.

Probably no other American boss can compete with the late Henry Ford in this field. Throughout his long reign Ford was a willful tyrant. Some of his cruder tactics have become legendary; for instance, having an unwanted executive's furniture piled outside his office and a sign "You're fired" hung on the hatrack. His more elaborate firing methods have been described vividly (although often inaccurately) in a memoir *(We Never Called Him Henry)* written by Harry Bennett, who was Ford's strong-arming, right-hand man for twenty-nine years until he himself was fired by the old man's successor, his son.

President John McCaffrey of International Harvester, for one, frankly admits, "We are not good at firing managers," and he thinks that in his company the necessity to fire them is largely avoided by sticking strictly to a policy of promotion from within. But a certain amount of executive turnover is inevitable in any company, and the process can be an excellent corporate tonic.

A really good executive today is more than likely to be adept at letting his colleagues go, while his skill in managing managers may greatly reduce the necessity for doing it. At any rate, if firing were not treated as an emergency operation but accepted as a continuing—and potentially helpful—fact of corporate life, executives might learn to do it better.

October 1954

Entrepreneurs

Joe Hirshhorn, the Brooklyn Uranium King

By EMMET JOHN HUGHES

Joseph Herman Hirshhorn, age fifty-seven, five feet four inches high, stands at the glittering top of a world he made by and for himself. He looks a bit like Al Smith, walks a bit like Groucho Marx, and thinks a bit (he hopes) like Bernard Baruch. He is bilingual: adequate English and fluent Brooklynese. One day early last May, he sat in his suite in Toronto's Bank of Nova Scotia Building, on the walls of which hang landscapes, still lifes, and abstracts (a part of his million-dollar collection of contemporary American art). For the occasion, there perched on Joe's desk a cake whose pink-and-green frosting proclaimed: "Rio Tinto–Hirshhorn E Pluribus Unum."

Towering at Joe's side stood the natty British figure of Roy William Wright, boss of the Rio Tinto Mining Co. of Canada Ltd. As the cake was cut, Joe sang, "I'll be loving you always and always." He had just traded Rio Tinto Ltd. his equity in a vast sweep of Canadian mining properties—uranium, gold, iron, copper, acquired over a period of two decades at a cost of some $4.8 million—for about $31 million in Canadian Rio Tinto stocks and debentures and the chairmanship of the Canadian company's board.

The story behind this event goes back half a century and to quite another world—to a village in Latvia, in fact, where Joseph Herman Hirshhorn was born in 1899, the twelfth of thirteen children, whose father died in Joe's infancy. Joe was six years old when by train and steerage, via Liverpool, he landed at Ellis Island to join his mother and the rest of her brood in a Brooklyn tenement. "I came out of a hellhole," Joe recalls. "And I was lucky—some of my playmates in that neighborhood found their way to the electric chair." His mother, Amelia, worked in a sweatshop pocketbook factory—twelve hours a day, six days a week, for $12 weekly. With such resources, she moved her family to a slightly more spacious slum on Humboldt Street.

Across the bleak scene flares one flaming memory: a three-alarm fire that in May, 1908, gutted the Humboldt Street tenement. Some upper-floor tenants died in flames—or were impaled on the fence below. The Hirshhorns survived, but Amelia was taken to the hospital while her children scattered around the neighborhood to get along as best they could. "I stayed alive on garbage," Joe murmurs. "Poverty has a bitter taste. I swore I would never know it again."

One day Joe had caught a glimpse on Manhattan's Broad Street of the New York Curb Market. "It fascinated the hell outta me," he remembers. "The wigwagging-like deaf-and-dumb signals between sidewalks and windows, the brokers with their colored hats." Three years later, still not knowing what it was all about, he went back to the Curb.

He was fourteen years old: "It was 1914. The exchanges were closed [at the beginning of World War I], and when I wandered onto the Curb," he recalls, "there were all these guys sitting around playing cards, and when I told them what I wanted, they just laughed at me. 'Hell, sonny, we're lookin' for jobs ourselves.'"

Joe patiently plodded through the offices of lower Broadway until he found a job with the Emerson Phonograph Co. as office boy and noon-hour switchboard operator. Such a start was less than spectacular, but it sufficed. Emerson's general manager was also editor and publisher of the *Magazine of Wall Street* and had an office with a ticker in it. "So after six months," Joe recalls, "I marched into his office and said I was no office boy, I wanted to be a broker." A fortnight later Joe was charting stocks at $12 a week.

At seventeen, he struck out on his own. He had, to start with, a sum of $255. Within a year, as a broker on the Curb, he had made his first fortune: $168,000. The Twenties saw him grow rich. In 1922 he married Jennie Berman, of Brooklyn, who was to bear him four children. In 1924 he quit the Curb to trade in unlisted securities, first in a short-lived partnership and a year later in his own J. H. Hirshhorn & Co. By 1928, Joe Hirshhorn, strictly a brokers' broker, was ringing up profits at a $200,000-a-month clip.

More memorable than the scaling of such heights, however, was Joe's tiptoeing back from the precipice that lay just ahead. In the glittering spring of 1929, he was thinking of paying over $500,000 for a seat on the New York Stock Exchange, but pulled back. He remembers it this way: "When it got to where doctors and dentists were quitting their jobs to speculate, you knew it was all crazy. I could see IT coming. I got scared. I sold everything I had in August." He got out with $4 million.

Meanwhile he had discovered Canada. He had been up there to look things over once or twice and he had been much impressed by what he had heard about Canadian gold. And early in 1933, J. H. Hirshhorn & Co., Ltd., opened its doors, to be one of the few brokers' brokers in Toronto. For quite a while Canada was anything but hospitable to Joe. Neither Toronto society nor its stiffly conservative banking fraternity could understand, much less like, the man who chattered like a Brooklyn peddler, and let his good spirits explode in such phrases as: "I feel felonious!"

Preston East Dome was a gold-mining company formed early in the century in the hopeful shadow of a great gold strike in the Porcupine area of northern Ontario. A fire had destroyed the company's installations, Preston East Dome was out of funds, and its stock certificates were selling for less than 5 cents on the Toronto exchange. Everyone had given up hope of making something of Preston, except a geologist named Douglas Wright who made his way to Joe's office. Joe liked what Wright told him and put up $25,000 for a drilling program. Within a few months, gold was struck. The mine today is grossing an annual $2.5 million. Last May, when he threw his Preston holdings into the deal with Rio

Sign language from the old Curb market:

Joe wants to "buy" . . .   *"one" . . .*

Tinto, they were valued at $7.55 a share. It was, as Joe says, quite a big ticket.

Thanks to such tickets, Joe, through the Thirties, found himself living in a world ever further removed from the bitter memory of Brooklyn. He now traveled a circuit of two apartments and three homes—the apartments in Toronto and New York, homes in Great Neck, Long Island, Miami, and the Poconos. To soften the hours spent poring over corporate balance sheets he installed a Capehart* in every house, and bought himself seven pianos. In the Poconos he built a splendid French provincial house on the 470-acre Huckleberry Hill Farm, with handball courts, Guernsey herds, and dormitories big enough to accommodate any twenty-four school chums his children might like to bring home. "It was built from the heart," Joe remembers. "But—I was the only Jew around for twenty-five miles. We were left alone." Finally, he sold Huckleberry Hill Farm to the Kress family for a third of what it had cost him.

*An expensive radio-phonograph console.

"thousand"   *at "500"*

In 1945, Joe's marriage ended in divorce. "To do what I did, you gotta work, you gotta work like crazy. I sacrificed my family, my relations with my wife and my kids." He married again, was divorced, and married again.

But through those troubled years Joe kept at his steady run. Some people thought they saw something reprehensible about it. Mining has notoriously held an attraction for penny-stock tricksters, the "hit-and-run" boys, the venal array that prompted Mark Twain to describe a gold mine as simply a big hole with a liar at the other end. Inevitably, many of the chances Joe took with his own and other people's money—a list of mining gambles with names like Anglo Rouyn, Armistice, Aquarius, Calder Bousquet—fell below high hopes. Yet Joe never quit on a company. When, for instance, Anglo Rouyn's gold petered out, Joe switched the company into Saskatchewan copper (Anglo Rouyn was one of the biggest Hirshhorn properties in the Rio Tinto deal). The verdict on Hirshhorn heard today in the Ontario Securities Commission's offices is that his financing has been sound, his geological advice the best, and his legal counsel responsible and respected.

The idea that Franc Joubin, a mining consultant, expostulated to Joe in 1952 was an explanation of the riddle of Ontario's Algoma Basin north of Lake Huron, a heavily explored area whose bush-shrouded acres had been tramped by prospectors and geologists. Everyone had seen his Geiger kick excitedly from time to time. All had taken samples for assays from the surface, where uranium was supposed to lie, but every assay had shown only negligible amounts. Everyone decided the Geiger readings must have come from thorium, for which there was no market.

Joubin decided to test an old Algoma ore sample for thorium itself—and found there was hardly any. He was sure then that he knew the answer: rain and snow and sulfur in the earth had leached away the radioactivity in surface outcroppings in the basin, and the Geigers had chattered the truth of big uranium-ore bodies *beneath* the surface.

"I bought on my faith in the man," Joe says. "That's what counts with me. I don't ask my grandmother or a fortune-teller." Joe put up $30,000. Joubin had an option to buy a 10 percent share of the deal. (His 10 percent was to make him a multimillionaire.) Drilling began in April, 1953. The core samples were sent to Vancouver for assaying. One morning in May, a bulky envelope came back to Joubin's desk. The report was that out of fifty-six samples, fifty contained uranium.

The area to be staked was filled with hunters and vacationers and lay close to a major highway and a Canadian Pacific rail line and the depressed little lumber town, Blind River; the risk of the operation's becoming known was enormous. Geigers, tents, sleeping bags, and tons of food had to be quietly assembled. Hirshhorn and his colleagues purchased mining licenses in scattered spots all over Ontario. Bases were set up at scattered points, one at South Porcupine, 200 miles above Blind River. Lawyers were lined up to draft claim papers as fast as the staking parties made their way through the bush.

When the expedition's pontoon planes took off from South Porcupine, they headed north, then swung southwest to Algoma, and there deposited in the bush some of the four-score stakers, who still did not know exactly where they were. For six weeks the crews snaked along a ninety-mile Z, following their chattering Geigers. A halt was called July 9. And on July 11, in mining recorders' offices all over Ontario, lawyers and engineers raced in to enter a total of 1,400 claims covering 56,000 acres.

Pronto Uranium Mines was formed. In August, 1955, Pronto's Blind River mill began operating—to break all Canadian records for a mine of this size. The Hirshhorn-Joubin staking rush was followed by the rush of other promoters. By 1957 it is expected that eleven mines will be operating in the Blind River area. Blind River signifies a good deal more than the climax of a Brooklyn boy's career; it means uranium-ore reserves estimated to be at least 100 million tons—and probably several times that.

The triumph of Blind River posed, for Joe, an old problem: Now that you've got it, what are you going to do with it? Two decades of speculating had involved him in operations spanning Canada—oil and real estate, gold, copper, iron ore ("In mining I have no favorites; I'll mine granite if it will pay"). Blind River, on top of all this, was, in a way, just too much. The moment obviously called for stocktaking in the fullest sense—combing all the corporations out of the pockets of Joe's old clothes, adding them up, and putting them together in some sane order.

The answer came in the shape of eighty-three-year-old Rio Tinto Co., Ltd., of London. Rio Tinto, in which the Rothschilds had large interests, had just finished selling the bulk of its great Spanish holdings in copper, sulfur, and iron pyrites, and it was especially interested in a uranium investment. Rio Tinto wanted permanent control over Hirshhorn's whole Canadian mining empire, and Joe needed a corporate package for all his holdings. The result, last May, was Rio Tinto Mining Co. of Canada, Ltd. Into this elegant new receptacle Joe dropped all of his holdings in forty-six different Canadian mining companies (one of which was itself a package of seventeen earlier companies). Although Joe did not get voting control, he owned the biggest single slice of equity (55 percent).

There were some memorable moments during the long months of negotiating that threw Hirshhorn of Brooklyn into a roomful of London's financial aristocrats. Joe would throw his feet on the furniture, chew his unlit cigar unremittingly, and jar leisurely British discourse to an end with a phrase like: "Let's cut the baloney and make a decision, eh?" But when the whole improbable encounter was concluded, there prevailed a mutual and affectionate respect.

Joe Hirshhorn is most impressive when—with unlit cigar jammed between tight lips—he reaches for a telephone. To Joe, the telephone is like a vital physical organ, certainly to be valued, for example, above one kidney, or some miscellaneous glands. This is not entirely figurative. His twenty-seven-year-old son, Gordon, recalls one night in 1947 when he and his sister were summoned to Joe's bedside in a New York hospital, where Joe lay gravely ill with peritonitis. Joe was coming out of the anesthesia, both arms pinned beneath devices for transfusion and intravenous feeding. As the children tiptoed into the room, the semi-darkness was rent with the scream: "Get this goddam thing outta my arm—I gotta make a phone call." The children softly retired, reassured.

The phone is the pulse of his whole office. Into the telephone rattles: "Not interested, pal, not interested—I don't wanna make any more money, get it? Take it to somebody else, PLEASE." To a charitable solicitation: "O.K., O.K., O.K., I got the idea—how much you want?" On being asked his opinion of an executive: "He's crazy. He is also a dope." To an exciting proposition: "I'm with you—put me on your team, kid—I wanna fix up the world too—just gimme a hammer and nails, and tell me what's to be done...."

There has never been any master design to Joe's course of action. There has simply been that spur to action, the passion of the born speculator. "Just to test my judgment—that's what gives me the great kick," Joe explains. "The money doesn't matter—not after the first million. How could it? You can't wear more than two shirts a day, or eat more than three meals."

But beyond that, according to one of Joe's friends, there is in him a fervor for making something out of nothing. "I'm not interested in the industrial or manufacturing picture," Joe explains. "That's strictly competitive, not truly creative. . . . No, I don't have a very high regard for Wall Street—it's parasitical—what does it *create?* But *resources*—that's something else. There you're in the world of the Harrimans and the Huntingtons and the men who really *built*. So look at Blind River. It took a lousy $30,000 to get it started—and now there's four, maybe eight, billion dollars in wealth there. But that isn't all. There will be 20,000 people making their living there by the end of next year. There are railroads. There are mills. There are homes. There are schools. The whole works. It's new. It's just born. And I'm glad I helped build it."

November 1956

Joyce Hall Is Thinking of You
By SEYMOUR FREEDGOOD

Not long after Hallmark Cards opened its resplendent new $8-million building in Kansas City, a couple of hard-faced men put the intellectual foundations of the company to a formidable test. Striding into the sumptuous lobby, the pair informed the receptionist that they wanted a Hallmark card ("When You Care Enough to Send the Very Best") to console a friend who was about to be executed in the state penitentiary. The firm, which prides itself on having a greeting card to suit any occasion, rose to this one. Memories have blurred, but the company's best recollection is that the men were offered Hallmark's all-time best-seller, the Pansy card—a 5-cent general-purpose "Friendship" item "To Let You Know I'm Thinking of You," although not specifying what. The customers were apparently satisfied, and so, the company hoped, was their friend.

The booming greeting-card industry has moved far from those simple times, less than a generation ago, when all but a tiny fraction of its trade was Christmas, valentine, and birthday cards. Today it still labors to put out new batches of "seasonals" to mark the major holidays and half a dozen minor ones. But no big publisher may rest easy unless his inventory also contains a broad range of designs and sentiments calculated to ring the changes on all "everyday" incidents from conception ("A Little Bird Told Me You Were Expecting") through all the triumphs and vicissitudes of the human condition to ultimate demise ("Heartfelt Sympathy"). There are, in addition, the great variety of Friendship cards— Hello, Good-bye, Thinking of You, Cheer Up, Why Haven't You Written. By way of the new "studio" cards (so called from the many little art studios that began to produce them after World War II), it is also possible to send hangover condolences or advise the boss to drop dead. The net result is that this year the industry will gross about $275 million from the sale of over five billion cards to retailers. At retail, sales will run to about $550 million.

Hallmark is a private corporation whose stock is entirely held by Founder, President, and Board Chairman Joyce C. Hall, members of his family, and a few top executives. Today its gross is believed to be bigger than the combined sales of its three major competitors. (As a privately owned company, it publishes no sales figures, but a reasonable guess at its 1958 volume would be about $80 million.)

The company's success in extracting hard cash out of the demand for soft sentiment is in large part due to the brilliant stratagems devised by the proprietor. Of these the most notable was his decision, unique in the industry, to begin advertising on the air: his TV spectaculars, for example—a long series of distinguished plays, including productions of *Hamlet* and *Macbeth*— have done much to identify Hallmark with "quality," and greeting cards with Hallmark.

Propelling and sustaining Hallmark's rise is a complex production and retail-supply organization. From their offices on the top floor of Hallmark's seven-story building, Joyce Hall and his small group of top managers oversee a 4,800-man work force involved in the planning, creation, manufacture, and sale of some 11,000 lines of cards and specialty items (gift wraps, ribbons, party decorations, paper hats, etc.), which Hallmark distributes to 18,000 dealers at the rate of over one billion a year. Every year 7,000 of the company's items are redesigned. To do this and to create new items, Hallmark maintains what it believes to be the biggest art department in the world: over 300 designers, tinters, letterers, etc., plus some thirty-five writers and editors. It also makes extensive use of outside talent—for example, such artists as Norman Rockwell, Saul Steinberg, Winston Churchill, and writers like Ogden Nash, Father James Keller (of the Christophers), and Dr. Norman Vincent Peale.

Founder Joyce Clyde Hall (to all but his most intimate associates he is *Mr.* Hall or, occasionally, "J.C.") is, at sixty-seven, an erect, urbane six-footer with an imperious manner, a calculating eye, and a prairie man's twang, who laid the groundwork for his $80-million corporation in 1910 when he rented a cubicle over a Kansas City shoeshine parlor and set up shop as a post card jobber. From that day on, his preoccupation with his business has been so great as to baffle—when it has not outraged—his competitors and many of his employees. Says a former executive, "Never in my life have I seen anything, except the worship of God, taken as seriously as J.C. takes greeting cards."

Hall is full of many apparent contradictions. He fervently believes that the child-labor laws "are one of the worst things that ever happened to this country. They've destroyed the pioneer spirit." On the other hand, he has set up what is perhaps the country's most liberal employee-benefit and profit-sharing plan for his staffers, over whom he rules as a stern yet beneficent father, supervising almost every detail of their working lives, including the food served them in the company's excellent cafeteria. Hall's international competitions for painters and his touring art exhibits have made him a major patron of the fine arts. His own taste in painters, however, runs to Norman Rockwell; and in poets to Edgar Guest, whose verses have adorned Hallmark cards since the 1920's.

Hall's possessiveness and "inconsistencies" create frustrations for his top managers, some of whom occasionally feel they could run the business better without him. "He won't delegate," one of his subordinates complained recently.

"I know I ought to give those fellows more authority," Hall observes. "But if I let go, who's going to pin them to the cross? That's what makes an executive. He's a guy like me who's got to police things and see that they get done."

Twice a day, Hall meets with his O.K. Committee to decide which of the latest crop of hand-painted designs are to go into production. Hall usually likes to be in on even the most minute of these decisions. To a considerable extent he relies on hunches, or "the vapor of past experience," as he likes to put it. "I know I know, and I know that I'm right—there's something in the past forty-eight years that's telling me."

However, accurate as Hall's intuitions usually are, he and the O.K. Committee lean heavily on market information from the dealers. With the sales history of each of their items on hand, Hallmark's researchers can analyze the design, motif, style, color, sentiment, etc., of all the best and worst sellers. This analysis has produced some useful insights: Hallmark's writers try to avoid the use of the word "mighty"—research has shown that it pulls down sales. Peacocks are unpopular; the old superstition that peacocks bring bad luck still prevails. In addition, the reports record changes in public taste—e.g., although the red rose continues to be the best flower seller, buyers are showing a rising preference for white and pink ones.

What the public still appears to want most is a card delicately illustrated with one or more babies, bunnies, cherubs, pussycats,

Santas, Easter eggs, hearts, or flowers, and carrying a folksy message. Thus, for a wedding-anniversary greeting "To a Swell Couple," Hallmark offers a card depicting a pair of ducklings:

> *Don't know who gets the credit*
> *For your happy married life—*
> *Must be a case of one swell guy*
> *Who's got a real swell wife!!*

A card presumably intended for a very young friend is illustrated with a basketful of blue-eyed kittens:

> *These kittens feel important—*
> *'Cause here's what they get to do—*
> *They get to bring this birthday wish*
> *Especially "FUR" you!*

To be sure, the taste for this kind of card is not universal. Nevertheless, the public appetite for pussycats appears to be insatiable.

To create the bulk of his cards, Hall has set up a production line staffed for the most part by young women—because, as Mrs. Jeannette Lee, Hallmark's art director, explains it, "Girls are usually happier working on cherubs and babies than men." When the planners decide that one of their cards must be redesigned, they send off a "ticket" indicating the general specifications of the card to be supplied—e.g., "15-cent Cheer, Humorous, For Moderately Sick Man." Two or three times a week the editorial department, which thinks up the ideas the illustrators will follow, receives bundles of such tickets. Three or four editors and writers may get together to brainstorm. From these exhausting sessions, during which the participants from long practice may communicate as often in verse as in prose, an idea will generally emerge. Not long ago there was a call for a 10-cent General Friendship card, humorously written and illustrated, which would enable just about anyone to inquire about the well-being of just about anyone else. A writer came up with the idea of having some limpid-eyed animal peer from the card with the message: "Just Little Ole Me . . . Sayn' How Ya Be?" But what kind of limpid-eyed animal? A giraffe? A Kodiak bear? The writers, in joint council with Hallmark's chief designers, decided (presumably on the basis of what the public was then buying most in the way of appealing animals) on a limpid-eyed hippopotamus.

The result of the brainstorming will go to Hallmark's art department. Talented men and women prepare the rough sketches for each card and indicate the exact tones needed for reproduction. Then "finishers" take over: deft, pretty young women who do the actual watercolor work. Perched in front of their drawing boards, many of them look astonishingly like the cherubs, if not the pussycats, they delicately paint.

There is a second art studio, sequestered from the first in a glass-enclosed room, where a small group of young men design the "contemporary" line. "We put them off in a special cage," Hall explains, "because we were afraid they'd be an explosive force on the others."

Eight years ago Hall warned that such cards might ruin the industry. The genre was originally designed to suit the needs of an "audience too literate and sophisticated ever to buy ordinary commercial cards." But by 1950 the market was flooded with "slam" and "insult" cards that were increasingly brutal, sexually suggestive, and (as the trade puts it) "sick." Many of the big publishers, who had been sniffing the trend toward greater sophistication, drew back. Hall, whose concern for the industry is second only to his feeling for Hallmark, decried the new cards as "vulgar" and "horrible."

Then in the mid-1950's data from Hallmark's dealers seemed to prove that a nationwide mass audience had developed for so-called sophisticated cards. Hall remained dubious. But he was more or less out of touch with the business at the time, having contracted polycythemia, from which he did not fully recover until 1955. By the time Hall returned to full duty, Robert McCloskey of the art department, to Hall's intense astonishment, had already developed several cards that soon became best-sellers. A number of people have come to share Hall's astonishment. One of the most successful of the new cards, for example, depicted a man perilously close to involutional melancholia and bore the legend, "Happy Monday." What had come over the American public? Sales began to climb, and, soon after, every major publisher followed Hallmark into the new market.

No man to fight a rising sales curve, Joyce Hall moved ahead briskly to satisfy the urge to be beastly. This February, Hallmark is releasing for the first time a line of "Sharp Dart" valentines. The

Sharp Darts, which Hall conceived a year ago and then bucked through the production over the objections of most of his subordinates, are plainly derived from the nineteenth-century "penny horrible" valentines, and many of them, like their predecessors, are (as one Hallmark executive puts it) "plain mean." Under the caption "What A Gossip," one card has this to say of a sleazy blonde who, equipped with field glasses, telescope, and telephone, leers near an open window:

> You never say a friendly word
> Just dirty gossip that you've heard
> You've really got a lot of gall
> No wonder you've no friends at all.

Hall admits some concern about the effect of the Sharp Darts on Hallmark's reputation for wholesomeness. "This whole line bothers me," he said recently. "I don't want to do anything destructive, but I know they'll sell jillions."

December 1958

Science

The Exploration of "Inner Space"

By GEORGE A. W. BOEHM

Imagine a team of scientists from another planet hovering covertly in Earth's overcast. From their spaceship a mile or so up, they are investigating this planet. They lower cameras through the clouds. They bring up a sampling of air polluted with fumes from a smelting plant and wonder, "What life can exist in this sulfurous atmosphere?" A small scoop on the end of a wire brings up the green scum from the surface of a stagnant pond, indicating that there is some kind of life. Meanwhile, they study the contours that are being traced on their radar screen—the ups and downs of hills and valleys—which they can translate into crude topographical maps. The situation of these unearthly scientists is comparable to the situation and the problems that confront oceanographers.

The men who are investigating the oceans down to the bottom ooze and the underlying crust of the earth are exploring an "inner space." Diving vessels are clumsy and unmaneuverable; oceanographers must grope blindly with instruments to measure pressure, temperature, and the chemical composition of water. At all depths the seas are in constant motion; even the deepest waters swirl in eddies or jiggle like jelly in a cup. A scientist can scarcely ever be sure whether his records are typical, or merely reflect some freak local condition.

Yet from millions of scientific measurements made from the pitching decks of small ships there is being gradually pieced together a picture of the oceans from top to bottom. Putting together cause and effect, scientists are beginning to explain the mighty forces that circulate the water, shape and reshape the ocean bottom, and pour energy into the air to drive the winds.

The oceans may, indeed, hold the keys to the survival of mankind. They can yield food for a world population that threatens to triple within the next century. They may, or may not, provide a safe dumping ground for the deadly wastes of the atomic age.

The oceans apparently are in constant motion at all levels. Oceanographers have detected flowing water down to more than 35,000 feet, as far as they have lowered their instruments, and photographs of the deep-sea floor reveal ripples in the sand and ooze.

Deep circulation is wholly unlike surface circulation; both the pattern and the causes are different. Winds have no direct effect below 300 feet. What sets the deep water in motion are subtle differences in density. Cold water is heavier than warm; salty water is heavier than fresh. In the North Atlantic, for example, surface water brought north by the Gulf Stream becomes chilled. Being exceptionally salty (because of evaporation as it passes through the tropics), it becomes slightly heavier than the surrounding water. It therefore sinks and slides southward under the warmer (and therefore lighter) water of the mid-latitudes. This sequence accounts for a broad sheet of water that flows toward the equator between the depths of 6,000 and 9,000 feet.

In an even grander and more leisurely way the oceans continually turn over, top for bottom. The motion is too slow to meter (a fraction of an inch per day on the average), but oceanographers infer the heaving from the distribution of oxygen in the sea. Surface water dissolves oxygen from the air; submerged water gradually loses oxygen. Thus every bottle of water hauled from the depths reveals the date when it was last at the surface. From tens of thousands of samples brought up from all levels oceanographers estimate that the Atlantic turns over once every 500 to 1,000 years; the Pacific takes perhaps twice as long.

This overturning may determine whether man can safely exploit atomic energy on a large scale. Every year tons of atomic wastes will have to be deposited somewhere while their radioactivity decays—a process that takes centuries. The ocean floor seems to be the only storehouse that is sufficiently large, well shielded, and remote to contain all the deadly garbage the atomic age is likely to produce. To be sure, wastes will be encased in sealed containers, but seals may leak and containers corrode and break. It clearly won't do to dump wastes in places where strong upward currents might carry them to the surface. Oceanographers will have to pinpoint stagnant areas on the bottom.

Even then there may be complications. Some animals concentrate certain chemical elements a millionfold or more; some microscopic beasts called foraminifera, for example, contain approximately four million times as much titanium as the water they inhabit. Such an animal might digest a considerable amount of radioactivity, then swim upward a few hundred feet, and be eaten by another animal. If this process continued, it is conceivable that a chain of animals, like a bucket brigade, might eventually bring to the surface dangerous amounts of radioactivity. Oceanographers will have to learn more about the eating and migrating habits of sea creatures before the radioactive disposal problem is solved.

November 1959

Labor and Government

The Next American Labor Movement
By DANIEL BELL

A political party is defeated; two men, Phil Murray and William Green, die; a third, Dan Tobin, retires—and a twenty-year era is closed. Not often do history and Providence join to mark so sharp a turning point. The era just ended was defined variously as "the new Statism," "the laboristic society," or even "labor rule." Suddenly, none of the definitions means much of anything. None describes the present quality of the relationships of U.S. management, labor, and government.

The salient fact today is that labor is on the defensive. The tangible evidence of a rising American living standard, and the steadily growing sense of social responsibility among corporations, have given the business community new prestige, indeed an ascendancy in society at large. The middle-class aspirations of U.S. workers, the desire and ability to own a house, a car, and other essential luxuries of middle-class living, have led to an acceptance of the capitalist system and its technology.

For those who saw unionism as a radical challenge to the social order, management's initiative in human-relations programs in the factory, in financing higher education, in community responsibility, etc., has instilled a sense of gloom. In one form or another, many labor intellectuals have accepted an image of the future that was stated baldly by Columbia sociologist C. Wright Mills. In a book written five years ago, *The New Men of Power,* Mills predicted a "bureaucratic integration of labor unions with business enterprises." In this view the labor movement was being taken into camp by the "sophisticated conservatives, represented by magazines like *Fortune.* . . ." Unlike the old-fashioned conservatives who want to break unions, "they [the sophisticates] hold that unions are a stabilizing force and should be encouraged as a counterforce against radical movements . . . they would have the trade-union leader end up in their personnel and public-relations departments as a junior lieutenant of the captain of industry."

The election confirmed and deepened this gloom. For the union intellectuals, the victory of Eisenhower and the "smart Dewey boys" around him represents the political triumph of the "sophisticated conservatives." Now they feel the labor movement will really be taken into camp. Says Sol Barkin, research director of the C.I.O. Textile Workers Union, "They will buy us off, splinter us, and contain us."

The gloom merges with a specific political dilemma. Labor unions, unlike a political party, can never array themselves in total opposition to the reigning Administration in Washington. While collective bargaining on money issues may in the future be settled without White House intervention, there is a whole range of issues in which labor has to bargain politically with the powers that be, whatever it thinks of the powers that be.

Some unionists have urged labor to stay out of Republican Washington. Short of all-out war, it is unlikely that unionists would participate in any new tripartite agency to regulate wages and enforce stabilization controls. But the advice to stay out of the government altogether is not likely to be accepted—the government is just too important and influential. The acceptance of this fact of life is only a beginning, however. How far should labor go in asking for "representation" in government agencies? Would such representation be window dressing, or would there be an effective voice in shaping policy? If labor took any responsibility for policy, how far would that hamper labor criticism of Eisenhower's general policies? If some of labor's legislative goals are reached, how much of a political payoff to the Republicans is required?

The guaranteed annual wage will be the next demand on labor's agenda. The g.a.w. is not a new notion, of course; in the past, however, it has been primarily a trading point. It now becomes a serious demand. The g.a.w. is in one sense a continuation of labor's historic drive for security. But to see it only as such is to miss the deeper, profoundly conservative significance of labor's quest for a status within capitalist society. The demand for an annual wage, another name for a salary, is a demand for equality with the managers, professionals, and white-collar workers.

The debate over the g.a.w. essentially repeats the great labor-management debate over pensions. Industry will argue that the g.a.w. creates a rigid labor force and a high fixed charge on corporate reserves. Labor will argue that with an established income, workers could plan expenditures and buy more evenly, in turn permitting steadier expansion in consumer-goods industries.

The guaranteed annual wage would create short-run cost burdens, as pensions and high wages have, for particular enterprises. But these labor demands have helped give U.S. capitalism the dynamic quality that has made it so different from the European model. By becoming costly, labor has spurred industry to more efficient planning and to mechanization. And U.S. mass-production unions by and large have not balked at large-scale technological change.

In this respect the industrial history of the last fifteen years has been a fruitful tension between "progress" and "equality." Management, through technology, has taken the lead in expanding production, creating, as Schumpeter put it, "short-run inequities for the sake of long-run rise in living standards." And the trade unions have fostered egalitarianism by their insistence on such innovations as grievance systems, seniority, pensions, and welfare benefits.

Labor's major problems in the next decade are not confined to its relations with government and industry. With the passing of the old labor tycoons, the new leadership inherits an internal "managerial problem" of staggering proportions.

In odd and lagging fashion, the structure and posture of Big Labor have often caricatured those of Big Business. After all, unionism too is a big business, with its own staff and line operations. The number of full-time labor officials is enormous. About 15,000 to 20,000 officials are employed by the national unions. Another 15,000 to 20,000 full-time functionaries serve some 70,000 local unions and 1,000 central labor bodies. It takes about 500,000 more people to fill out the line of union organization; a large proportion of these serve as union stewards or committeemen and receive plant compensation for time spent on union grievances, collective bargaining, etc.

Surveying their huge and often inchoate domains, the new labor leaders face a problem akin to one faced thirty years ago by those who gave character to the American corporation. The modern corporation was the creation of a group of "organizers," the Sloans, Teagles, Swopes, and Giffords, who took the sprawling enterprises flung up by the empire builders and gave them organizational cast and continuity. In the next few years the labor movement will have to "rationalize" and create, in the neutral meaning of the word, a "bureaucracy" that will give big unionism a cast and continuity of its own.

April 1953

GSA: Washington's Most Durable Mess
By HERBERT SOLOW

Three years ago the Republican party asked for a chance to "clean up the mess in Washington." One aspect of the mess was the giant General Services Administration, purchasing agent and property manager for much of the U.S. Government. GSA's 25,686 employees buy, sell, construct, rent, lease, maintain, design, research, mine, manufacture, transport, store, and otherwise "service" most federal agencies outside the Pentagon (and in some respects the military, too). GSA holds almost $9 billion in land, buildings, automobiles, clerical supplies, and other physical assets ($4 billion more than General Motors' assets). Its purchases in fiscal 1954 came to $1 billion. GSA is, in effect, a vast, diversified commercial-industrial corporation in the government, and its operations touch thousands of enterprises outside the government. And GSA is in just as much of a mess today as it was in 1952.

The irony of this situation is not confined to the fact that the Republicans campaigned against messes. The mess that Truman left behind in GSA was especially susceptible to a businessman's cleanup, and the Eisenhower Administration is full of businessmen. To enrich the irony, the very conception of GSA as a consolidated service agency was Republican in origin, created on the recommendation of the first Hoover Commission.

It is the most durable mess in Washington. It would take a congressional investigation to light up the whole of it. It involves great U.S. corporations and marginal operators; oriental swindlers and Caribbean grafters; Chicago politicians; Washington influence-peddlers and fixers; and, above all, time-serving bureaucrats who are neither Republicans nor Democrats, nor yet honest mavericks, but just job holders, glowing with contempt for the U.S. taxpayer.

Happily, the cast also includes some honest, capable, GSA employees, men harried, half underground, and hoping for better days.

September 1955

Regulation by Elephant, Rabbit and Lark
By GEORGE BOOKMAN

Chief Judge E. Barrett Prettyman, of the U.S. Circuit Court of Appeals for the District of Columbia, is not only a distinguished jurist but also one of that noble breed of Americans, a Virginia gentleman. As such, he is of course a good judge of corn whiskey and horseflesh, and also possesses that other mark of good breeding—a sprightly ability to express his thoughts in clear, pungent English. In the course of a lecture series appropriately titled "Trial by Agency," delivered at the University of Virginia Law School, Judge Prettyman summed up his impressions of government administrative agencies, after a lifetime of studying them as a practitioner and later as a judge. "To a purist in the theory of American government, an administrative agency is a hybrid, indeed a monstrosity," he observed. "It is part elephant, part jack rabbit, and part field lark."

Currently, Congress and the President are deeply concerned about the administrative agencies, whose loosely defined powers cut across the three principal governmental branches: legislative, executive, and judicial. The problem centers around the seven major agencies, designated as "independent" by Congress, which have such aggregate power over business that they have been called the "fourth branch of the government." Their writ runs into every facet of the economy, as their names imply: the Interstate Commerce Commission, Federal Trade Commission, Federal Communications Commission, Federal Power Commission, Securities and Exchange Commission, Civil Aeronautics Board, and National Labor Relations Board. Without sanction of these agencies, no railroad, no airline, no interstate trucker, no pipeline or barge line may introduce a new service, discontinue an old service, or set a rate; no radio or television station may operate; no gas producer may market his fuel or figure its price in interstate commerce; no interstate public utility may build a power plant; no sizable firm may market a new security, or safely plan a merger.

The agencies that administer these vast powers have been a problem to the President and Congress virtually since the first one, the ICC, was established in 1887. They were invented for an inherently difficult task: to lay down practical rules for business, under broad policy statutes from Congress, without taking over from businessmen functions that are rightfully theirs in a free marketplace. Working in the fluid field of administrative law, the agencies were invented to make decisions that would be swift, sure, and expert both on events already past (i.e., adjudicating cases) and also in anticipating the future by making rules to cope with the ingenuity of businessmen and the effects of new discoveries in science and technology. The agencies were supposed to be as weighty and dispassionate as courts, yet not so rigid in procedures; as active as the executive branch, but not so political in outlook; as responsive to the public interest as Congress, yet able to dart quickly into the details of the changing industrial scene.

June 1961

Economics

Capital Goods: The Critical Factor
By GILBERT BURCK and SANFORD PARKER

The best economic news in years is that the often-predicted and much-feared post-Korean slump in capital goods has failed to materialize, and that the capital-goods market appears to be expanding once more. This good omen, which has gone practically unnoticed in all the jubilation about the current improvement in general business conditions, contains the real key to the national economic destiny. Let only this trend strengthen, and the nation's growth and prosperity automatically and quickly gain strength. But let the trend begin to disintegrate, and the nation's economic health begins to disintegrate.

The trend is turning up despite the fact that American business has spent no less than $300 billion on capital goods in the nine years since World War II. The probability is that capital-goods spending over the next five years will at worst average no less than the near-record $36 billion of 1954, and it may rise as much as a third higher. Between now and 1959, the U.S. will probably spend around $200 billion on capital goods. This is a truly stupendous prospect.

There are three reasons why the behavior of the capital-goods market is of surpassing importance:

1. Capital goods are the "procreative property" of industrial society—the manufactured goods whose sole function is to produce and distribute other goods and services—and as such they are basically responsible for rising productivity and national wealth. The chief economic difference between primitive and civilized man lies in civilized man's facility in creating and using capital goods. A nation must learn to create and increase a stock of those goods if it wants to progress; a nation that fails to replace or increase its stock begins automatically to retrogress.

2. Capital goods in themselves constitute a sizable and important part of the U.S. economy; last year their sales came to $37 billion—more than the factory value of all new cars, new homes, and other durable goods for consumers taken together.* They include the innumerable machines, buildings, and equipment that make, process, transport, and display the nation's goods and services; and the five million people who make them are scattered over nearly every industrial area of consequence. Tick off a few of the important capital goods and you are soon calling the roll of America's oldest and newest factory towns—the locomotives, forgings, and transformers of the great Delaware Valley industrial complex; the machine tools of Bridgeport, Connecticut, and Cincinnati; the turbines and generators of Schenectady, New York, and Lynn, Massachusetts; the pumps and irrigation machines of Alhambra, California.

*Capital goods as defined in this article include only business expenditures on plant and equipment—no government armaments, roads, or other public works; no personal-consumption spending even on autos or other durables.

3. This is not all. What is vastly more important, capital goods play an economic role all out of proportion to their dollar volume. For they not only *exaggerate* but *accelerate* and sometimes lead the pace of the economy as a whole. When business in general falls off, the capital-goods business tends to decline much more and thus intensify the general decline; when business in general advances, the capital-goods business tends to race ahead of it and thus to intensify the general rise.

Economists of such widely varying stripe as Karl Marx, Wesley Mitchell, and John Maynard Keynes have agreed that the eccentricity of the capital-goods market is a critical factor in business cycles, and their theories about it in the main differ only as to why and how the tendency occurs. Some economists have built whole theories of the business cycle on the concept of the "acceleration principle," originated by Columbia's J. M. Clark. This principle says capital-goods buying is affected merely by the *rate* of change in national output—i.e., even if national output is growing, a decline in the rate of its growth will result in a decline in the volume of capital spending.

Fully formulated in all their intricate and prolix splendor, the theories based on the "acceleration principle" probably try to cover too much ground, but there is no doubt about the two assumptions on which they rest: not only does capital-goods volume accelerate the swings of the economy as a whole by fluctuating more than the economy as a whole, but the total stock of capital goods cannot increase faster than consumption very long before a general decline sets in. History, indeed, has put its cachet on these two assumptions. Capital-goods buying fell much more than general business in the panic of 1907, the recession of 1921, and in the Great Depression of the 1930's. In doing so, it intensified all those declines.

It is no wonder that the state of the capital-goods market became a prime subject for the "postwar planning" movement that gathered way a dozen years ago, even when World War II was at its very height; no wonder that the age-old notion of "stabilizing" business investment has caught the imaginations of businessmen as well as economists since the war.

September 1954

Six Prophets

Today Is Only a Fumbling Prelude
By DAVID SARNOFF

On the day when the first issue of *Fortune* was published, television, nuclear energy, jet planes, penicillin, nylon and dacron fabrics were unknown or incubating in laboratories. . . .

The temptation, at least for someone who, like myself, has been in touch all his life with such spiraling wonders, is to continue the inventory of what is coming. The very fact that electronics and atomics are unfolding simultaneously is a portent of the amazing changes ahead. Never before have two such mighty forces been unleashed at the same time. Together they are certain to dwarf the industrial revolutions brought about by steam and electricity. There is no element of material progress we know today—in the biological and chemical fields, in atomics and electronics, in engineering and physics—that will not seem, fron the vantage point of 1980, a fumbling prelude.

The most futile intellectual exercise is the discussion as to whether an industrialized society is "desirable." We might as reasonably argue whether the tides and the seasons are desirable. The genie of science could not be stuffed back into the bottle even if we so wished.

January 1955

A Major Factor Will Be Confidence in the Dollar
By GEORGE MAGOFFIN HUMPHREY

A goal that may overshadow all others in importance to our nation is the maintenance of confidence—living, enthusiastic confidence both for today and for the future. It must be shared by everyone—businessmen, workers, investors, and consumers alike.

How can this essential confidence be maintained and strengthened during the next twenty-five years?

A major factor in the maintenance of national confidence is people's confidence in what the dollar is worth. During the decade prior to 1953, the severe decline in the purchasing power of the dollar robbed people of nearly half the value of their savings. This inflation has been brought to a virtual halt, and during the past two years consumers' prices have remained practically unchanged.

We must make sure that the inflationary trends do not reappear. We must work to ensure that the dollar of 1980 will buy at least as much food and clothing as the dollar will buy today—preferably and properly more. If that is done, all will share the benefits of increased productivity, and the saver who puts away a dollar for his retirement, to buy a house, to educate his children, for an emergency, or for any other purpose, will still have a dollar that is worth a dollar when he needs it.

April 1955

Energy Is the Great Need for Our Survival
By CRAWFORD H. GREENEWALT

There is one goal, the attainment of which I fear is a long way off, its distance measured in decades rather than in years. How is mankind to supply his ever increasing requirements for energy? By this I mean energy in its broadest sense—not only the energy to drive our turbines, power plants, and automobiles, but the food energy required by the human body.

Over the years many have forecast the exhaustion of our sources of coal and oil. To be sure, they have all been overly pessimistic, as our supplies of these fuels still seem ample. It seems quite certain, however, that they will indeed be exhausted someday, and it is essential for our survival that we be ready with as good as an alternative as possible.

There is much talk these days about atomic energy as the answer to this problem. So it may be, and I have no doubt that we will in due course have central stations powered by the atom. As with coal and oil, however, there is a limit to the earth's supply of fissionable material, and so I am inclined to think that atomic energy, while important, will be only an interim solution.

What we must devise eventually is some way of utilizing more fully the energy that comes to us from the sun. There is a *really* worthwhile chain reaction—conveniently placed so one need not fear lethal radiations—generous in its output—and so long-lived that the day of its exhaustion lies in the inconceivably remote future. I wonder what our position would have been today had amounts of money and effort equivalent to those expended on atomic energy been devoted to the utilization of solar energy. Idle speculation—but the solution of the solar-energy problem cannot fail to be of more lasting benefit to mankind.

May 1955

We Are Running Out of Room
By JOHN VON NEUMAN

The great globe itself is in a rapidly maturing crisis—a crisis attributable to the fact that the environment in which technological progress must occur has become both undersized and under-organized.

In the first half of this century the accelerating industrial revolution encountered an absolute limitation—not on technological progress as such but on an essential safety factor. This safety factor, which had permitted the industrial revolution to roll on from the mid-eighteenth to the early twentieth century, was essentially a matter of geographical and political *Lebensraum:* an ever broader geographical scope for technological activities, combined with an ever broader political integration of the world. Within this expanding framework it was possible to accommodate the major tensions created by technological progress.

Now this safety mechanism is being sharply inhibited; literally and figuratively, we are running out of room. At long last, we begin to feel the effects of the finite, actual size of the earth in a critical way. . . .

The limit is now being reached, or at least closely approached. The advent of nuclear weapons climaxes the development. Now the effectiveness of offensive weapons is such as to stultify all plausible defensive time scales. As early as World War I, it was observed that the admiral commanding the battle fleet could "lose the British Empire in one afternoon." Yet navies of that epoch were relatively stable entities, tolerably safe against technological surprises. Today there is every reason to fear that even minor inventions and feints in the field of nuclear weapons can be decisive in less time than would be required to devise specific countermeasures. Soon existing nations will be as unstable in war as a nation the size of Manhattan Island would have been in a contest fought with the weapons of 1900.

June 1955

The Divinity That Exists in Man May Save Us
By ROBERT EMMET SHERWOOD

It seems self-evident that all prophecy or speculation concerning the next twenty-five years—or the next millennium—must be entirely dependent upon the ability of our own and other nations to prevent calamitous war.

If the objective of disarmament is not achieved by 1980—long before 1980—then we may as well write *finis* to the human story. When we consider what deadly scientific progress has been made in the sixteen years since Albert Einstein wrote a letter to Franklin D. Roosevelt about the potentialities of nuclear fission, we may well be appalled by contemplation of what might be produced during another few years of fierce competition in military preparation between rival nations, rival ideologies. If we have not already reached the ultimate in the capacity for mutual destruction, we shall be reaching it soon.

What can we do about it? All I can do is express the belief—or, if you will, the faith—that before 1980 the threat of a third world war will be a malodorous memory, existing only on the library shelves, and not on the front pages. If you ask me for convincing reasons for my optimism, I can provide no facts or figures, no blueprints, no statistics or charts or expert analyses. I can say only that my confidence in the future is founded on the fact that I believe in God.

I believe in the assurance, given in the first chapter of the first book of the Bible, that "God created man in his *own* image." (The italics are the Bible's.)

That is the most important statement in the recorded history of the human race. It has provided both the inspiration and the justification of all of man's progress. The essential concept of the divinity that exists in man is the force that impelled man out of the jungle and along the ascending path that leads to the stars.

Thus believing, I find it inconceivable that man is about to destroy himself with the products of his own God-given genius.

July 1955

Will God Never Let Us Alone?

By HENRY R. LUCE

One day, a year or so ago, Margaret Bourke-White asked to see me. That meant that she had some big and probably wild and expensive project to propose. I wondered what it could be, for it seemed to me she had already done everything including the North Pole, to say nothing of the darkest depths of coal mines and of Africa. When she came into my office she proceeded in a matter-of-fact manner to register her request. She wanted a promise that it would be she and no other who would have the assignment to go to the moon. Taking her quite seriously, I said yes.

Naturally, we will be happy to have the Trip to the Moon in *Life*— and an analysis of its economic consequences in *Fortune*. But I began to ask myself in the following days: Do I myself want to go to the moon? I mean even after Miss Bourke-White has got back

David Sarnoff

Robert Emmet Sherwood

George Magoffin Humphrey

Crawford H. Greenewalt

Henry R. Luce

safely, and regular service has been established? I have concluded that I do not really care about personally going to the moon. This conclusion has been a little disturbing to me, since up to now there has never been any place that I didn't want to go to. I have never had my fill of traveling this earth and visiting its inhabitants. Human destiny is here—is it not?—and it is this which has fired my curiosity and aroused my concern. But if men and women are soon to be tripping to the moon, that surely will radically change the whole outlook on the human adventure, which will have passed beyond any grasp I might have of its meaning and purpose.

But still, I further reflected, it will continue to be the *human* adventure. And if that adventure does, as I believe, have meaning and purpose; if it is true, as Lord Tennyson sang, that "thro' the ages one increasing purpose runs," then none of us will be alien in any new and vaster age. Occupationally obsolescent I may be; but not personally alien. So—on to the moon! In mental reach, if not in physical fact!

Furthermore, if Lord Tennyson is right, then going to the moon is significant because man gets there by his own efforts, by the use of his God-given faculties. It is significant because when man gets to the moon, it is because God may want him to get there to see what he has never seen before, to see everything in literally a new light.

How painful it is to see things in a new light! When only a few centuries ago the suspicion dawned with Copernicus that our earth was not the center and greater part of the universe, it was frightfully upsetting. Human life has never been the same since. And when, in our great-grandfathers' time, the Darwinian rumor ran, all too plausibly, that Adam and Eve were not created in B.C. 4532, and that we came from a long line of monkeys—that half-truth brought spiritual derangement to millions. Will God never let us alone for an aeon or two to get used to enjoying the half-lights of the world we have? Evidently not.

The actual day-to-day conditions of human life on this planet are changing faster in our lifetime than in all times past. And the lights change the way people see things. Not only the atom is probed, but also the psyche; both are "disintegrated."

With all these shocks of change, the wonder is that we—speaking especially of Americans—hold so firmly to the sense of purpose in human life. Why do we so stubbornly refuse to believe that life is meaningless? Science discloses no "meaning" or "purpose." Our artists and our novelists have disintegrated the human personality into the most miserable shreds of degradation. But we persist in talking of "human dignity." Is our talk a last collective shout in a cosmic graveyard? Twenty-five years from now, will men believe still, or more than ever, that there is in life a "dignity" infinitely precious—that liberty wagered against death will win and is forever worth winning—because indeed "thro' the ages one increasing purpose runs"?

Such questions will never be answered with universal satisfaction. But these are the questions around the answers to which human life has always been organized.

December 1955

The Sixties

It is evident from scenes in the Sixties that changes in an American society under Capitalism are becoming not only rapid but radical. In monetary affairs, abandonment of the gold standard is having a far-reaching effect. Drastic changes are demanded. Business is better than it has ever been in the past 30 years, but there are matters crying for solution, etched in despair in the Appalachian hills, drawn in turbulent black and white lines in the cities, against which mansions of vested wealth stand as an anachronism. Capitalism is confronted by an insistence on higher standards of behavior and tougher penalties for not living up to them. Here also are portraits of people trying to deal with statistics, the arcane language of economics, expense accounts, the game of advertising. Once again Capitalism copiously supplies military goods, this time for the war in Vietnam. And the moon looks down on a conspiracy of industry and science that is shooting at it, creating a breathtaking and bizarre scene.

The Era of Radical Change
By MAX WAYS

Within a decade or two it will be generally understood that the main challenge to U.S. society will turn not around the production of goods but around the difficulties and opportunities involved in a world of accelerating change and ever widening choices. Change has always been part of the human condition. What is different now is the pace of change, and the prospect that it will come faster and faster.

The condition is man-made; and everybody has some share of responsibility for it, not the least, the U.S. industrialist. For many changes come about through the business system. Within corporations hundreds of techniques, arising from scores of separate scientific and technological disciplines, are drawn together through complex management structures. An intricate mediation of values and purposes occurs in "the market," meaning thousands of interconnected markets, where the public exercises ever increasing power through billions of daily decisions.

Not long ago Alvin Pitcher, of the University of Chicago's divinity-school faculty, writing with anguished eloquence in the *Harvard Business Review,* asked, "How much flux can man stand?" Not this much, he said, calling for a slowdown of automation and other socially disruptive and "needless" changes. Pitcher's anxiety was broader than the usual fear of such economic consequences as unemployment. He associated the present unprecedented mobility of American society with juvenile delinquency, with the dissolution of communities, with a barrenness in individual life. Man, who needs a measure of order and stability, is being dehumanized, he said, by excessive change.

Most American political and social issues today arise, like Pitcher's protest, out of concern over the pace and quality of change. In many cases, the protest is accompanied by proposals that government restore order by taking some additional degree of control. Historically, it would be ironic if the long struggle of the individual versus the state should issue as a program for protecting the individual by having government take charge of change.

But that isn't the real choice. In Jefferson's day organizations other than government were thin on the ground, small and simple. In the last 150 years they have proliferated in numbers, grown huge in size, and, most important, have so evolved as to widen the scope of individuals working within them and of individuals dealing with them from outside. Organizations making up this "middle tier" between the government and the individual include, in addition to business corporations, voluntary organizations, labor unions, philanthropic foundations, and universities. These last generate in their research centers most of the scientific discovery that is later transferred into technological change. They also educate nearly all the managers of the sister organizations and the intellectuals who try to express the patterns of value emerging in the society—or to improve those patterns by criticism.

Changes can be categorized to show how different the present condition is from anything in the past:

Gradual change. Immense alterations in the human condition have occurred in the past without much occurring in the life of any one man. A language, for instance, can evolve from the most limited and primitive form to one rich and complex without any generation's being aware of the process.

Revolution and major disruption. These occur in all periods of history and the changes involved can be both rapid and general. But from the beginning a revolutionist thinks he knows the order he wants to establish. The wheels will turn and come to a point of rest. Subsequent politics are efforts to restore an equilibrium.

Rapid change. The period 1800 through 1950 in some Western countries saw for the first time an open vista of rapid and general change. No terminal point was in view once "the method of invention" had been invented. From 1850 until 1914, there was a growing tendency to see "progress" as a kind of inevitable and beneficent tide, lifting up all the familiar patterns of society as if they were a colony of houseboats, leaving them unchanged in themselves and in relation to one another.

Radical change. The break between the period of rapid change and that of radical change is not sharp; 1950 is an arbitrary starting date. More aspects of life change faster until it is no longer appropriate to think of society as mainly fixed, or changing slowly, while a tide flows around it. So many patterns of life are being modified that it is no longer useful to organize discussion or debate mainly around the relation of the new to the old. So many old landmarks have been set in motion that they have become misleading as guides. Newness has become an even more treacherous beacon. In the late nineteenth century or early twentieth century, "to be up to date" was a boast. In 1964 the very phrase sounds dated, for everyone knows that to be up to date means to be on the verge of becoming out of date.

Robert Oppenheimer has expressed the break with former eras this way: "This world of ours is a new world. . . . One thing that is new is the prevalence of newness . . . so that the world alters as we walk in it, so that the years of man's life measure not some small growth or rearrangement or moderation of what he learned in childhood, but a great upheaval."

Charles de Gaulle put it this way: "The world is undergoing a transformation to which no change that has yet occurred can be compared, either in scope or in rapidity."

The Angel Gabriel in *Green Pastures* put it more succinctly, "Everything nailed down is coming loose."

Yet there is a danger in that word "everything." If it means the particular works of man as we see them around us, it is true: most of these (e.g., old buildings, old machines) will quickly disappear. But if "everything" is taken to include, say, the continuity of man's quest for order and right and truth and harmony, then it is not true. There are, indeed, two different ways in which we can blind ourselves to the meaning of the radical change around us: either we comfort ourselves with some such piece of obsolescent wisdom as "the more it changes, the more it stays the same," or else—and this is worse—we assume that the flux is total, that past, present, and future have nothing to do with one another, that no purpose is feasible because the "winds of change" are beyond control and, anyway, human values now have no endurance, no footing. Both these escapes from thinking tend to deny or diminish human responsibility, the first by assuming that the order "built into" society is beyond man's ability to destroy or improve, the second by confusing radical change with absolute randomness. To speak of change, however radical, presupposes some constants, some continuities, some patterns in that which is changing. The greater the change, the harder the reach needed to establish the patterns.

In looking for patterns, we do not start from scratch. Neither men nor society determines objective truth, and a change in society will not change truth. But the perception of truth by men— what they perceive and how they perceive it—is surely affected by changes in society. Many truths of history, science, philosophy, and religion have been perceived as transcending change. In a time of great social flux the truths perceived as transcendent may be fewer—and therefore more precious.

May 1964

Gold

A Prodigious Error

By JACQUES RUEFF*

A grave peril hangs over the economy of the West. Every day its situation more and more resembles the one that turned the 1929 recession into the Great Depression. The situation was neither created, nor even expressly desired, by the U.S. It is the product of a prodigious collective error, an error that will go down in history as cause for stupefaction and scandal.

For more than a century, except for a few periods, the solidarity and relative stability of the civilized world were based on the monetary convertibility that was assured by the gold standard. Since all national currencies could be exchanged for a specified weight of gold, they were exchangeable at a fixed rate among themselves. What gave the arrangement its solidity was the fact that no country could create money except against gold or its own national credit (i.e., government bonds).

The U.S. retained gold coinage and full gold redeemability of currency until 1933; thereafter, the use of gold was restricted to international payments. During World War I, Europe suspended the gold standard and afterward returned to a gold-bullion standard, which meant that redeemability was limited to a set minimum quantity of gold—one kilo (about thirty-five ounces).

*Jacques Rueff was monetary adviser to Charles de Gaulle.

The European powers made one other historical change in the gold standard and this is the one that chiefly concerns us here. Back in 1922, long before the U.S. went off the gold standard, the International Economic Conference in Genoa passed its famous Resolution 9, which recommended adoption of an international convention embodying "some means of economizing the use of gold by maintaining reserves in the form of foreign balances." This recommendation brought into existence the "gold-*exchange* standard," which was gradually grafted on the old gold standard throughout most of the Western World. The gold-exchange standard collapsed in the great depression of the Thirties but came to life again after World War II. It dominates the monetary picture today.

Under this standard, central banks consider themselves authorized to create money not only against gold or government bonds, but also against any foreign currency that is considered as good as gold. (The English term "gold-exchange standard" is used by economists everwhere. It is an odd misnomer, for under this arrangement the exchange of gold is actually discouraged.)

The country with a key currency (i.e., the U.S.) is in the deceptively euphoric position of never having to pay off its international debts. The money it pays to foreign creditors comes right back home, like a boomerang. When foreign central banks received dollars or dollar credits as a result of the American balance-of-payments deficits, they were not compelled to demand the gold to which their dollars entitled them. Instead, they left a large portion of these dollars on deposit in the U.S., where they were generally loaned to American borrowers. The central banks welcomed this new arrangement all the more enthusiastically because it substituted in their accounts revenue-producing assets for entirely unproductive gold bullion or coins. The functioning of the international monetary system was thus reduced to a childish game in which, after each round, the winners return their marbles to the losers. The built in stabilizer is removed.

In this way the gold-exchange standard wrought a vast revolution. It imparted to countries whose money had international prestige the marvelous secret of the deficit without tears. In the U.S., the gold-exchange standard had the effect of encouraging the generous program of foreign aid, and a blithe disregard of the deficit that ensued. The giver had the pleasure of giving, and the receiver the joy of receiving.

The replacement of the gold standard by the gold-*exchange* standard has had three basic consequences:

First of all, under the gold-exchange standard, the volume of internal purchasing power is not at all affected by a balance-of-payments deficit. By disconnecting the internal volume of purchasing power from the external balance of payments, the gold-exchange standard removes one of the regulating influences that used to operate under the gold standard.

The second consequence is a veritable duplication of credit bases in the world: the dollars that go abroad as a result of U.S. balance-of-payments deficits return to the U.S. as sight deposits or short-term investments. This becomes a powerful instrument of worlwide inflation when there are large international movements of capital from countries with key currencies. This was tragically illustrated by the events that led up to and followed the 1929 Depression. The financial reconstruction of Germany after the Dawes plan in 1924 and of France after Premier Poincaré's reforms in 1926 caused a massive flow of capital from the U.S. and Britain into those two countries. With both Germany and France operating under the gold-exchange standard, this influx of capital gave the 1929 boom its unprecedented dimensions and its dreadful climax.

Similarly, movements of capital from the U.S. to Germany and France in 1958, 1959, and 1960 accounted for the abnormal rise in share prices in financial markets on both sides of the Atlantic. When capital flows from one country to another, the effect can be expansionist in the latter without being recessive in the former. With nothing tending to brake the boom, all the countries operating under the gold-exchange standard find themselves carried along on a wave of inflationary economic and stock-market expansion.

The third and most serious consequence of the gold-exchange standard is the deceptive character of the credit structure it brings about. The $17.5-billion U.S. gold reserve is doubly committed. Some $11.5 billion of it is pledged as the reserve that must be maintained, under law, against Federal Reserve currency and deposits. Meanwhile all of the reserve constitutes a guarantee against about $20 billion now held by foreigners in short-term or sight assets.

It is not the value of the dollar that is cast in doubt. The real cause for concern is that the gold-exchange standard, working at a time of large international movements of capital, puts a double mortgage—and a very high one—on the U.S. gold stock. If foreign holders of dollar assets were suddenly to demand full payment in gold, they could topple the whole U.S. credit structure.

There is unfortunately only one way to rid ourselves of the risks that are the West's legacy from fifteen years' operation of the gold-exchange standard. This is to pay off in gold all the dollar assets held by central banks outside the U.S. Only such a drastic step can banish the danger of sharp deflation or collapse that is inherent in the double-credit structure now based on the U.S. gold reserves.

The difficulty is that this would suddenly deplete the U.S. gold reserve below what must legally be held in reserve against Federal Reserve notes and deposits. This problem is less serious than it looks, for the reserve requirement can be changed by law, and besides the government has other resources at its disposal to bolster its reserves, such as its ability to draw on the International Monetary Fund. Moreover, if the liquidation of the gold-exchange standard is not undertaken in panic—and this is precisely what must be avoided—it can be carefully organized to take place gradually.

The liquidation of the gold-exchange standard poses difficult questions for political art and monetary technique. These questions demand deep study and discussion. In preparing for this discussion it is worth observing that the problems to be resolved are not exclusively or even essentially American. Their solution can be found only in a profound modification of the system now in force for the settlement of international payments, hence of the very rules governing central banks.

If the gold-exchange standard is principally responsible for prolonging the U.S. balance-of-payments deficits, it must be remembered that it was not the U.S. which established this standard, but the Genoa Conference of 1922, at which the U.S. was not even represented.

What one international conference did, only another international conference can undo. But it is essential that the undoing occur without delay. A monetary crisis would compromise the financial rehabilitation that has at last been accomplished in all the Western countries. It would expose their economies to a grave recession, and the threat of another 1929.

July 1961

Social Stresses

The Road to Hazard

By JOHN DAVENPORT

The Appalachian Mountains lack the ruggedness of the Rockies or the ultimate cruelty of the Andes, but they contain some tough country—tough topographically and tougher in terms of the human condition. Enter this region, say from Lexington, Kentucky, and the landscape at first has a deceptively pleasing mien. This is the Bluegrass, large estates, for the most part, with neat white fences, and behind the fences grazing cattle or grazing horses whose owners and guests will drink bourbon juleps on Derby Day. Farther on, however, the road begins to climb through the western spurs of the Appalachians, and the farms are pressed into the narrow bottom lands. Here, if a man owns a precious allotment for tobacco, he may do pretty well—eking out perhaps as much as $1,000 from a single acre. But up the "hollows" are many less fortunate, earning a precarious $400 or $500 per year in cash from hillsides so tilted that as the moonshiners say, "The only way you can get corn down from those hills is in quart jars." Eastern Kentucky and much of Appalachia is full of this kind of subsistence farming where men are "underemployed" as surely as they are in many parts of the deeper South. Says one who knows the region well: "The people in these low-income farms don't come within the province of organized labor, which would dramatize the situation. If you have 5,000 unemployed in Dayton the uproar is terrific. But 50,000 underemployed on the farms and no one cares about it." There are, as a matter of fact, easily one million farm families in America living below subsistence levels, and the rugged regions of eastern Kentucky have their full quota of this undramatized poverty.

Turn southward now into Leslie County, and as the road passes a cliff face, dark streaks—coal—appear in the rock and driving becomes more hazardous due to thundering coal trucks, tearing downgrade from strip and auger mines to deliver their black burden to a railhead. Mining is temporarily flourishing in Leslie County, where employers, having broken with John L. Lewis's United Mine Workers, are paying $10 to $15 a day to miners in the small seams (as against $24.25 a day in the deep mines where the union holds sway). But coal is a fickle master. Beyond Leslie County the country roughens still more; the dump heaps of abandoned cars beside the roadway multiply, as do the signs, "Are you ready to meet God?" Come then to Hazard, county seat of Perry County, and well named. Hazard too was once a boom town, but those days lie in the past. The sign on the road leading into town reads: Population 6,850; but the population in fact is now down to about 5,500. Not so many years ago there were a dozen or more major coal companies operating in and around the town including the Blue Grass Mine, Black Gold Coal, Columbus Mining, and Four Seam Coal. Now most of these deep mines are closed down, caught between falling prices for coal and rising costs due to union pressure on wages and also to exhausted or semi-exhausted seams.

All that remains of the famous Blue Grass Mine, right across the Kentucky River from Hazard, is a dark hole in the hill's face and a smashed and rusting tipple. Below the mine the Blue Grass mining camp still stands—thirty or more houses in various stages of dilapidation laid out with specious precision on deeply mudded streets. Mining families still live here, some on pensions, and some finding other work. Others have been less fortunate. In the vincinity of Hazard a small shack clings to the side of the mountain, supported on one side by long stilt-like poles, with an errant mountain stream nearby. The boards on the front porch are rotting, and the glass of one window is broken and papered over. An extraordinarily fine-looking woman opens the door, and ushers the visitor into a bedraggled room with an open coal stove. At one side is a tumbled bed with two children lying on it. There are four more children at school; an older son and daughter have moved away. The father, an unemployed miner, is seeking work "somewhere in Ohio" and can contribute little to the family. How does the woman live? "I get surplus food when they pass it out—flour, corn meal, and the like. I don't eat much meat myself, sometimes buy a little for the children." She plants a garden in the summer months. She belongs to the Holiness Church, and the meetings mean a great deal to her. "I don't expect to be around too long,"

People and Places in Trouble
A portfolio by Walker Evans

On these pages are pictures made in the winter of 1961 in pockets of new unemployment and old poverty lying often in the midst of prosperous regions. The people shown here are not the hundred neediest cases—or the million. Mostly they are just laid-off citizens.

"We have to get out of here next month . . ."

"I read a lot of books now from the library . . ."

"Laid off November 9. Even the 1958 cutback didn't hit me . . ."

"I was in coke. They use oxygen and natural gas now . . ."

Quietly, these are the things that are said—not much more.

Johnstown, Pennsylvania, in January.

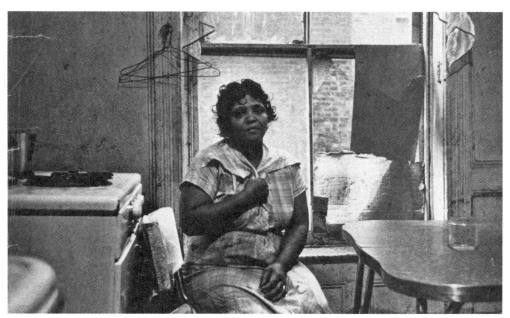

On the "wrong" end of Fifth Avenue, New York.

she says. "You've got to be ready to go." And again, brooding: "Life ought to be forward—a widening out." Her voice trails off. The door opens and closes, and one is outside again in the harsh snowbanked valley.

March 1961

The City and the Negro
By CHARLES E. SILBERMAN

"The approved way to talk about cities these days," Paul Ylvisaker of the Ford Foundation has observed, "is to speak solemnly, sadly, ominously, and fearfully about their problems. You don't rate as an expert on the city unless you foresee its doom." Doom is easy to foresee in the spreading slums, the increasing crime rates, the public disaffection of almost every large city.

For this to happen, however, city planners and civic leaders will have to understand better than they now do what their cities' greatest problem is. It is not, as so many assume, to bring the wandering middle class back from the suburbs. Cities always have had to create their own stable, cultivated citizenry out of whatever raw material lay at hand. For the American city during the past 150 years, the raw material was the stream of immigrants pouring in from Britain, Ireland, Germany, Norway, Russia, Italy. The city needed these immigrants to do all the dirty and menial jobs that older residents disdained. But the city did more than use its newcomers; it equipped them to take their place as fully participating members of U.S. society—always the principal business and glory of the American city.

But it isn't any longer. The newcomers are from a host of American towns and hamlets with names like Memphis, Tennessee, Sunflower, and Rolling Fork. Between 1950 and 1960 the twelve largest U.S. cities lost over two million white residents; they gained nearly two million Negroes.

When city officials talk about spreading slums, they are talking in the main about physical deterioration of the areas now inhabited by Negroes. And when they talk about juvenile delinquency, or the burden of welfare problems, they are talking principally about Negro adjustment to city life. For the city is not absorbing and "urbanizing" its new Negro residents rapidly enough; its slums are no longer acting as the incubator of a new middle class.

One reason for this is that city planners have been more interested in upgrading the value of the city's real estate than in upgrading the lives of the human beings who inhabit the real estate—driving lower-class Negro residents out and bringing middle-class residents in.

The Negro population outside the Deep South has increased fivefold since 1910; it has nearly tripled just since 1940. Most of the Negroes have crowded into the slums of the twelve largest cities, which today hold 60 percent of the Negroes living outside the Deep South. Since 1940 the Negro population of New York City has increased nearly two and one-half times, to 1.1 million, or 14 percent of the city's population. The Negro population of Los Angeles County has jumped a phenomenal sixfold since 1940, from 75,000 to 464,000.

The Negroes, to be sure, are not the only disadvantaged peoples coming into the large cities. In New York the Puerto Rican population swelled from perhaps 100,000 in 1940 to over 700,000 in 1960. And other cities have received a steady stream of impoverished whites from the southern Appalachian Mountains. These, the oldest and purest of U.S. stock, have at least as much initial difficulty adjusting to the city as do the Negroes and Puerto Ricans. But the Negro problem is what city planners and officials are really talking about when they refer to the City Problem.

Migration to the large city has always involved a heavy cost in family dislocation, pauperism, crime, delinquency, and urban blight. Immigrants bring with them housekeeping and other habits that clash with city standards; and the impersonality of city life tends to erode the social relationships that regulated behavior in "the old country."

But the Negro is unlike the European immigrant in one crucial respect: his color. The Irishman could lose his brogue; as soon as he was "Americanized," his problem was resolved. But the Negro cannot escape so easily.

There are other differences. The European peasant, no matter how depressed his position, had roots in a "whole society" with a

stable culture and stable institutions and above all a stable family
life. The Negro does not. Slavery made a stable family life (and a
stable culture) impossible. Husbands could be sold away from
wives, children from parents. Such family life as did exist centered
almost entirely around the mother.

What slavery began, prejudice and discrimination have helped
perpetuate. Family disorganization is endemic. Negro women
frequently find it easier to get jobs—e.g., as domestics—than
Negro men, thus making them the financial center of the family.
The inability of Negro men to find jobs that confer status and
dignity, together with the servility required of them in the South,
have led Negro men to sexual promiscuity, drinking, and violence
as means of asserting their masculinity. Family disorganization is
compounded by the overcrowding and dilapidation of their
housing.

Hence the Negro, all too often, is trapped in a vicious circle from
which he cannot extricate himself. Little in the Negro boy's
environment is likely to give him any sense of aspiration or any
direction; he has no male model to follow and little reason to
assume that education offers a way out of the slum. His lack of
education and aspiration, in turn, makes it virtually impossible for
the Negro youth to find a job with dignity and status, even where
discrimination is absent. All too often, therefore, he decides that
there is no point in trying, and he loses the capacity to take
advantage of such opportunities as do arise. In the jargon of the
social worker, he "develops a self-defeating mode of living" that
keeps him trapped in the slum forever.

To make matters worse, the gap is widening between Negro
education and training, on the one hand, and the requirements of
the labor market, on the other. The Europeans immigrated during
periods of rapidly expanding U.S. demand for unskilled labor; no
great transfer of skill was needed to enable an Irish or Italian
peasant to find a job on a construction gang. But in the U.S. today,
the demand for unskilled labor is shrinking relative to the total
labor force. Since 1947, employment of white-collar workers—
executives, entrepreneurs, professional and scientific employees,
clerks, and salesmen—has gone up 43 percent compared with only
a 14 percent gain in blue-collar and service-worker employment.
By 1970 a substantial majority of workers will be in white-collar or
highly skilled blue-collar jobs—in jobs that characteristically require real training and thought. Three out of four nonfarm Negro

male workers, however, are in unskilled or semiskilled occupations, compared with only one in three among white workers.

In this new world of specialized skills, Negroes have more and more trouble finding and holding jobs. The unemployment rate among Negro men is more than twice that among white men. In some cities as many as one Negro male in three is out of work. The problem is particularly acute among Negro youths.

It would be a serious mistake to equate the Negro's apparent apathy and lack of motivation with a sense of contentment. It is a lot harder for today's Negro to bear his poverty and lack of status than it was for the European immigrant, who arrived at a time when the great majority of the population was poor. The Negro migration, by contrast, is occurring in an affluent society. Like the underdeveloped peoples everywhere, American Negroes have been fired by the revolution of rising expectations. In Harry Ashmore's phrase, Negroes have seen "the other side of Jordan"; they are in a hurry to cross. Among a good many Negroes, especially the college students involved in the sit-in movement, impatience with their rate of progress has conquered apathy and led to direct, disciplined, and frequently courageous action to improve the Negro position. But among the great mass of working-class Negroes and a large part of the middle class, apathy exists side by side with a growing, festering resentment of their lot. These Negroes are more and more convinced that they should have a better life; they are less and less convinced that they themselves can do anything about it.

Impatience is turning into bitterness, anger, and hatred. The danger is not violence but something much deeper and harder to combat: a sense of permanent alienation from American society. Unless the Negro position improves very quickly, Negroes of whatever class may come to regard their separation from American society as permanent, and so consider themselves permanently outside the constraints and the allegiances of American society. The Negro district of every large city would come to constitute an American Casbah, with its own values and its own controls—and a deep hostility to the white community. In such a situation, communication between the races would become impossible. And life in the large city would become unbearable.

March 1961

Mansions of a Dynasty
By CHARLES J. V. MURPHY

When Richard King Mellon was a boy, the founding generation of the Mellons was still all in view in Pittsburgh. His grandfather Judge Thomas Mellon lived in a rambling brick house at 401 North Negley Avenue that he had built more than half a century before. The houses of his sons were close by. The Mellons were closely knit. Richard remembers the festive gatherings at his uncles' homes at Christmas and Thanksgiving, and the respectful processions to his grandfather's house on New Year's Day.

The home in which Richard grew up yielded to no other in untrammeled extravagance: sixty-five rooms and eleven baths, marble floors and marble stairways, brave turrets, leaded casement windows, and a billiard room. It was much more cheerful and informal inside than its granite walls looked to be from the outside. In the foyer stood a magnificent hatrack intricately constructed of buffalo horns, mother-of-pearl, and slabs of glass; and brooding over the drawing room with the Louis Quinze chairs and tables was an enormous buffalo head. In his youth, Richard's father, Richard Beatty Mellon, had been a rancher and banker in Bismarck, in the Dakota territory, and splendid lithographs and chromos of the famous Indian chiefs of that day—Sitting Bull, John Grass, Running Antelope, and Rain-in-the-Face—graced the library walls.

The house mirrored Richard Beatty Mellon's affluence and earthiness. His wife, the former Jennie Taylor King, was a spirited, plump, loquacious woman with bright red hair, who in the first years of the Great Depression put out word that passers-by who were hungry would be welcome in her kitchen; beyond question, it was the most finely appointed free-lunch counter in the nation.

Richard's cousin Paul was born in a house on a five-acre wooded hillock on Forbes Avenue on what this past summer became the campus of the Carnegie-Mellon University. His father, Andrew, who would become Secretary of the Treasury, built the house in 1900 for his twenty-one-year-old British bride, Nora McMullen, daughter of a prosperous Hertfordshire brewer. The household staff included a cook, a kitchen maid, a butler, a parlor maid, an upstairs maid, a nurse, a laundress, and a coachman learning to be a chauffeur. "The house," Paul has written, "was late Victorian and very dark—the halls were dark, the walls were dark, and outside, Pittsburgh itself was very dark." But Paul recalls most vividly the fine paintings on the walls. "My father was a collector of paintings—his interests were mainly in the Dutch seventeenth-century and English eighteenth-century schools. There were one or two English landscapes, and about ten of those formal protraits, large and small. These very urbane and always self-confident personages in their classical landscapes and autumnal parklands smiled down at me with what seemed a warm and friendly glow."

The glow was not warmth enough for Nora McMullen. The city's harsh climate, its dinginess, the press of Mellon relatives, her husband's endless preoccupation with business proved too much for a sensitive young woman. They were divorced in 1912, after which Andrew Mellon acquired a mansion of forty rooms on Pittsburgh's Woodland Road, a mixture of red brick, fieldstone, and heavy timbers standing among oaks, willows, and formal gardens; inside, a ballroom, fireplaces framed in marble or carved oak, a bowling alley, and a swimming pool.

November, December 1967

Stormy Weather

The Incredible Electrical Conspiracy
By RICHARD AUSTIN SMITH

As befitted the biggest criminal case in the history of the Sherman Act, most of the forty-five defendants arrived early, knocking the snow of Philadelphia's Chestnut Street from their shoes before taking the elevator to federal courtroom No. 3. Some seemed to find it as chill inside as out, for they kept their coats on and shifted from one foot to another in the corridor, waiting silently for the big mahogany doors to open. As a group, they looked like just what they were: well-groomed corporation executives. On the other side of those doors was something none of them relished: judgment for having conspired to fix prices, rig bids, and divide markets on electrical equipment valued at $1.75 billion annually. The twenty indictments, under which they were now to be sentenced, charged they had conspired on everything from tiny $2 insulators to multimillion-dollar turbine generators and had persisted in the conspiracies for as long as eight years.

The courtroom doors opened and everyone trooped in to be confronted by Judge J. Cullen Ganey, chief judge of the U.S. District Court. It was clear almost immediately that he took a stern view of the conspiracy: "This is a shocking indictment of a vast section of our economy, for what is really at stake here is the survival of the kind of economy under which this country has grown great, the free-enterprise system."

The first targets of his censure were the twenty-nine corporations and their top management. He acknowledged that the Justice Department did not have enough evidence to convict men in the highest echelons of the corporations, but the "real blame" should be laid at their doorstep: "One would be most naïve indeed to believe that these violations of the law, so long persisted in, affecting so large a segment of the industry and finally involving so many millions upon millions of dollars, were facts unknown to those responsible for the corporation and its conduct. . . ."

Many of the individual defendants he saw "torn between conscience and an approved corporate policy . . . the company man, the conformist, who goes along with his superiors and finds balm for his conscience in additional comforts and the security of his place in the corporate setup."

Gray-haired Westinghouse Vice President J. H. Chiles, Jr., vestryman of St. John's Episcopal Church in Sharon, Pennsylvania, got thirty days in prison, a $2,000 fine . . . William S. Ginn, $135,000-a-year vice president of General Electric (indicted in two conspiracies), thirty days and a $12,500 fine . . . G.E. Vice President George Burens, $4,000 and thirty days. "There goes my whole life," said this veteran of forty years with G.E., waving his arm distractedly as he waited to telephone his wife. "Who's going to want to hire a jailbird? What am I going to tell my children?"

By lunchtime the second day it was all over: seven jail sentences and twenty-four suspended jail sentences handed down, $1,924,500 of total fines, $372,500 against Westinghouse, $437,500 against G.E., the biggest company of them all and the one without which the conspiracies could not have existed. What was behind these industry-wide derelictions?

When Ralph Cordiner took over the presidency of G.E. from Charles E. Wilson in December of 1950, it was clear that the corporation was in for some changes. He spread the word to some 6,000 G.E. executives. First, he said, G.E. was in sorry shape; it was dedicated principally to "security, complacency, and mediocrity"; second, decentralization and rewards based on performance were going to be relied on in the rapid transformation of this "sinecure of mediocrity" into a dynamic corporation—G.E. would be split into twenty-seven autonomous divisions comprising 110 small companies and run just as if they were individual enterprises; third, G.E.'s new philosophy of decentralized management specifically prohibited meeting with competitors on prices, bids, or market shares. Charlie Wilson's instructions on compliance with the antitrust laws, first issued in 1946, were very much in force.

Cordiner subsequently reiterated the instructions in the earlier antitrust directive, 2.35. There was good reason for stressing this last point. Antitrust was then a very sore subject at G.E. In the decade just ended (1940–50), the corporation had been involved in thirteen antitrust cases, the offenses ranging from production limitation and patent pooling to price fixing and division of markets. Moreover, G.E. had long been something of a battleground for two schools of economic thought. One school was dedicated to the concept that corporate progress, like national progress, was best secured by freedom of private initiative within the bonds of justice.

The second school held that competition, particularly price competition, was for the birds. It was considered easier to negotiate market percentages than fight for one's share, less wearing to take turns on rigged bids than play the rugged individualist. Besides, the rationale went, they were all "gentlemen" and no more inclined to gouge the consumer than to crowd a competitor. Admittedly, all of them knew they were breaking the law—Section 1 of the Sherman Act is as explicit as a traffic ordinance. Their justification was on other grounds. "Sure, collusion was illegal," explained an old G.E. hand, "but it wasn't *unethical*. Those competitor meetings were just attended by a group of distressed individuals who wanted to know where they were going."

One reason for the influence of G.E.'s anticompetition school was a change that occurred in the electrical industry after World War II. Smaller companies were becoming bigger and they were broadening their product lines. Customers had a wider choice of heavy electrical equipment, alike in quality and design. Price, consequently, became the decisive selling point. To turn this situation to their best advantage, buyers adopted a new technique: the competitive bid. This produced serious instability in the market and made profit planning difficult. The collusionists themselves like to think nine G.E. executives out of ten shared their point of view.

Now, despite what Cordiner said about overall company policy on cartels, under his decentralization plan the head of each of the 110 units comprising the company was being given power to set his own marketing policies and to raise or lower prices as he saw fit. Anyone might have foreseen the results.

G.E.'s heavy-equipment division, accounting for some 25 percent of G.E. sales, was the oldest division, and the foundation upon which the whole company had been built. Moreover, it was the stronghold of the collusionists.

During OPA days, some thirty to forty heavy-equipment men in the industry gathered regularly at meetings of the transformer section of the National Electrical Manufacturers' Association in Philadelphia's Penn-Sheraton Hotel with the N.E.M.A. secretaries from New York. But when the N.E.M.A. secretaries had departed, the company men reassembled within the hour for a cozier meeting. The talk then was about prices, OPA-regulated prices, and how the industry could best argue Washington into jacking up the ceilings.

These price klatches continued after OPA's demise. But instead of discussing pricing under government controls, the conspirators turned to fixing prices among themselves. The agreements seemed to some of the participants to put them no more outside the law than agreements under the OPA, until company lawyers put everyone in G.E. on notice that it certainly was illegal to discuss prices with competitors, whether the public was gouged or not. The head office followed this up by barring anybody who had anything to do with pricing from attending N.E.M.A. meetings. This situation continued for about nine months. Then, abruptly, "word came down to start contacting competitors again," one G.E. executive remembers. "It came to me from my superior, but my impression was that it came to him from higher up. I think the competitive situation was forcing them to do something, and there were a lot of old-timers who thought collusion was the best way to solve the problems. That is when hotel-room meetings got started. We were cautioned at this time not to tell the lawyers what we were doing and to cover our trails in our expense-account reports."

In the manufacture of circuit breakers the annual sales total amounted to roughly $75 million: the sealed-bid business (between $15 million and $18 million per year) done with public agencies, city, state, and federal; the private-sector business conducted with private utilities and totaling some $55 million to $60 million per annum.

An agreement was made, in so far as the sealed-bid business was concerned, to rotate that business on a fixed-percentage basis among four participating companies, then the only circuit-breaker manufacturers in the U.S. G.E. got 45 percent, Westinghouse 35, Allis-Chalmers 10, Federal Pacific 10. Every ten days to two weeks working-level meetings were called in order to decide whose turn was next. Turns were determined by the "ledger list," a table of who had got what in recent weeks, and after that the only thing left to decide was the price that the company picked to "win" would submit as the lowest bid.

Apart from this group was a second tier of conspirators who dealt generally with market shares in the yearly $55 million to $60 million worth of private-sector business. Once each week, certain general managers and vice presidents would get the word to each other via intercompany memo. A different executive would have the "duty" over each thirty-day period.

The conspiracies had their own lingo and their own standard operating procedures. Meetings were known as "choir practices." Companies had code numbers—G.E. 1, Westinghouse 2, Allis-Chalmers 3, Federal Pacific 7—which were used in conjunction with first names when calling a conspirator at home for price information ("This is Bob, what is 7's bid?"). At the hotel meetings it was S.O.P. not to list one's employer when registering and not to have breakfast with fellow conspirators in the dining room. The

G.E. men observed two additional precautions: never to be the ones who kept the records and never to tell G.E.'s lawyers anything.

Things were not always smooth even inside this well-oiled machine, for the conspirators actually had no more compunction at breaking the rules of the conspiracy than at breaching the Sherman Act. "Everyone accused the other of not living up to the agreement," one conspirator recalled. The most constant source of irritation occurred in the sealed-bid business, where chiseling was difficult to detect. But breaks in book price to the utilities in the open-bid business also generated ill will and vituperation. Indeed, one of the many ironies of the whole affair is that the conspiracy couldn't entirely suppress the competitive instinct. Every so often some company would decide that cutthroat competition outside was preferable to the throat-cutting that went on in the cartel; they would break contact and sit out the conspiracy for a couple of years.

What prompted their return? Chronic overcapacity, for one thing, that put a constant pressure on prices. An executive, who ebulliently increased capacity one year, a few years later might join a price conspiracy to escape the consequences of that increase.

A more human explanation of why the conspiracy snarled on for eight years was corporate pressure to perform.

For G.E. 1954 was a bad year, as it was for the rest of the industry. The result was that Cordiner and Robert Paxton, executive vice president for industrial products, began putting more heat on one division after another.

"We were told," as one general manager remembered it, "that G.E. was losing business and position because our prices weren't competitive."

So things went for some eight years.

On the morning of September 28, 1959, a urgent long-distance call came in to G.E.'s vast Transformer Division at Pittsfield, Massachusetts. It was for Edward L. Dobbins, the divisional lawyer, and the person on the line was attorney for Lapp Insulator Co. He wanted to say that one of Lapp's officers, subpoenaed by a Philadelphia grand jury, was going to tell the whole story. "What story?" said Dobbins pleasantly, then listened to an account that sent him, filled with concern, into the office of the divisional vice president, Raymond W. Smith.

Smith was a big man in G.E., veteran of twenty-eight years with the corporation; he was also a big man in Pittsfield, where the Transformer Division employs 6,000 people out of a population of 57,000, director of a local bank, active member of the hospital building board. Smith heard Dobbins out, and began pacing back and forth. "It's bad," he said, "very bad."

The story which the man from Lapp was about to spill was that Paul Hartig, one of Smith's departmental general managers, had been conspiring with Lapp Insulator and a half-dozen other manufacturers to fix prices on insulators. Such news was unsettling enough, but Smith's alarm had its roots in something deeper than the derelictions of a subordinate. He was himself "Mr. Big" of another cartel, one involving $210 million worth of transformers a year. Nevertheless, he concluded that he had no choice but to report the trouble to Apparatus Group Vice President Arthur Vinson, in New York.

That very night, despite a storm, Vinson flew up to Pittsfield. Boss of G.E.'s nine apparatus divisions, Vinson was used to hearing the word "trouble" from his general managers, but the way Smith had used it permitted of no delay. He listened to Smith, his own concern centering immediately on the extent of G.E.'s involvement. He asked Smith whether the Transformer Division was itself involved in a cartel and received assurances to the contrary.

By sheer coincidence, Chairman Ralph Cordiner showed up in Pittsfield the next day. He had come, ironically enough, to hear an account of how, by cutting the formidable costs of custom-made transformers, Smith's Transformer Division expected to beat the ears off the competition, foreign and domestic.

Told of Hartig's involvement in the insulator cartel, Cordiner reacted with shock and anger. He had reason to think his general managers were making "earnest efforts" to comply with both the spirit and the letter of the antitrust laws; he had so testified in May before a congressional antitrust subcommittee. When the Tennessee Valley Authority had complained that it was getting identical bids on equipment, and the Justice Department had begun to take an active interest in this charge, he had sent G.E.'s amiable trade-regulation counsel, Gerard Swope, Jr., son of the company's former chief executive, to Pittsfield. Swope considered it his mission to explore "a more dynamic pricing policy to get away fron the consistent identity of prices." He had, however, ventured to say, "I assume none of you have agreed with competitors on prices," and when nobody contested this assumption, he came away with the feeling that any suspicion of pricing agreements boiled down to a competitor's voicing a single criticism at a cocktail party. Cordiner had been further reassured by a report from G.E.'s outside counsel, Gerhard Gesell of Covington & Burling, who had burrowed through mountains of data and couldn't find anything incriminating.

But what Cordiner heard about the insulator department was only the beginning. G.E.'s general counsel, Ray Luebbe, was brought in, and within a matter of days Paul Hartig was in Luebbe's New York office implicating Vice President Ray Smith.

Smith made a clean breast of things, detailing the operation of the transformer cartel: bids on government contracts were rotated to ensure that G.E. and Westinghouse each got 30 percent of the business, the remaining 40 being split among four other manufacturers; book prices were agreed upon at various meetings; secrecy was safeguarded by channeling all phone calls and mail to conspirators' homes, and by destroying written memoranda upon receipt.

Then Smith implicated a second G.E. vice president, William S. Ginn, forty-one, head of the Turbine Division. Ginn was considered a comer in the company. Unfortunately for him, he was an important man in *two* cartels, the one in transformers, which he had passed on to Smith, and the one in turbine generators, which only the year before had aroused the suspicions of TVA by bringing about some very rapid price increases.

The involvement of divisional Vice Presidents Smith and Ginn put G.E.'s whole fifteen-man Executive Group—a group including Cordiner and Paxton—in an understandable flap. By now, the corporation was plainly implicated in four cartels.

The Justice Department had got started on the case because of TVA's suspicions and because Senator Estes Kefauver had threatened an investigation of the electrical industry if the government didn't get on with the job. Robert A. Bicks, the most vigorous chief of Antitrust since Thurman Arnold, had plenty of will to get on with the job, but the way was clouded. The Antitrust Division had once before—in 1951–52—tried to find a pattern of collusive pricing in the maze of transformer bids, but had wound up with no indictments. Now proof of collusion seemed as elusive as ever.

The tactics of the Antitrust Division now were to use grand juries to subpoena documents, and then, after study of these, to subpoena the corporation executives who would logically have been involved if a conspiracy existed. Justice Department attorneys had begun ringing doorbells across the land. As the trust busters took testimony under grand-jury subpoena, apprehension ran through the industry. Everyone was only too well aware that an Ohio judge had recently clapped three executives behind bars for ninety days for participating in a hand-tool cartel.

Back at G.E., meanwhile, Cordiner had issued instructions that all apparatus general managers were to be interviewed by company attorneys. Most of the guilty lied, and Cordiner, accepting their protestations of innocence, began to formulate what he thought would be G.E.'s best defense. It would have two principal salients: the company itself was not guilty of conspiracies; whatever had occurred was without the knowledge of the chairman, the president, and the Executive Office. G.E.'s corporate position on antitrust compliance was a matter of record, embodied in Cordiner's own antitrust directive. Illegal conduct of any individuals was clearly beyond the authority granted to them by the company, and therefore the company itself should not be held criminally responsible.

But, the legal basis of G.E.'s not-guilty stance was shaky to say the least. Its lawyers felt bound to inform the Executive Office: "The trend of the law appears to be that a business corporation will be held criminally liable for the acts of an employee so long as these acts are reasonably related to the area of general responsibility entrusted to him notwithstanding the fact that such acts are committed in violation of instructions issued by the company in good faith. . . ." Under the decentralization policy, distinguishing between an "innocent" corporation and its "guilty" executives would be tough—Cordiner himself had given the general managers clear pricing powers.

The Cordiner position had another weakness: it was based on the assumption that G.E. was involved in only four cartels—at the most. Yet wider involvement could reasonably have been expected. That very month general counsel Luebbe had been warned by one of the general managers who had confessed that collusion would be found to have spread across the whole company front. ("I tried to tell Luebbe to stop the investigation," reflected the general manager, "and try to make a deal with the government. I told him in November, 1959, that this thing would go right across the board. He just laughed at me. He said, 'You're an isolated case—only you fellows would be stupid enough to do it.'") Thus when wider involvement actually did come to light—the four cartels multiplied into nineteen and accounted for more than 10 percent of G.E.'s total sales—the company found itself in the ludicrous position of continuing to proclaim its corporate innocence while its executives were being implicated by platoons.

But vulnerable or not, G.E.'s posture was officially established, and management moved to put it into effect. Raymond Smith was summoned to Arthur Vinson's office and told his job was forfeit and his title too. There was a spot for him abroad, at substantially less money, if he wanted to try to rebuild his career in General Electric. Smith was stunned. He had finally leveled with the company to help it defend itself, and there'd been no hint of punishment then or in the succeeding two months. He decided he'd had it, at fifty-four, and would just take his severance pay and resign.

It was probably a wise move. Those conspirators who didn't quit on the spot had a very rough go of it. Initial punishment (demotion, transfer, pay cuts) was eventually followed by forced resignation. But the extra gall in the punishment was the inequality of treatment. William Ginn had been implicated at the same time as Raymond Smith, yet he was allowed to continue in his $135,000 job as vice president of the Turbine Division—until he went off to jail loaded with the biggest fine ($12,500) of any defendant.

Widespread resentment over this curious partiality to Ginn and over the meting out of discipline generally was destined to have its effect: G.E. witnesses soon began to turn up at the trust busters' camp. Lawyers began popping up trying to get immunity for their clients in return for testimony. Scarcely a week went by that Bicks didn't get information on at least two new cases. Then the trust busters hit the jackpot in switchgear.

Switchgear had been particularly baffling to the Antitrust Division, so much so that in trying to establish a cartel pattern in the jumble of switchgear prices the trust busters got the idea they might be in code. A cryptographer was brought in to puzzle over the figures and try to crack the secret of how a conspirator could tell what to bid and when he'd win. But the cryptographer was soon as flummoxed as everyone else. One of the government attorneys in the case, however, had made a point of dropping in on a college classmate who was the president of a small midwestern electrical-equipment company. This executive didn't have chapter and verse on the switchgear cartel but what he did have was enough for Justice to throw a scare into a bigger company, I-T-E Circuit Breaker. Indicating that subpoenas would follow, antitrust investigators asked I-T-E to supply the names of sales managers in specific product lines. When the subpoenas did come, a pink-cheeked blond young man named Nye Spencer, the company's sales manager for switchgear, was resolutely waiting—his arms loaded with data. He had decided he wasn't about to commit another crime by destroying the records so carefully laid away in his cellar.

There were pages on pages of notes taken during sessions of the switchgear conspiracy—incriminating entries like "Potomac Light & Power O.K. for G.E." and "Before bidding on this, check with G.E."; copies of the ground rules for meetings of the conspirators: no breakfasting together, no registering at the hotel with company names, etc. Spencer, it seems, had been instructed to handle some of the secretarial work of the cartel and believed in doing it right; he'd hung on to the documents to help in training an assistant. But the most valuable windfall from the meticulous record keeper was a pile of copies of the "phases of the moon" pricing formula for as far back as May, 1958.

Sheets of paper, each containing a half-dozen columns of figures, they immediately resolved the enigma of switchgear prices in commercial contracts. One group of columns established the bidding order of the seven switchgear manufacturers—a different company, each with its own code number, phasing into the priority position every two weeks (hence "phases of the moon"). A second group of columns, keyed into the company code numbers, established how much each company was to knock off the agreed-upon book price. For example, if it were No. 1's (G.E.'s) turn to be low bidder at a certain number of dollars off book, then all Westinghouse (No. 2), or Allis-Chalmers (No. 3) had to do was look for their code number in the second group of columns to find how many dollars they were to bid *above* No. 1. These bids would then be fuzzed up by having a little added to them or taken away by companies 2, 3, etc. Thus there was not even a hint that the winning bid had been collusively arrived at.

With this little device in hand, the trust busters found they could light up the whole conspiracy. The new evidence made an equally profound impression on the grand juries. They handed down seven indictments. Forty companies and eighteen individuals were charged with fixing prices or dividing the market on seven electrical products. Switchgear led the list.

Allis-Chalmers thereupon decided to play ball with the government. The trust busters were willing to go easier on Allis-Chalmers *if* the company came up with something solid. It did. Thousands upon thousands of documents were turned over the the government. New indictments were added for collusion in power transformers, power-switching equipment, industrial controls, turbine generators, steam condensers.

So, executives from every major manufacturer in the entire electrical-equipment industry came to sit in the crowded Philadelphia courtroom and hear Judge Ganey sentence seven executives to prison; put twenty-three others with suspended jail sentences on probation for five years; and impose nearly $2 million in fines.

Twenty-nine companies received fines ranging from G.E.'s $437,500 and Westinghouse's $372,500 down to $7,500 each for Carrier Corp. and Porcelain Insulator Corp. The others, for the record, were: Allen-Bradley Co., Allis-Chalmers Manufacturing Co., A. B. Chance Co., Clark Controller Co., Cornell-Dubilier Electric Corp., Cutler-Hammer, Inc., Federal Pacific Electric Co., Foster Wheeler Corp., Hubbard & Co., I-T-E Circuit Breaker Co., Ingersoll-Rand Co., Joslyn Manufacturing & Supply Co., Kuhlman Electric Co., Lapp Insulator Co., McGraw-Edison Co., Moloney Electric Co., Ohio Brass Co., H. K. Porter Co., Sangamo Electric Co., Schwager-Wood Corp., Southern States Equipment Corp., Square D Co., Wagner Electric Corp., C. H. Wheeler Manufacturing Co., and Worthington Corp.

The causes which underlay the electrical comspiracies, however, are still as strong as they ever were. Chronic over-capacity continues to exert a strong downward pressure on prices. Corporate pressure is stronger than ever on executives, who must struggle to fulfill the conflicting demands of bigger gross sales on the one hand and more profit per dollar of net sales on the other.

"One thing I've learned out of all this," said one executive, "is to talk to only one other person, not to go to meetings where there are lots of other people." Many of the defendants look on themselves as the fall guys of U.S. business. They protest that they should no more be held up to blame than many another American businessman, for conspiracy is just as much "a way of life" in other fields as it was in electrical equipment.

But top executive officers of the biggest companies, at least, have come out of their antitrust experience determined upon strict compliance henceforth. G.E. and Westinghouse, without which cartels in the industry could never endure, are taking more elaborate preventive measures. Both are well aware that any repetition of these conspiracies would lay them open to political pressure for dismemberment.

The problem does not start and stop with the scofflaws of the electrical industry or with antitrust. Much was made of the fact that G.E. operated under a system of disjointed authority, and this was one reason it got into trouble. A significant factor also was the disjointment of morals.

April, May 1961

The Perils of the Conglomerates
By GILBERT BURCK

Lammot du Pont Copeland, president of Du Pont, was asked not long ago why his company wasn't going conglomerate or diversifying into new lines, as so many other U.S. corporations were doing. "Running a conglomerate," Copeland replied dryly, "is a job for management geniuses, not for ordinary mortals like us at Du Pont."

Multi-market companies, the most portentous business phenomenon of the postwar era, derive a certain strength from their disparate union; even if things go bad in one division, the company's total performance may hold up very well, and the resources of the combination can be marshaled to cure division ailments. But a multi-market company is also by definition a multi-adversity company. As corporate history testifies abundantly, a single-market company, even in good times, runs into troubles that can strain if not floor the most gifted managers.

This has not discouraged the conglomerates. With the development of new techniques like scientific decision-making—and par-

ticularly "exception" reporting, the profit-center concept, and
computerized information systems—managers are confident that
they can handle these aggregations. They do not go so far as to say
they can take over any kind of business. They do prefer their
acquisitions to have some "mutuality of interest" or "con-
centricity," both of which designate some kind of meaningful
relationship. Another of their favorite words is "synergy," sometimes described as the two-plus-two-equals-five effect, or the
combination of two things whose joint effect is greater than the
sum of the parts.

An enthusiastic body of thought has dubbed the multi-market
firm the "free-form company," and hailed it as one of the greatest
happenings of our time, made possible by the postwar profession-
alization of American management. The new techniques have
generated a breed of young, ambitious, creative free-form managers, possessing an uncommon degree of generalized management talent (the argument goes), adaptable and versatile, with
minds spacious enough to see beyond the company and yet
disciplined and informed enough to solve its special problems—
and with an uncanny eye for growth situations, especially those in
new technologies. They use jet planes like taxis and are peren-
nially inspecting plants the world over, soaking up wisdom here
and discharging it there. They can handle several businesses at
once, more effectively, not to say more brilliantly (they say), than
the old-time specialists handled a single business. The enthusiasts
see the free-form company with its free-form managers as the
prototype of all sizable firms a generation hence.

What makes this all sound plausible is that some multi-market
corporations have so far shown a high capacity for increasing their
earnings; e.g., Litton, Textron, FMC; over the past six years Litton's
sales have quintupled, those of Textron and FMC have tripled, and
their profits have at least kept pace with sales.

The prophets of the free-form corporation define it as basically
scientific, professional, and entrepreneurial. They distinguish it
from what they call the General Motors School, which one market
letter alludes to as the "obsolete world of Alfred P. Sloan." Sloan
showed how a certain amount of decentralization within G.M.
could be used to strengthen headquarters control. What G.M.'s
management was to the past, the letter implies, free-form management is to the future.

The question is whether there is really a substitute for the manager with years of specialized experience. Two who think not are Joel Dean, professor of business economics at Columbia, and Winfield Smith of the University of Chicago. "The belief that managerial ability is general and transferable," they have written, "appeals not only to journalists, novelists, politicians, and the general public, but to successful managers as well. We believe the weight of evidence is to the contrary, that managerial ability is generally tied quite closely to the particular industry setting in which it develops and operates. A good manager's intuitions, like those of a good card player, come from his long experience with the special rules, technology, and markets of a particular industry.

The multi-market companies have been favored so far by good times—times in which steadily rising demand has enabled many second-rate and even marginal companies to turn in good performances. But competition inevitably increases, either because competitors become more proficient or because demand temporarily tapers off, or both. The going inevitably becomes harder, and many an acquisition that looked like a sure moneymaker runs into unforseen trouble.

The history of corporate diversification is not lacking in examples. Back in 1956, after Olin Mathieson moved into new markets in an offensive of acquisitions, the company's executives predicted sales of $1.2 billion and net of $111 million by 1960; today, after five years of heroic "restructuring," the company has still not reached that goal. Blaw-Knox, the steel-mill-equipment manufacturer, was making $4.16 a share in 1956, when it diversified into road-building and food-processing equipment and construction contracts for chemical and petroleum plants. By 1965 profits had slid to $1.61 a share.

But the conglomerate tide, as *Fortune* began to report two years ago, seems virtually unstoppable. The targets of aggression are some of the most upright, prudent, powerful, and self-assured corporations in the land. Proud old names have already been taken over, and dozens of veteran executives have been sacked. Foreboding, frustration, and even fear are epidemic in perhaps three out of five big corporate headquarters. Anguished executives who should be minding the shop are instead spending long hours counseling with lawyers, management consultants, proxy specialists, and public-relations men skilled in the art of forfending takeovers.

Conglomeration enthusiasts are shedding few tears of sympathy, and taking every opportunity to discharge homilies on the mission of the conglomerate. It is ridding the economy of backward, stuffy management "that doesn't deserve to have control of all those assets." It is revitalizing complacent enterprises that have grown fat and sluggish. Conglomeration means a freer, more flexible, and on the whole a more competitive economy. And they're all sure they are in the main groove of economic history. Nicholas Salgo, the Hungarian-born ex-realtor who started Bangor Punta with a potato railroad and an expropriated Cuban sugar company, predicts that in ten years there will be only 200 major industrial companies in the U.S., all conglomerate.

The fact remains, however, that the process of putting conglomerates together tends to expand stock prices long before it expands the economic values on which stock prices ultimately depend. In 1967 the average aggressor company paid eighteen times earnings for the average target; last year the figure shot up to twenty-five. Sometimes, moreover, the acquiring company adds sweeteners that boost the price still further. It trades, say, $75 million worth of stocks for another company's stock, and guarantees stockholders that their shares will be worth $100 million in a year. If the shares haven't risen that much, the acquiring company issues enough new ones to bring the payment up to $100 million.

The news that a merger is in the works tends to send stock prices up, sometimes explosively. Grumman rose 8½ points in two days because it was rumored that Gulf & Western, City Investing, Curtiss-Wright, Walter Kidde, and Fairchild Hiller were all after it. This can give the appearance of growth where none exists, and often produces a chain-letter effect whose terminal stages may be painful. Generally the acquirer is a company whose stock is selling at a relatively high price-earnings ratio. Usually the p/e is high because the company has demonstrated a capacity to grow at an exceptional rate—although frequently an outfit skilled in public relations, by talking imaginatively about its plans and prospects, can command a much higher p/e ratio than actual performance warrants.

Any time such a company—for that matter any company—buys another with a lower price-earnings ratio, earnings per share of the merged company in the first year of its existence will, other things being equal, be higher than those of the acquiring company in the previous year. Contrariwise, any time a company buys another with a higher price-earnings ratio, the combination will turn up with lower earnings per share. This sounds incredible. It says that a conglomerator is better off—or *seems* better off—merging with an inferior organization than merging with a superior one. Yet it is so.

Assume Company A has a million shares earning $1 each; they are selling at $30 a share because the market judges A's growth favorably. Now assume Company B also has a million shares earning $1 each; they are selling at only $10 a share becuase B shows no internal growth at all. So A generously offers B's stockholders $15 a share, either in cash, which it can easily raise, or preferably in A's own stock, which has the advantage of exempting B's stockholders from an immediate capital-gains tax. In other words, A trades 500,000 of its own shares for all of B's million shares. So the new company is capitalized at 1.5 million shares earning $2 million. This works out not to $1 a share, as before the merger, but to $1.33. Although nothing really has changed in the companies and the economy is certainly no richer, earnings per share are a third higher. On the strength of this showing, the market bids the new stock to an even higher multiple.

The stockholders rejoice. Remarkable! And in a way it is re- markable. For the increase occurs *even if A is not growing internally at all*. So long as A can buy a company with a lower p/e (and thus at a per-share price lower than its own valuation), it can raise the new company's earnings per share. And so long as the conglomerate, even if not growing, can keep on buying other companies with lower p/e ratios, even if *they* are not growing, its earnings per share will continue to rise. But the day inevitably comes when such a conglomerate runs out of acquisitions. Then, if there has been no internal growth in earnings, earnings per share will fall steeply and the market price of the company's stock will probably fall even more. The stockholders who are in at the end are left holding the bag.

Sheer size of the target is no longer an obstacle to a takeover. A year or two ago, Wall Street jokers remarked that only General Motors and A.T.&T. were safe, but now some of the experts aren't so sure about G.M. "General Motors," argues one visionary financier, "is in many ways an ideal target. It has a low price- earnings ratio, relatively slow growth, large asset base, lots of cash, and high net worth. It is also shamefully underleveraged. Like Du Pont, from which it inherited its financial policies, G.M. has little debt. G.M. is thus practically a partner of the federal government, which takes more than half its gross profit. As a matter of fact, some have argued G.M. should have borrowed billions and bought in a lot of its own stock. This would have provided leverage—would have enabled earnings per share to rise faster than earnings as a whole.

"Well, G.M. didn't take on a lot of debt. Now suppose some hero conglomerator printed up $15 billion worth of debentures and maybe another $10 billion in stock and warrants. G.M. stock, which pays $4.30, is selling at around $80. Our hero would offer, say, $125 worth of his securities, paying, say, $5 or $6, for every share of G.M. Once G.M. stockholders realized that i.o.u.'s would really be paid out of G.M.'s own pocket, with the federal government footing part of the bill, they probably would trample over one another in the rush to exchange their shares. This may sound unthinkable. But things just as unthinkable are happening all the time.

February 1967

Voices

We're Drowning in Phony Statistics
By DANIEL SELIGMAN

In an otherwise admirable speech in Athens, Georgia, last spring, Attorney General Robert F. Kennedy declared: "Ninety percent of the major racketeers would be out of business by the end of the year if the ordinary citizen, the businessman, the union official, and the public authority stood up to be counted and refused to be corrupted." The underlying thought here was certainly praiseworthy, but the statistic, "90 percent," was, to put it bluntly, phony. There is no general agreement on what a "major racketeer" is or agreement on what constitutes standing up to be counted. This may seem like nit-picking. But unless somebody does a lot of nit-picking soon, we are going to be engulfed by phony statistics.

They come in two varieties. One is the Meaningless Statistic— ordinarily meaningless because a figure is used in conjunction with an undefined term, so that it is quite unclear what is being added up to arrive at the figure.

The other kind is what might be called the Unknowable Statistic. In this case, the meaning may be perfectly clear, but the alleged fact is something that no one could possibly know—e.g., "the American girl kisses an average of seventy-nine men before getting married," which was a contribution of Dr. Joyce Brothers to *This Week* magazine. (She never answered the letter I sent asking for the source of her information.)

Many Unknowable Statistics concern animals, ones about rats being especially popular. For years newspaper feature writers have put New York City's rat population at eight million. An issue of the *Nation* raised the figure to nine million, possibly to help the authors make the point that, "symbolically," there were more rats in New York City than people. I discussed the rat figures with Clinton A. Garvin, who is the Rodent and Insect Consultant to the city's Health Department. He pointed out that the only real study of the city's rat population had been made in 1949, when some investigators had actually gone out and counted rats in certain areas. Extrapolating their findings for the entire city, they had concluded that there were, at most, 250,000 rats in it, or one rat for every thirty-six persons. However, Dr. Garvin noted that there had been a Department of Interior study which suggested that, on the average, cities in the U.S. had one rat for every five persons. On balance, Dr. Garvin thought, the truth probably lay somewhere between the one-in-five and the one-in-thirty-six figures. He added that counting rats is very hard work. "You can count a rat on the eighth floor of a building, and then another on the seventh floor, and then another when you get to the sixth—but after all, you may just be seeing the same rat three times."

One of the first phony statistics that I consciously identified as such appeared in the New York *Times* in an article on the traffic problem: traffic jams in 1956 had "cost the nation $5 billion." The statistic is Unknowable. It is meaningless because it is unclear what is being added up to arrive at a total of $5 billion—the aggregate value of the output that would have been produced if a certain amount of manpower had not been tied up in traffic or shipments that went undelivered because of traffic jams? Or what?

I had a little better luck tracking down a figure on the cost of traffic *accidents*. Last year the Associated Press quoted General Henry J. Hoeffer, assistant general manager of the National Safety Council, as predicting that by 1966 the "economic loss" from traffic accidents would be $7 billion a year. In response to my letter, General Hoeffer replied that he hadn't made the statement, but that it seemed in line with past experience. He included some Safety Council literature breaking down the cost of traffic accidents in 1959, when it had totaled $6.2 billion.

A recent book, *The Operators,* by Frank Gibney, is a treasure-trove of statistics which tend to be Unknowable rather than Meaningless. For example, the volume of kickbacks, payoffs, and bribes is running at an annual rate of $5 billion. The American people dribble away $500 million on home-repair frauds, another $500 million on worthless health and nutrition programs, $100 million on "mail-order robbery," another $100 million on fake reducing preparations, and between $50 million and $200 million on other "fraudulent or half-fraudulent" medications. Nor is that all. We citizens are taken for $500 million to $1 billion worth of bad checks every year and blow $75 million getting degrees from phony colleges. "Stock operators" take us for $200 million and real-estate men working the "advance-fee racket" for another $50 million. And society as a whole is taken for $5 billion or $10 billion by chiselers who underpay their income taxes by some such amount. The total of these drags on society (using the higher end of the range where there is a range) is $17,725,000,000.

That is only the beginning. Vance Packard says in *The Waste Makers* that Americans "waste" $25 billion a year on disposable packaging. James Jackson Kilpatrick says in *The Smut Peddlers* that we throw away $500 million a year to the "organized obscenity racket." Thomas E. Snyder, a research associate at the Smithsonian Institution's Division of Insects, was recently quoted in several newspapers to the effect that termites do $250 million of damage a year (up from $100 million a decade ago). Several witnesses testifying last year before the House Appropriations Subcommittee on Department of Labor and Health, Education, and Welfare, and Related Agencies Appropriations suggested that juvenile delin-quency cost the U.S. $2.6 billion a year; $115 million of this was the value of money and goods stolen or destroyed, while the remainder represented the cost—presumably the gross cost—of providing police protection, correctional institutions, etc. Disposable packaging, smut, termites, and juvenile delinquency, together with the traffic mess and Gibney's assorted drags, get the loss to the economy up to $57,275,000,000.

Let us go on. Three years ago J. Edgar Hoover said in a speech that the total cost of crime in the U.S. was running at a $22-billion annual rate. However, Mr. Hoover has never either broken down the figure or updated it or explained how it was derived in the first place. Was Hoover talking about all criminal offenses, or only about *organized* crime? And in the latter case, how organized does crime have to be to be included? What about the "more than $1 billion" in cash that dishonest employees embezzle each year (according to Continental Casualty Co.)? What about the $25 million that is taken from supermarkets in shopping carts? (The figure, supplied by the Super Market Institute, includes the value of the carts themselves.)

Also, among the illegal activities that "cost" the U.S. large amounts, we must face up to gambling. Many gambling statistics seem to have come out of the Kefauver Committee's 1950 investigation of organized crime in interstate commerce, which has reported, "conservatively," that "$20 billion changes hands every year in the United States as a result of organized illegal gambling, a not inconsiderable portion of which stays with the promoters and operators of this illicit activity." The reference to $20 billion that "changes hands" suggests that this amount is lost by bettors to organized gamblers; but that involved reference to the "not inconsiderable portion" seems to say that only *some* of the $20 billion is lost. In another context, the committee referred to the figure as "the annual turnover" in the U.S. which doesn't seem to help much either. A witness at the recent McClellan Committee investigation of gambling held out for $50 billion.

To resume the count of all the statistical drags on the gross national product: In addition to the $57,275,000,000 mentioned above, we now have $22 billion as the cost of crime in general, $1 billion for embezzlement, $25 million for consumer theft via shopping carts, and $50 billion for gambling. The drag thus far, then, is $130,300,000,000.

That is not the end, of course. I also have in my possession statistics on the alleged cost to society of fires, hurricanes, and dog-bites.

Hurricane Donna was originally reported to have destroyed "well over $1 billion." How this estimate was derived, and what it meant—i.e., did the $1-billion figure refer to original cost, depreciated value, or replacement cost?—was never very clear; what *was* clear was that someone had taken insurance-company claims estimates of $135 million and proceeded from this figure, somehow, to a total cost, including uninsured property, of $1 billion. Later, the claims estimate was reduced to $100 million. Most hurricanes are like that.

The methodological problems with fire losses are roughly the same. The basic data here are the claims figures compiled by the National Board of Fire Underwriters, which adds to them its own estimate of unreported losses. For 1960 it reported that total losses had been $1,107,824,000.

I picked up one Unknowable Statistic from a short item in the New York *Times* which quoted the U.S. Public Health Service to the effect that in 1957 "medical costs resulting from dogbites" had been $5 million. Favorably impressed by the three-year time lag, which suggested forcibly that the U.S.P.H.S. did not shoot from the hip in these matters, I wrote to the service demanding the details. In reply, the Acting Chief of the Public Inquiries Branch of the service's Office of Information sent me a study which had been published in *Public Health Reports.* This made it clear that some kinds of dogbite information are available in endless and stupefying detail. The study showed, for example, that in Pittsburgh during July and August of 1958 there had been 947 reported dogbites (507 of them in July), and it broke these down by the race, occupation, sex, and age of the victims, the sex, age, and breed of the dogs, the time of the day and day of the week when the dog bit, the events immediately preceding the bite (the victim's side of the story only), and the "anatomic location and severity" of the bite. The study also mentioned an estimate that about 611,500 Americans had been bitten during 1957.

But the article in *Public Health Reports* was not so persuasive about the *cost* of dogbites. It stated, with apparent confidence, that the dogbite charge is about $1 million a year for "animal losses" and—as the *Times* had reported—$5 million more for "medical and public health expenses." The source of this information was given, in a footnote, as the *Journal of the American Medical Association* for May 10, 1952. In that publication I read an account of a speech delivered some time earlier to the Minnesota Veterinary Society by Dr. James

H. Steele, then of the U.S.P.H.S., in which the $1-million and $5-million figures had been mentioned—as "conservative estimates." Turning back to *Public Health Reports*, I could find no reason for coupling these 1952 cost estimates with the 1957 reported-bite estimate. Actually, one of the most striking facts to emerge from the study is the wide fluctuation in reported dogbites; in Pittsburgh, they went from 434 in July and August of 1957 to 947 in the same months a year later. The authors attribute this rise to better reporting rather than more biting. This is certainly an optimistic view of the case, but it suggests that there must be a sizable, and Unknowable, bill for unreported dogbites. And, of course, the fluctuation proves that the figure for the cost of reported dogbites cannot be a constant $5 million.

We can now add $1 billion for Hurricane Donna, $1,107,824,000 for fire losses, the $5 million for treating dogbites, plus the additional $1 million for "animal losses" resulting from dogbites. These figures get us to $132,413,824,000.

This list of drags on the economy is far from comprehensive, but I do not want to end it without adding two more phony statistics. One of these need only be mentioned, since it seems to be Unknowable on the face of it, and I undertook no correspondence to confirm that impression. This is the allegation, made by the Yale Center of Alcohol Studies, and reported in a 1958 National Industrial Conference Board publication, *Studies in Personnel Policy*, that excessive drinking costs U.S. business $1 billion annually. The cost is said to show up in the form of absenteeism, accidents, turnover, lost production, lowered morale, and "bad decisions"; however, no dollar breakdown has been offered by the center.

The second statistic commanded my special attention because it was not qualified by any "about" or "at least" or any of the other hedges that peddlers of phony statistics usually throw in: "Each year moths destroy $400 million worth of fine clothing and material." This appeared in an advertising folder published by the Lane Co. of Altavista, Virginia, manufacturer of cedar chests.

A gentleman in the company's advertising department replied to my inquiry that the "probable origin" of the figure was a bulletin prepared by the Stored-Product Insects Section of the Biological Sciences Branch of the Agricultural Marketing Service of the U.S. Department of Agriculture. The bulletin, which he sent me, said: "Estimates of the damage caused each year by clothes moths and carpet beetles in the United States range from $200 million to $500 million." I wrote to the Stored-Products Insects Section to ask where it had got these figures. I got a reply which said, in part: "There has not been an authentic survey of the damage caused annually by clothes moths and carpet beetles in the United States. It is difficult to conduct such a survey because of . . . the widespread occurrence in individual homes, factories, wholesale and retail outlets, government stores, etc. . . . and the difficulty in appraising the actual loss in the value of the article. . . ." Having confirmed my impression that we were talking about something Unknowable, my correspondent then confused me by adding: "We selected the figures of $200 million to $500 million because they appeared to us to be the most realistic of the estimates available."

In any case, excessive drinking and moths bring the total of all the drags on the economy to $133,813,824,000. This is more than 25 percent of the G.N.P. The list could, of course, be expanded considerably, and it might even be possible to get the total to something higher than the G.N.P. There are a lot of people around who would take it seriously.

November 1961

Extinction of the Last Simple Graces
By CHARLES J. V. MURPHY

Many corporations have forbidden their representatives to buy first-class tickets with company expense money. Murphy's letters to his editor belong in the debate over luxurious expense-account living.

Lima, Peru
Dear Colleague:
This morning's flight, since it spanned a mere 1,100–1,200 miles, or about three hours in jet time, I dutifully, even cheerfully, made for the rear of the vehicle, a section which in more forthright times would have been called the steerage. The spectacle was one of unrelieved misery and anguish. Upwards of fourscore human beings of both sexes, young and old, representing all aspects of the condition of man to be found in the New World and Old, were bestially compressed inside a narrow aluminum cylinder, the cubic

area of which could have tolerated but half their number in moderate comfort.

The mere mechanical business of cramming so many people into so little space was itself an engineering feat of a high order. But to have kept them alive through a long journey required corporate talents—a capacity for cunning, a diabolical understanding of the last wafer-thin calculations of the margins of human endurance of the sort we have not seen since the end of the slave trade. Even so, when I got aboard at Bogotá it was plainly touch and go whether the captain would reach Lima with a live cargo.

The condition of the passengers was pitiful in the extreme. Directly across from me was an elderly gentleman whose bearing and grooming, in the degree that these characteristics could still be discerned through the woefulness that enveloped him, were clearly those of a Spanish aristocrat, possibly even a grandee. At this lamentable point, however, only a knowing eye would have recognized him for what he was. He had begun his journey in Europe, and eight hours of jet economics had utterly beggared him. His fine suit was rumpled and stained. A blotch of what I took to be a second-class claret spread across his once immaculate shirt. Truly I was appalled. Here was a gentleman who in his own experiences and through his noble line had emerged proud and erect through the centuries from the conquest of a continent, from under the heel of Napoleon, from wars on land and sea. Nevertheless, eight hours in a jet tourist seat were quite sufficient to transform him into a shapeless piece of flotsam.

I felt my reason being unseated, steeled though I was for the test by my affection and regard for our company's accounting department. Bulging beside me, in the adjoining seat, was a bearded character who may well have been freshly graduated from Fidel Castro's training camps for guerrillas. He was puffing furiously on a large cigar. Before long I became aware, along with the smell of something burning, of a fiery sensitivity spreading below my knee. On investigating in a gingerly way—it is difficult in such crowded quarters to move one's person more than an inch or two in any direction—I discovered to my horror that the left leg of my pants was briskly afire. I might well have been consumed in the holocaust—the suit was one I acquired in Hong Kong and therefore highly inflammable—had not the Fidelista thrust down a huge paw to quench the flame. The burnt area, happily, is not large; nor do I believe that the cost of having the vanished part restored by

reweaving will be substantially more than the amount I will have
theoretically saved by going, to use that misleading term, "economy class."

Up front, whenever the dividing curtain parted, as it occasionally did to allow the passage of one of the attendants, the scene was
one of utter tranquility, of well-ordered leisure. The floor was free
of orange peel, discarded newspapers, and the debris of meals that
tortured men could no longer keep down. To me, the measure of
difference between the two worlds seemed, if not planetary, then
certainly oceanic.

Reflect well, my dear friend, on this experience of mine. Technology is no longer being shaped in the interest of fortifying man
in dignity and erectness. It has been coldly and cunningly warped
toward the end of returning him to the savagery of technically
contrived destitution. What an outcome for the once glorious
promise of the Air Age.

Your friend,
Charles

Rio de Janeiro, Brazil
Dear Colleague:

It has been my good fortune through this long day, on the
occasion of my passage from Lima, to return once more to the
amenities associated with a first-class passage. This privilege I
conferred upon myself only after grave deliberation.

I am concerned, as you know, with the question of how a man
past his prime, yet with some considerable experience in withstanding the rigors of an earlier era of travel, can best secure for
himself certain minimal measures of comfort in the face of what is
being falsely and equivocally hailed as "technological advance." It
may be your special fate and mine, sir, in the twilight of our
careers, to witness the extinction of the last simple graces and
amenities at the hands of the corporate technologists and accountants.

But to continue: the vehicle which I entered this morning at
Lima was identical in all physical respects with the one that had
transported me there. I entered the vehicle through the rear, which
presented a scene as appalling as that which I described in my
previous letter. Fortunately, there was no longer need for me to

linger in this forlorn pit. Closing my ears to sounds such as might last have been heard when the Irish were being herded into the cattle boats at Queenstown to build the railroads in the American West, I thrust my way forward, but not without a momentary embarrassment. A child lay half in the aisle, half under its mother's leg. My instinct would have been to raise the child gently and restore it to the mother. But I have learned from harsh experience in the so-called tourist section that to yield to a compassionate gesture, however heartbreaking the circumstances, is to expose oneself to social obligations of the most costly nature. Just as in China where a motorist stands liable for the lifelong support of all dependents if he is so rash as to stop to give succor to a pedestrian whom he has run down, so in the tourist section of an airplane any passenger who unwisely extends sympathy to a stranger in the same fix is certain to find himself saddled with an unwanted acquaintanceship for whatever time remains of the awful journey. I had no real choice, therefore, but to boot the poor child aside and project myself with all possible dispatch toward the dividing partition.

My dear friend, what a change! As the partition, a plastic curtain of no particular strength, slid open to admit me, I was filled with a sense of wonder. The first impression was one of untrammeled spaciousness, of well-ordered leisure, the calm of a New England sunset. The only sound was the popping of champagne corks and of a butter knife molding caviar to the delicate circumference of a cracker. Female attendants in fetchingly abbreviated garments hovered about, geisha fashion.

I had no difficulty whatsoever in fitting myself into circumstances so agreeable to the spirit. My sense of the fitness of things was altogether assuaged by the realization that I was once more, if but fleetingly, one of the "happy few" in the first-class end of the new technology. To the degree that I may have yielded to the qualms of conscience, it was only from an initial notion that the poor devils in the rear might be driven, in the extremity of their desperation, to batter down the flimsy partition between the two worlds, as the French masses once stormed the palaces of their kings. The notion proved groundless, to my rising satisfaction.

Thus the hours fled, at a cost (by my crude mathematics) of a mere $40 an hour.

Your friend,
Charles

En Route to Caracas
Dear Sir:

Your rather peremptory note of the 16th instant came to my hand this morning just before I left my hotel to board the jet vehicle in which I am to be confined for the next five and a half hours.

Having long observed your disposition as an executive to live by the book, I was not really surprised to have you remind me, with a sternness I consider altogether unjustifiable, that there is to be no appeal whatsoever from the ruling of our beloved controller that all company travel is to be done in the "economy" end of the airplane. Let me state, for the record, that this is where I am at this very instant. I am there against my better judgment, certainly against my self-interest, my various members adroitly telescoped. The wisest traveler of all is one no taller than than five feet two inches and weighing no more than 115 pounds.

Until the recent past—before, that is, the advent of the jet technology as rationalized by unscrupulous economists—a voyage in a flying machine could be an immensely satisfying experience. The operators vied with one another in inventing schemes for making more comforts available to travelers. A staple vignette in the airline advertisements of this golden era was the picture of a businessman snoozing in what looked like a club chair, his legs stretched out into uncluttered space, his briefcase with its important papers safely tucked under his arm. Forget all that. Comforts of this sort no longer exist in the new steerage. Among the traditions that have evaporated is the notion that travel is broadening. A moment ago, our captain announced in a cheerful voice that the Amazon was at that moment some six miles below us. By squirming around, it is possible for a small, agile person to obtain a slanting view of the world below such as might otherwise be vouchsafed by peering through a partially lifted manhole cover. But even this glimpse was lost to me. The gentleman directly in front of me, perhaps because of some private anguish of his own, chose that fleeting moment to thrust back in his seat with such violence as to jam my briefcase against my Adam's apple. Except for a stoppage of breath, which fortunately lasted but a few seconds, I am in no immediate discomfort, although quite unable to move. While I missed the chance to see the Amazon, I do not doubt that it continues to flow to the sea.

Your obedient servant,
Charles

May 1963

What Is Marion Harper Saying?

By SPENCER KLAW

Marion Harper, Jr., a large, high-domed, forty-four-year-old New Yorker who is chairman and president of McCann-Erickson, Inc., is an advertising man of a new and formidable type. Harper's stock in trade is scientific communication, and the image he projects, to use a handy trade expression, is that of a man who has transcended old-fashioned trial-and-error methods and put the art of commercial persuasion on something like a scientific footing. Furthermore, Harper rejects as obsolete the idea that advertising men should stick to advertising. He likes to describe McCann-Erickson as a "marketing-oriented communications service for advertisers." By this he means that McCann-Erickson, in addition to writing a client's advertising, is prepared to help him repackage, rename, and even redesign his products, change his price structure, get more shelf space in the supermarkets, write inspirational literature for his salesmen, and improve his corporate personality. It is Harper's aspiration, in short, to be the blender of what he often refers to as "the total marketing mix."

Harper has, of course, no exclusive right to the role of scientific communicator and all-around marketer. Most advertising men these days bombard clients with research, and it is a poor agency that can't afford at least one house psychologist. Moreoever, in the age of self-service, when so many manufacturers have to coordinate their advertising campaigns with coupon deals, store promotions, product publicity, and the like, advertising agencies have been forced to interest themselves, willy-nilly, in all facets of marketing.

But Harper did a lot to create the role of the total marketer, and he plays it with matchless authority and style. When he has lunch with a client, or someone he would like as a client, he is apt to construct a conversational launching pad of unchallengeable truths, and then whoosh off into a philosophical and psychological stratosphere where few, if any, of his competitors are equipped to follow him. "Marion can talk the client's own language," a former associate says. "First he talks about accountability and control and system and organization. This is very soothing to a lot of executives. It eases their tensions and fears. They listen to Marion and they think, 'By God, here's a fellow who sees things our way.' *Then* he gives them a good whiff of psychology."

He might discuss a couple of McCann-Erickson house specialties: the Relative Sales Conviction Test, say, and the Purchase Proposition. Then, with his conversational rockets developing full thrust, he might turn to an analysis of the coming Information Revolution, come out boldly for "holistic" techniques in corporate public relations, explain how men and situations are linked by "event loops," and coast into orbit with an account of the wonders of "co-creativity," a form of super-brainstorming that Harper has been experimenting with lately. To keep his idea inventory at a high level, Harper leads a life engineered for maximum cerebration. When he gets up in the morning, for example, he pedals the equivalent of one to four miles on a stationary bicycle, and while pedaling he improves his mind by reading a book propped up on the handle bars. Moreover, to free his mind for higher things, Harper has tried to eliminate the element of conscious choice from much of his daily routine. Thus he dresses unconsciously, automatically selecting a suit whose color matches his mood—brown when he feels cheerful, gray when things look terrible. "Sometimes I don't really find out how I feel until I notice what I have on," he explains.

Harper's unremitting mental application made him president of McCann-Erickson in 1948, when he was only thirty-two. At the time, McCann's billings (roughly, the volume of advertising it handled) totaled $54 million, and it ranked fifth in size among advertising agencies. Last year billings were close to $330 million, and McCann-Erickson, with offices in twenty-two countries, did more business than any other agency except J. Walter Thompson. As a business getter, Harper is perhaps the most successful advertising man of his generation.

Harper's success owes much to his early realization that advertisers are eternally eager for assurance that they are spending their money in the right way—and to his discovery that science can often help allay anxieties on this score. To this end, he has established a department at McCann-Erickson called the Institute of Communications Research—to "formulate better systems . . . practices, and principles through the courageous study and research required to change the fundamental knowledge of communications beyond existing frontiers."

Among the projects under way at the institute is a study of how people's eyes move when they look at an ad or a commercial. (For instance, do they watch Betty Furness or the refrigerator?) The institute is also attempting to predict the relative sales appeal of different slogans by flashing them briefly on a screen with a device called a tachistoscope, and seeing which slogans people remember. Harper himself is especially enthusiastic about a study that is being made of pupil dilation. It stems from the discovery by a University of Chicago psychologist, now working under a grant from McCann-Erickson, that when people look at a picture that interests them, the pupils of their eyes dilate in proportion to their interest. Further study of this phenomenon is expected to help find better ways of pretesting advertisements.

At the moment, Harper is greatly excited about his experiment in what he calls co-creativity. To carry it out, he launched last year a satellite of McCann-Erickson bearing the name Jack Tinker & Partners. Tinker was formerly in charge of creative services (art and copy) at McCann, and his partners are three other high-salaried McCann-Erickson veterans, among them Dr. Herta Herzog, a leading authority on motivation research. Harper has freed them of administrative duties, and set them up in an elegantly appointed duplex apartment in midtown Manhattan. Their exact mission is hard for many to grasp, but seems simple enough to Harper. "We focus a lot of attention on the problem of the individual creator at McCann-Erickson," he said recently. "But there's this whole new dimension of co-creativity. What happens when you blend different skills at a very high level? We're conducting an experiment to learn whether through co-creativity you can produce better, neater, brighter, hotter, more creatively. . . ."

Harper has also given the group the job of figuring out what to do about the term "corporate image." A few weeks ago he spent a morning exploring the subject with the partners. "The corporation has to be seen in the context of its being," Harper said at one point, chopping the air with the edge of his hand. "You have to look for the inward truth." They all agreed that McCann-Erickson should start talking about either corporate "identity" or corporate "commitment." In the end, "commitment" got the nod. "Now let's see if we can get a philosophical base for this," Harper said as he departed for lunch with a client, "and then we can try to bring it into operational reality."

January 1961

Beyond the Horizon

The Vietnam War: The Costs

By WILLIAM BOWEN

With about 235,000 U.S. servicemen now in South Vietnam, the costs to the U.S. of the war are running at a yearly rate of more than $13 billion. The war, it appears, will get bigger. U.S. Senators who know what Defense Department witnesses say in closed congressional hearings have predicted a U.S. buildup to 400,000 men, or more. General William Westmoreland, the U.S. commander in Vietnam, has reportedly requested a buildup to 400,000 by the end of December. With that many U.S. servicemen in South Vietnam, the cost of the war would run to $21 billion a year—even more if bombing and tactical air support increased in proportion to the buildup on the ground.

Costs per man run much higher than they did in the Korean war. The pay that servicemen get has gone up more than 40 percent since them. Some matériel costs have risen very steeply since Korea. The F-86D fighters in Korea cost about $340,000 each; the F-4C's in South Vietnam cost nearly six times as much. Ammunition use per combat soldier is very much higher than in the Korean war. The M-14 rifle fires up to 150 rounds per minute, and ten rounds per minute at a sustained rate. The M-16, carried by some Special Forces troops, can use up ammunition at a full-automatic rate of 750 rounds per minute. The M-79 grenade launcher fires grenades as if they were bullets.

The nature of the war contributes to making it peculiarly expensive for its size. Technologically sophisticated military forces, magnificently equipped to kill and destroy, are employed against meager or elusive targets. In Korea, there were visible masses of enemy forces to shoot at, and the U.S. superiority in weapons could be exerted efficiently; in Vietnam the enemy hits and runs, and moves under cover of darkness or foliage. With their abundant firepower, the superb U.S. fighting men in South Vietnam clobber the Vietcong in shooting encounters, but the U.S. forces run up huge costs—in troop supplies, fuel, helicopter maintenance—just trying to find some guerrillas that they can shoot at.

There is an almost profligate disparity between the huge quantities of U.S. bullets and bombs poured from the air upon targets in Vietnam and the military and economic damage the bullets and bombs do, in the aggregate. In North Vietnam the U.S. has debarred itself from attacking economically valuable targets such as port facilities and manufacturing plants. From bases in Thailand, F-105's fly over North Vietnam and drop their mighty payloads on or near roads, rail lines, ferry facilities, bridges. The costs to the enemy of repairing the damage are picayune compared with the costs to the U.S. of doing the damage. Machine guns mounted on helicopters and on A-47's (elderly C-47's, modified and fitted with three guns) fire streams of bullets into expanses of jungle and brush that are believed to conceal Vietcong guerrillas. The thought of an A-47 firing up to 18,000 rounds per minute into treetops brings to mind that bizarre image in Joseph Conrad's *Heart of Darkness*, of the French warship off the African cost: "There wasn't even a shed there, and she was shelling the bush . . . firing into a continent."

B-52's, operating at a cost of more than $1,300 per hour per plane, fly a ten-hour round trip from Guam to South Vietnam to strike at an enemy that has no large installations or encampments visible from the air. The B-52's have been fitted with extra racks that increase their payloads to more than sixty 750-pound bombs, about $30,000 worth of bombs per plane. "The bomb tonnage that is resulting is literally unbelievable," said Secretary McNamara at a Senate hearing last January. Several weeks later, at a press conference, he said: "Our consumption in February . . . of air-delivered munitions alone in South Vietnam was two and a half times the average monthly rate in the three years of the Korean war." But much of that "literally unbelievable" bomb tonnage merely smashes trees and blasts craters in the earth.

Only a rich nation can afford to wage war at ratios so very adverse. But the U.S. *is* a rich nation. If there is a great disparity between the bomb power dropped and the economic value of the targets, there is also a great disparity between the wealth and power of the U.S. and of the enemy. The cost of the bombs is small in relation to the G.N.P. of the U.S., and the damage they do is sometimes substantial in relation to the G.N.P. of North Vietnam, or to the resources available to the Vietcong. But the costs of winning are going to be unpleasantly large, and are going to get larger, creating new economic strains.

The official position of the Defense Department is that it does not know what the costs of the war are, and that it does not even try to compute them. As a Pentagon official put it: "We have no intention of cost accounting the war in Vietnam. Our business is to support the conflict there. Our business is not cost accounting."

April 1966

The Monsters of Huntsville

By PAUL O'NEIL

The biggest loudspeaker in the world is oystery white in color, has a square, rather querulous mouth that is thirteen feet across, and is mounted on a high, four-legged tower atop a grassy hill at the George C. Marshall Space Flight Center near Huntsville, Alabama. It was built two years ago to "transmit pure tones at a sound pressure level of 141 decibels" —which means it is the damnedest hi-fi set in existence—but it is difficult not to suspect that it is actually the gullet of some huge and unfortunate beast, removed by surgery too hideous to contemplate and still hurting. The great, blind, throatlike device turns slowly through a full 360 degrees when in use, and as it eeks and oinks, howls and whistles, moos and rumbles, and on occasion roars like three Niagaras, it seems actuated by some vast fund of helpless animal fright rather than by a spool of magnetic tape.

The horn has been erected to serve as a guinea pig for machines far bigger, far more cunning, and vastly more powerful than itself—the family of 1.5-million-pound-thrust Saturn rocket boosters, which have been conceived to provide the U.S. with more lift than the Russians and which are currently being fabricated at Huntsville. The Saturns have dreadful voices. When one of them is held captive in the space center's towering static stand and test-fired on the ground, the noise it generates travels for great distances through the broad valleys and rolling hills of the country round, and sometimes does so with startling eccentricity. Low clouds or even temperature inversion in a clear, blue sky can reflect and concentrate sound as a concave mirror reflects and concentrates light, and can fling it down in torrents far from its point of origin. It is the horn's demeaning duty, thus, to give imitations of the ear-splitting tones that are combined in Saturn's basso roar, and determine whether conditions are safe. As the loudspeaker bays at the horizon during the hours before a test, a group of technicians known locally as the "noise boys" courses the countryside with decibel counters to make sure no outlying hamlet is getting more than its inevitable share of sound effect.

But this is simply overture. The horn eventually falls silent and turns its cheek away from the steaming, metallic monster on the next rise of ground. Amid the hush it is impossible not to meditate on the Saturn's size, its spurious impassivity, and its disconcerting independence of man; on the little electronic brain that is thinking away beneath its big, pointed moron's skull, on its electronic nervous system, and its tubular digestive system, and the Nero-like lust with which it vomits the contents of its nine aluminum bellies. Its tanks are now topped. They contain 39,000 gallons of kerosene and 56,000 gallons of liquid oxygen. The Saturn will spew the whole explosive mess out through its eight engines in 120 flaming seconds. What is its mood? Does it hate us all?

The last of its white-overalled human attendants scuttle off and hide from it. Half a mile away, behind a steel wall, spectators— among them a pair of nuns, local merchants, a knot of French army officers, a scattering of housewives and secretaries—jam up, shoulder to shoulder, and peer at it through a series of four-inch slits. Their voices die away. A soundless waterfall begins foaming on the canted steel deflector at the base of the stand. Gongs, muted by distance, ding monotonously in the eerie quiet. Saturn springs to life in one match-in-the-gas-tank instant; its base is suffused with a wild glare, its engines pour incandescence, and a vast whoosh of orange fire curves up and out to flail for a hundred yards in the air beyond the test stand. For the space of a heartbeat, perhaps two— as streamers of saffron smoke rise above the fire and dark birds circle crazily in the foreground—the spectator feels a curious sense of anticlimax. Then he drowns in arriving sounds—a thunderous, blistering blowtorch roar that invades the viscera and the throat and trembles away inside the body as though the inner tissues had turned to aspic.

It is easy enough for anyone riased on *Buck Rogers in the Twenty-fifth Century* to get the gist of U.S. plans for space travel. Actually believing them is something else again; they sound so much like excerpts from old science fiction that anyone conditioned by the immortal Buck is plagued, in the presence of space scientists, by the unreasonable but recurring idea that he has fallen in with maniacs or comedians. The Saturn cures him. In its malevolent presence he instantly abandons the conditioned skepticism of a lifetime. The spectator, gripping the edge of his viewing slot like a man in a hurricane, knows in his very liver that the moon is really only sixty hours from Earth.

June 1962

The Seventies

We come now to the fifth decade. This is a room of moderns, quite impressionionistic—of unfinished sketches; of corporate landscapes that had once been lush with profits now looking bleak; of portraits of blemished heroes; of still lifes of professors who wear helpless expressions at the surprising motions of the American economy. Most alarming is a picture of industry, which had won World War II and supplied all that was asked for in Vietnam, now falling behind the Soviets in total production of military power, although not through failures of Capitalism but as a result of political decisions. What might be taken as a symbol of the Seventies is a lurid picture of buildings in our cities collapsing. There are artifacts, however, to lift our spirits: a laser that shoots a tentative beam of hope into one aspect of the country's future; a device the size of a tenpenny nailhead that can make 100,000 calculations a second. Withal, a Mr. Greenspan exhibits a modestly cheerful countenance.

How Social Responsibility Fits the Game of Business

By JOHN McDONALD

Many executives in U.S. business are suddenly meeting a whole array of social issues—pollution, racial discrimination, consumerism, and the like—that seriously and directly affect their corporate operations. This may be the first time in U.S. business history that so much *conscious* thought has been given to reconciling what happens in markets with what is happening in society.

Until quite recently no public opprobrium attached to dumping waste chemicals into rivers, or refusing to hire uneducated blacks. Businessmen never had to speak the language of corporate "social responsibility." But with social standards changing, they are forced to remember an old but muted truth: although the corporation in its markets pursues hard economic goals headed by profit, it lives and breathes in society.

Milton Friedman, the leading fundamentalist of classical economic thought today, has accused corporate executives who talk about "social responsibilties" of something akin to fraud and subversion of free enterprise. He maintains that since executives are fiduciaries enjoined to make money, they are misappropriating the shareholders' investments and usurping the functions of politics and government if they choose to get involved with pollution control and urban problems. Friedman does acknowledge that, in seeking to maximize their profits, businessmen must abide by law and "ethical custom," but he does not seem to see the new issues that have arisen in this area.

The awkward thing about the standard mode of economic thought has always been that it is forced to contend with a vast region of exceptions—kinds of behavior that are not in fact controlled by an impersonal market mechanism. These have come to be regarded as "market failures."

When the classical market fails, the situation becomes grist for the game theorists. Modern game theory goes back to the great work of John von Neumann and Oskar Morgenstern in the 1940's, but what it has to offer in understanding economic and social issues is still not widely appreciated. Although it is creatively mathematical and its developments have been closeted in that special world, it is an art of understanding, not a science.

Game theory is earthy and uninhibited. It looks for whatever might happen under any rules or lack of them. Co-operative game theory deals with what happens in both hard economics and a wide variety of social-economic arrangements. Von Neumann and Morgenstern, by recognizing standards of behavior as integral components of economic life, broadened the scope of economics to take in its whole social setting.

Of all the large social issues pressing on business today the most novel bears upon the changing standards concerning the environment. The issue looms large not only because industry has produced more undesirable goods (i.e., pollutants) along with the increasing amount of desirable ones, but also because the basic U.S. philosophy of economic growth is no longer accepted without qualification.

Although most chief executives take for granted that the consumer will pay for pollution control in the end, they also recognize that that doesn't say much about what is happening or may happen to them in business as a result of the solutions adopted or in prospect. The chief of a leading forest-products company described a common view of some of the internal complexities of the problem: "We want to clean up air and water, but we don't want to be at a competitive disadvantage. Suppose you've already put money into pollution control while others in the industry haven't, and along comes a proposal for a new state standard. I might be better off with a higher one, because it would put my competitor at a disadvantage. But everybody knows the public is going to force it, and big polluters know that they're going to have to do something about the problem, that it's only a question of timing. I think much of this will have to be settled by federal law. You've got to go outside of industry to do it fairly."

Society appears no longer to want industry to allocate the social costs of production to society at large. Not being a player in this game at the economic level, society can only seek political solutions. That means a rule change—a new game. Business, too, is going the political route to obtain some influence over what the new game is to be.

This may be the only option it has left. But other solutions, developed by a new generation of game theorists, are also possible. One of these (called "the core") emphasizes cooperative hard economics. Its line of thought can be illustrated by the situation on

Lake St. Clair, Michigan, where pollution by business is interfering with business; hundreds of fishing and resort enterprises have been damaged, most seriously by mercury from one industrial polluter. The lake was also being polluted by the victims themselves, who included thousands of pleasure-boat owners. The market failed to offer a solution, and there was no new standard of behavior to rely on. Now that the damage is done, the victims are seeking relief at government levels.

As in most pollution situations, no effort by any one individual would avail. Voluntary cooperative economic action to control the pollution at its sources was not actually considered. But such an approach might have given the victims a way of getting a clean lake even in the absence of a social standard and without having to resort to politics. Cooperative action would involve trying to find the economic basis of a lake coalition. For the effort to work, the advantages to each member would have to be commensurate with the cost to each. This could happen if the loss each suffered as a result of pollution were greater than what each would have to spend to clean up his own effluent; or if those who gained disproportionately to their costs would offer a settlement to those who gained less than their costs.

In this case, the fishing and resort businesses might have found that they could afford collectively to reimburse the industrial polluter, who otherwise had little motive to join the lake coalition and control his effluent. Either arrangement would internalize the economics of the pollution cooperatively and would be stable.

Each player or group of players should be willing to join the overall lake coalition if each does better that way. If this is the situation, the *total* lake society is doing the best it can. This solution doesn't say precisely what distribution of costs and benefits will finally be made; other game-theory solutions can carry it further— for example, through the bargaining process.

The lake coalition will have stability if it has control of a decisive amount of pollution. If there is one holdout whose pollution is decisive, the solution falls apart. In sum, unless the lake businesses arrive at a voluntary cooperative arrangement with this kind of hard economic rationale, or the rationale of a standard of behavior, they will be vulnerable to a coercive resolution by politics and law, over which they would have some influence but not control.

December 1970

CATS AND DOGS
Some 31 million families now own pets, and almost half of them buy specially packaged food for their animals. Sales of pet food will total $1.4 billion this year, and have been increasing by an average of $120 million annually since 1965. The chances are that this trend will continue, for the dog population is increasing by over one million annually, the cat population by something over 300,000.

December 1971

Uncertain Times

When the Arabs Changed the Oil Business
By GURNEY BRECKENFELD

For most of the twentieth century, the preponderant strength lay on the side of the big oil companies. Dealing separately with weak, quarreling, and often ignorant regimes in the oil-producing countries, they frequently drove one-sided bargains. If one country bucked the system, more oil could be pumped up somewhere else. However, a combination of economic and political circumstances ended all that in 1970. Newly militant and unified, the predominantly Arab oil-producing countries turned the ten-nation Organization of Petroleum Exporting Countries into an effective cartel and forced the oil companies into major bargaining battles—with six Persian Gulf members, Iran, Iraq, Saudi Arabia, Kuwait, Abu Dhabi, and Qatar; and with Libya in North Africa.

In response to the OPEC challenge, the oil companies banded together for the first time to negotiate as a team, managing to obtain an unprecedented waiver of U.S. antitrust laws. Even so, they proved no match for the oil countries' monopoly. Partly by threatening an embargo of essential petroleum supplies and partly by threatening to legislate higher tax rates and other terms unilaterally, the producers forced the rich and proud companies to submit to most of their demands for a greatly enlarged share of oil revenues. The Libyans were the big victors. They won a 46 percent increase in income per barrel of crude, to $2.01.

The most immediate consequence is that consumers in Western Europe and Asia have begun to pay more for gasoline, fuel oil, and other petroleum products. In the U.S., which imports from the Middle East only 3 percent of the oil it consumes, prices have been little affected so far, though the outlook is not encouraging. The balance-of-payments drain will be felt in Europe; Britain, which depends on the Middle East and North Africa for 83 percent of its oil, will pay out an extra $250 million this year. The Common Market countries and Japan will be similarly affected.

What matters for the long run is that oilmen have lost effective control over an indispensable portion of industrial civilization's basic sinew. The "hurricane of change," as oil consultant Walter Levy calls it, seems likely to confront the international oil companies with a considerably different set of business circumstances. Their role as concession holders, entitled to develop and exploit oil reserves around the world, seems destined for severe shrinking. Peru has yet to pay a penny for the holdings of Jersey Standard that it seized in 1968. Last February, Algeria, an OPEC member and the world's tenth-largest oil producer, seized a 51 percent interest in French oil operations.

Mohammed Reza Pahlavi, the increasingly independent Shah of Iran, talks of taking over the European-U.S. consortium in Iran when its present concession expires in 1979, even though the consortium has a contractual option for three five-year renewals. "It is ridiculous for a rapidly industrializing country such as ours to

*Defense Secretary
James Schlesinger*

*Sheik Ahmed Zaki Yamani,
Saudi Arabian oil minister*

have foreign countries take our oil from the well to the tanker," says the Shah. "We can do this ourselves now." Barring an unexpected reversal of the trend, it is a fair bet that almost all international oil companies' foreign subsidiaries in North Africa and the Middle East will face nationalization by the late Seventies or early Eighties.

Far more is at stake for industrial nations than the fortunes of major corporations. The approaching twilight of Western oil empires coincides with—and owes some of its imminence to—the increasing Soviet presence in the Middle East and North Africa. As British and French military power has diminished or been withdrawn entirely, the Soviet Union has moved cautiously into the vacuum. At the end of World War II the entire region from Morocco to southern Iran was firmly under Western control or influence. Today, eight of the sixteen Arab regimes have truned "revolutionary" and "socialist."

Oilmen have every reason to be concerned about such political instability in a strategically crucial—and increasingly anti-Western—region. Historically, great powers must control their sources of food and fuel, by either diplomacy or conquest. In private, some executives express fears that Middle Eastern turmoil contains the seeds of nuclear war. That danger cannot be dismissed, but on the evidence so far, both the U.S.S.R. and the U.S. seem inclined to avoid a collision that could lead to mutual self-destruction. The more subtle hazard is the possibility that the U.S.S.R. will gain an economic stranglehold over Europe's and Japan's oil supply through future coups that bring more Arab countries into the Soviet orbit.

August 1971

How We Blew 1973
By CAROL J. LOOMIS

The problems of the U.S. economy have an unnerving tendency to be something different today from what you thought they were yesterday. Not long ago, for example, we were agonizing about such matters as getting the federal budget under control, keeping labor's demands in check, making the U.S. "competitive" in world trade, and strengthening the dollar. Well, the budget has lately been under control, the unions have for some time been temperate in their demands, our trade balance is solidly in the black, and the dollar has suddenly become a tower of strength. And the nation's economic problems? They are the worst in decades.

The fact is that we have a whole new set of problems to agonize about. Or, more precisely, we have a new set of reasons to be concerned about the central problem, inflation. We have other economic problems these days, including an extraordinary array of shortages and supply dislocations, but inflation seems at once the most vexing and most intractable. The inflation keeps flaring up in new and different ways, for new and different reasons, and with consequences never imagined a while ago.

Only a year ago the Council of Economic Advisers, making its annual report to the President and the nation, stated, apparently with some confidence, that the rise in the G.N.P. deflator, a measure of inflation in the entire economy, would be held to 3 percent in 1973. As things turned out, the deflator rose by slightly over 5 percent—the worst performance for a peacetime year since 1948. The consumer price index ran up by over 6 percent. Food prices were up some 15 percent.

One might suppose that the entire economics profession would be stepping forward to advise us on how to get out of the mess. Unfortunately, most economists are acting as though they were shell-shocked by events. One of their number, Walter Heller, says that 1973 must be recorded as "a year of infamy in price forecasting."

Not so many years ago economists were talking as though they had finally unlocked the secret of managing our economy; some, indeed, were talking about their newfound ability to "fine-tune" it. In 1973, by contrast, many were acting as though they had simply given up on inflation, or, at least, resigned themselves to numbers that would once have been considered unthinkable. Heller himself figures we might as well start getting used to 4 percent.

After listening to a litany of downbeat forecasts as a recent session of the Joint Economic Committee, Representative Hugh Carey, who represents a Brooklyn district, looked unhappily at a distinguished panel of economists testifying before him and said he was reminded of that hapless gang, the 1962 New York Mets. "You make me think of Casey Stengel's question," Carey said. " 'Can't anybody here play this game?'"

Well, what went wrong? Just how did we move so quickly—in a controlled economy—from forecasts of 3 percent inflation, to a record of more than 5 percent, to a situation in which even the optimists cannot see how we are to get much below 4 percent?

It is important to bear in mind that the origins of the great inflation are quite unmysterious. In the mid-1960's, we tried, on top of an increasingly powerful business boom, to finance the Vietnam war without a tax increase, and the predictable result was a torrent of demand that washed away stable prices. Then the brakes we had stepped on began to grab on the economy itself. By the end of 1969, the U.S. had entered a period of recession, its first in nearly a decade.

In retrospect, what was shocking about the recession was that it proved so appallingly ineffectual. Recessions are supposedly the blood enemy of inflation. According to the script, they subdue spending, increase unemployment, drive down wage demands, and put out the fire under prices. In the 1969–70 recession, a year-long affair, spending and unemployment behaved according to the rules, but that was as far as things went. Wage increases slowed hardly at all; instead, labor demanded, and got, higher new levels of pay that would allow it to "catch up" on inflation.

The higher labor costs were, in turn, a hypodermic needle that pushed up prices, conferring on us bone-chilling inflation rates of 5.5 percent in 1970 and 4.7 percent in 1971. The recession had basically accomplished nothing.

Many businessmen and economists were driven to the view that a major structural change had come upon the economy, and that it now had built into it irresistible tendencies toward higher inflation rates. Those inclined to this view ascribed the change to shifts in the composition of the labor force and/or the growing clout of labor. They noted the rise of government unions, the shift of power from union leaders to a more militant rank and file, and a cluster of trends—rising affluence, working wives, unemployment insurance for strikers in a couple of states—that made long strikes more tolerable for labor.

Other students of the economy argued against the idea that there had been any fundamental change at all. As they saw it, there was indeed a problem with labor when inflation rates got above a certain level—say 2.5 percent—because labor was then driven to anticipate *future* price rises when it bargained on wages, and this process itself raised costs and prices still further. What was needed, on their analysis, was not any great structural reform, but simply to get the rate of price increases back down to the point at which inflation was no longer feeding on itself. Unhappily, this whole argument remains unresolved.

The U.S. had some further inflationary surprises in the shape of food prices, exports and imports, and plant capacity. All were of such a size and character that no amount of intelligent foresight could have been expected to prevent them entirely. They were made harder to deal with because they crashed into an economy already stretched tight.

The country worked itself into this shape in 1972. It was an election year. Wage and price controls were in place, and through most of the year they seemed to be working fairly well; they provided a framework in which measures to stimulate the economy could presumably be undertaken with confidence that the country would not blow apart. And though the economy was moving upward nicely through the year, there was a continuing rationale for stimulus: the unemployment figures were staying disturbingly high.

The advent of price controls, furthermore, had apparently caused the American public to relax a bit about inflation and start worrying more about unemployment. The shift in sentiment showed up, for example, in a Louis Harris study done at the beginning of 1972, in which the respondents were asked if they would rather see a reduction in unemployment or a reduction in the cost of living. The preference, by a fair-sized margin, was a reduction in unemployment.

That was also the Federal Reserve's preference in 1972. It gave the unemployment problem priority over inflation throughout the year and pursued a policy of very significant ease. The Fed's expansiveness permitted the money supply to grow, by one measurement, at a startlingly rapid rate of 8.3 percent, a clear record for the twenty-six years during which the statistic has been compiled.

Fiscal policy was also, under the approving eye of both President Nixon and Congress, doing its considerable bit to stimulate the economy. Part of the stimulus came from the elimination of excise taxes on cars and trucks and from some reduction of income taxes. A still bigger part came from federal spending, which began to accelerate rapidly in early 1972 and didn't slow down until about a year later. The deficits that ensued could once have been expected to drive Richard Nixon, a conservative at heart, up the wall; in 1972 it seemed just fine to him, and to most Democratic economists, upset about a continuing high unemployment rate and persuaded that the economy still had plenty of room to expand. They did nothing but egg on the Administration to even greater heights of stimulation.

One of those who perhaps can claim not to have been a member of the gang is Henry Kaufman of Salomon Brothers, who has for some years criticized the government's economic policies as undisciplined. Kaufman's unhappiness in 1972 was not so much with monetary policy. Rather, he focused on the budget, describing it as early as May as "excessively stimulating." In 1973, with the U.S. ensnarled in an unmanageable boom, Kaufman also began complaining about the "unprecedented" growth of money. And, of course, he soon came to be joined by all sorts of critics suddenly endowed with perception.

Adding all this up, it now seems clear that the Administration's biggest mistake in 1972 was to adopt a posture that was overly risky. It was especially risky because of a great surge of expansion that was taking place in other areas of the world. By early 1973, all the major countries in Europe, and Japan also, were riding waves of prosperity—though these, in every case, were accompanied, and marred, by inflation experiences worse than our own. To have everyone responding in unison to an upswinging baton was a situation not seen since the early 1950's, and this time the crescendo was much more powerful. It proved to be staggering in its effects. As Marina Whitman, until recently a member of the Council of Economic Advisers, states it, "We got reminded last year that we are a part of the world." The forces that hit us can be interpreted as mainly bad luck. But they may also be viewed as the harbinger of problems that will continue to vex us in the future. We have learned, at least, that the more a country becomes a part of the worldwide market, the more it loses control over events.

Our experience with food prices during the last couple of years is a compelling example of that proposition. In 1972, and even more in 1973, a ravenous worldwide demand for food landed on a world supply situation that was incredibly tight. Whether the ensuing price upheaval represented a single dose of bad luck, or the beginning of a new era, is a new question of some moment.

It will be recalled, perhaps fondly, that for most of the last forty years we have been struggling with problems of oversupply in farm crops. In 1972 the basic policy of the Department of Agriculture was still to hold down supply and keep prices up. The U.S. thus came into the worldwide supply crunch with an enormous number of available acres *not* under cultivation. Following the rules that would make them eligible for crop payments, farmers had "set aside" these acres. And because of other rules, designed to keep the supply of cattle down and their prices up, most of these acres could not be used for grazing either.

These policies were certainly no secret in 1972, and they came under considerable attack as meat and grain prices rose. Beginning in the late spring, for example, the Price Commission campaigned for changes that would increase supply. But very little got done, even after the crop shortfalls abroad, even after the now-famous Russian wheat deal made it clear that U.S. supplies were going to be coveted.

In a way, it wasn't surprising that the Department of Agriculture still held firmly down on supply. DOA has always had its constituency, and it is made up of farmers. Furthermore, the election was very much on the Administration's mind, and Nixon presumably took it as axiomatic that presidential candidates need the farmers' support.

In fairness to the President, however, it must be added that much of the information the White House was getting about food prices in 1972 was not too alarming. In a forecast that deserves to be carved in Jell-O, the Department of Agriculture predicted in November that food prices for the nine months ending in June, 1973, would be up by 2.6 percent. They actually rose by 11.5 percent.

Just after that forecast was made, wholesale prices jumped an eye-popping 5 percent. The Administration was galvanized into action. Secretary of the Treasury George Shultz, who had just been given authority over agricultural economic policy, immediately moved to do away with wheat "set-aside" requirements that Secretary of Agriculture Earl Butz had imposed in July. Shultz also suspended the remaining export subsidies for foods.

But none of these measures was able to contain food prices in 1973. Demand grabbed hold of the prices and swept them upward. During the year ending in August, 1973, wheat prices rose by 186 percent, corn by 163 percent, broilers by 158 percent.

The surprises and forecasting problems involved in being "a part of the world" have also been illustrated in the recent history of the dollar and U.S. trade. The first devaluation of the dollar, in

December, 1971, reduced its value by 11 percent (i.e., in terms of the currencies of our major trading partners, weighted by their importance in U.S. trade). This currency realignment was designed in part to make U.S. goods cheaper, and therefore more attractive in world markets, and also designed to make goods imported into the U.S. more expensive.

But neither exports nor imports behaved quite as expected. The anticipated export growth came very slowly and remained disappointing (except for agricultural products) through almost all of 1972, with dollar volume for the year rising only 13 percent and prices of exported goods rising only slightly. Meanwhile, the prices of imports did not go up nearly as much as expected; foreign suppliers and importers, it appears, were unimpressed by the demand for their goods, were anxious to keep their U.S. markets intact, and so held prices down by cutting profit margins. Both of these developments lulled the Administration into thinking that devaluations, insofar as their effect on prices was concerned, were no big deal.

But a second devaluation, of 6 percent, turned out to be a very big deal indeed. This time suppliers and importers, luxuriating in a powerful worldwide demand for goods, raised their prices almost immediately. They continued to raise them as the dollar, now "floating" in a new international currency system, lost additional value in the exchange markets. As a result, import prices jumped by a sizzling 17 percent in the first three quarters of 1973—a rise in prices costing the economy at an annual rate of about $11 billion. To supply perspective, that amount is more than consumers pay annually for appliances, television sets, and radios combined.

On the export side, the reverberations were equally loud. Cut-price U.S. goods, now responding to powerful world-wide demand, suddenly began to leave the country at record rates. Foodstuffs, obviously, were high on the list of most-wanted goods, but the demand extended to a broad range of commodities. All this had its wonderful side. Exports last year were up by about 40 percent over 1972, and by July the U.S. could claim, for the first time in nearly two years, a favorable balance of trade. But the effect on U.S. prices was not so wonderful at all. Prices charged to foreign customers were not (and are still not) controlled, and so export prices naturally swept upward in response to demand. Some domestic prices went along—e.g., those of products *not* under control, such as nonprocessed food.

What is ultimately most alarming about this inflationary chronicle is that it seems, even in retrospect, to have been largely unavoidable. It is hard to see how *any* control program could have effectively bottled up prices in the face of the overpowering demand that was everywhere in the 1973 world economy.

We also learned in 1973 that we lacked a clear understanding of our ability to produce what the world was after. That discovery emerged out of our problems with plant capacity. Almost everything about our capacity problems was a surprise. Through most of 1972, economists rather persistently took comfort from a presumption that the economy had a lot of elbowroom; we were not short of labor, they said, not short of capital, not short of anything. Scarcely anyone even mentioned plant capacity as a problem.

The official statistics on capacity utilization—i.e., on operating rates—supported this relaxed assessment of the case. Figures compiled by the Fed showed all during 1972 that there was plenty of unused manufacturing capacity; in fact, the proportion of capacity being utilized didn't rise above 80 percent until the fourth quarter, and then it got only to 81.5 percent.

And yet toward the end of 1972 the National Association of Purchasing Management was beginning to get some feedback that suggested things were not so comfortable. The N.A.P.M. said its members noted that there were now twelve items on its list of goods in short supply, compared with three a year before, and added: "Shortages are threatening to become a major concern of the current expansion." From there on in, its monthly reports reflected growing astonishment and dismay. "Members speak of the current shortage situation as the worst since World War II."

The reason is that basic materials capacity has been growing at a very slow rate. Since 1965, the Fed's figures show, total manufacturing capacity has risen by 50 percent, major materials capacity by only 35 percent. And why this lag? Economist Alan Greenspan believes that many older plants once devoted to production of basic materials have been made uneconomic by high wage rates—and have been excised from the capacity figures. An alternative, or supplement, to this view is the widely held theory that pollution controls have caused the closing of many major-materials facilities and impeded construction of new ones.

In one sense, it doesn't matter whether our capacity problems spring from rising labor costs or rising environmental costs. Both kinds of costs look as though they will be rising some more in the years ahead—and so, on either theory, there remains a question whether our industrial capacity will be adequate.

The energy crisis, which has recently preempted so much discussion of U.S. economic problems, will involve costs that are similar in many ways to those associated with the environment. In both cases, i.e., to avoid higher fuel costs and to avoid pollution, there are insistent new pressures to operate less efficiently.

One likely outcome is a drag on productivity. Its extent is immeasurable but its general significance to the questions about inflation is clear enough. The inflation rate is to some extent a "resultant" of trends in wages and in productivity, and any enduring slowdown in productivity gains would raise as serious a new question as can be imagined.

Any questions about productivity would seem to be especially compelling right now. It can be argued that 1973 was a key year— maybe *the* key year—in our fight against inflation. We had behind us a year of progress and we seemed close to establishing the notion that our inflation might really be brought under control. Organized labor was obviously trying to be helpful; its demands for over a year have been so moderate as to cause general amazement. Unfortunately, we weren't able to take advantage of this remarkable circumstance. We managed, with a combination of bad luck and bad policy, to blow the year.

January 1974

A Testing Time for America
By JAMES R. SCHLESINGER

A specter is haunting Europe: not the specter of Communism evoked in these famous words by Karl Marx in 1848, but the specter of Soviet hegemony. That specter arises from the steady expansion of the military of the Soviet state. Margins of the Eurasian continent—Japan, Korea, the Middle East—are exposed to the growing reach of Soviet military power and the psychological aura it increasingly conveys. Such power may be employed directly for intervention or seizure, but is more likely to be exploited indirectly to extract political, economic, or military

concessions. To avoid such concessions, deterrence through coun-
tervailing military power remains an indispensable requirement.
In the area of the Persian Gulf, the resources of which remain
critical to the economies of the industrialized world, the possibility
of Soviet military proponderance poses not only a direct threat, but
also, through potential control of energy supplies, an indirect
threat to the independence of the economies and the social order of
the industrialized world.

At no point since the 1930's has the Western world faced so
formidable a threat to its survival. As it was then, the military
balance is deteriorating, but the trend in large measure goes
unnoticed because the Soviets today speak in less bombastic and
threatening terms than the Nazis did. For too many Americans,
security—not only the physical security of the United States and its
closest allies, but also the security of the delicate web of economic
relations—has come to be accepted as the order of nature. The
illusion is widespread that America can obtain the benefits of
international order without paying the costs. Americans are com-
forted either by a belief that the nation's power has not declined or
by a belief that its power can decline without untoward consequences.

These soothing notions represent a flight from reality. The
United States today still represents the only potential counter-
weight to the military and political power of the Soviet Union.
There is no one else. We may resent that fate, but it remains the
fundamental reality of global politics.

Lord Acton's dictum that power tends to corrupt has, to be sure,
an abiding relevance for the actions of individual men and of
institutions. Yet, in the larger context of the affairs of nations, it is
readily misapplied, for it neglects an equally important truth.
Weakness also corrupts—and can do so fatally.

For the Soviet leadership, the accretion of military power is an
indispensable element in the success of the Soviet state. It is
reflected in the persistent rise in real Soviet military expenditures—at 3 or 4 percent per year.

In the Soviet view, detente itself is a *consequence* of the growth of
Soviet power, which has forced the West to grant concessions. Far
from sharing the Western view of detente as gradual reconciliation,
with hope of ending the possibility of conflict, the Soviets view
detente as rich with opportunities for major gains. There is little
here of a live-and-let-live attitude—with principal emphasis on
vistas of expanding trade and peaceful exchanges.

Among our leadership groups, the business community has been particularly utopian regarding the prospects of detente. Historically the business community, focusing on the narrower problems of production and sales, has been inept in politics generally, and insensitive to the clash of social forces. For the Soviets the innocence of Western businessmen (reflected in the gibe attributed to Lenin, that the bourgeoisie would glady contract to sell the rope with which to hang themselves) remains a byword and a source of steady amusement. Trade is no panacea for achieving international stability. The sale of refrigerators, soft drinks, or consumer goods generally will solve no political problems.

The share of public spending that the U.S. devotes to defense is at the lowest point since two years before Pearl Harbor. Since fiscal year 1968, U.S. military manpower has declined by 1.5 million men. It is now approximately 600,000 below the pre-Vietnam level. Indeed, it is almost 500,000 men lower than during the Eisenhower years, when the nation possessed overwhelming nuclear strength and declared its reliance upon a military strategy of massive retaliation. Even during the pell-mell demobilization following World War II, and during 1949–50, when Secretary of Defense Louis Johnson was "cutting fat and not muscle" before the Korean war, this nation maintained a higher ratio of its population under arms. In constant dollars, defense investment has shrunk to less than half of the 1968 level and 35 percent below the pre-Vietnam level.

The strength of the Navy is perhaps the most dramatic case in point. In the face of a major expansion of Soviet naval forces, which has altered the character of the naval balance, the size of the U.S. fleet has diminished sharply. In fiscal year 1968 the Navy had 976 ships. This fiscal year it will be down to 483 ships. The shrinkage reflects the disappearance from the fleet of vessels constructed during the World War II period, some thirty years ago. It also reflects the postponement of naval constructtion during the Vietnam war, and the present lack of shipyard capacity. Naval commitments in the Far East and in the Mediterranean have not shrunk commensurately. As a result, the smaller fleet of today is overworked in the attempt to maintain those commitments. The consequence has been a distressing decline of the material readiness of the fleet.

The decay in the condition of the fleet was dramatically underscored during the response to the *Mayaguez* incident. The thirty-one-year-old carrier *Hancock*, which has been operating without one of its four shafts, limped belatedly from Subic Bay toward the Gulf of Thailand at twenty-three knots, but never reached the scene. The helicopter carrier *Okinawa*, with part of its boiler plant off the line, crept along at thirteen or fourteen knots; it also never arrived at the scene. The escort vessel *Holt*, the first ship at the scene, had power-supply problems, and consequently its main battery was down the night before the engagement.

Since 1965 the character of the Soviet Navy has been altered in significant ways. Previously it had been designed primarily as a coastal-defense and interdiction force. Now, with the introduction of more capable classes of ships, it has become a formidable blue-water navy challenging that of the United States. Soviet fleets operate increasingly in the Indian Ocean, have begun to edge out the United States in the seas around Japan, and in certain respects have become a match for the U.S. Sixth Fleet in the Mediterranean, formerly an American lake.

Since 1960, Soviet military manpower has grown from approximately three million men to 4.4 million—more than twice the size of the U.S. military establishment. In every category of military hardware except helicopters the Soviets are outproducing the United States—dramatically so in the area of ground-forces equipment, in which the ratios run about six to one. Even leaving aside the massive Soviet reserve structure, the Soviet combat ground forces outnumber those of the United States by roughly three and a half to one.

The United States continues to have a significant qualitative edge in tactical air. Yet in recent years the Soviets have begun to deploy newer types of aircraft in substantial numbers. By the end of the decade, their tactical-air order of battle will be an impressive one. In fighter aircraft, production rates exceed those for the U.S. Air Force by a factor of four. (The USAF this year procured a total of 181 aircraft of all types: at that rate it would be unable to maintain a modernized fighter inventory.) In addition, the Soviets have been upgrading their airlift capabilities as part of a dramatic improvement of their mobility forces, which in the future will be able to intervene well beyond the boundaries of the Soviet Union—in areas such as the Middle East.

In the aggregate, the CIA estimates, the Soviets outspend the United States on defense by about 45 percent in dollar equivalents. In this era of conjoined illusion and skepticism, the hope has been expressed that such estimates are on the high side. To the contrary, my own experience in developing these estimates suggests that the procedures employed are highly conservative—and undoubtedly result in understatement of the Soviet effort. For one thing, the Soviet defense ministry receives a lot of external support. Soviet industry bears the cost of the massive reserve establishment. Other ministries absorb much of the costs of health, education, and housing for defense personnel—costs that are internal to the U.S. Department of Defense. Inclusion of such items would appreciably increase the estimate of the Soviet defense effort relative to our own.

Even more significant, however, than the existing discrepancy in expenditures are the relative budget trends. While the Soviet Union has been increasing its military expenditures in real terms at 3 percent or more per year, the United States has in recent years been shrinking its expenditures at approximately the same rate. Because the estimate for the Soviet Union is necessarily an approximation, one can question the precision of the figures for any single year. No one, however, can validly challenge the overall trends or their long-term implications.

The United States, of course, is not alone. Its NATO allies maintain forces far more potent than the forces maintained by the Soviet Union's Warsaw Pact allies. In terms of the overall balance, moreover, the estrangement between the Soviet Union and the People's Republic of China has probably been the single most significant strategic development of the last decade. It has meant that the worldwide military balance has not yet been upset. But it has made the Western position dependent upon continuing Soviet-Chinese tensions.

Does the tipping of the military balance matter? As the military balance tips more directly toward the Soviet Union, its neighbors will increasingly recognize the imbalance of power and some will become more willing to acquiesce in demands or to offer concessions. The gradual disappearance of American strategic nuclear superiority has reduced the inhibiting influence on Soviet policy those forces once provided.

Further weakening of American and allied general-purpose forces also means that we must accept increasing reliance on the threat of early recourse to nuclear weapons in the event of major conventional assault. That is a strategy we should seek to push further away, rather than to embrace. Because of its ostensibly low cost, it is a poor man's strategy, but it might better be characterized as a rash man's strategy. It would certainly require courage, if not rashness, to employ nuclear weapons in response to less than all-out assault.

Moreover, because there will be doubts regarding the will to use such weapons, such a strategy could invite the very types of confrontations that we should seek to deter. A potential opponent could reasonably conclude that nations lacking the courage to tax themselves sufficiently to provide the conventional elements of an adequate deterrent posture might well lack the courage to employ weapons inherently so much riskier and more destructive.

Yet beyond these basic issues of force structure and strategy, of military posture and military risks, of the actions necessary over the long run to maintain deterrence and a military balance, lies a question even more fundamental. The deterioration of the military balance both draws upon and contributes to the loss of will. In that loss of will—with all that it reflects regarding the decline in confidence and moral stamina—lies the not-so-hidden crisis of Western civilization.

Some years ago, in the final words of his memoirs, Arthur Krock confessed to a visceral fear "that the tenure of the United States as the first power in the world may be one of the briefest in history." On the basis of the present evidence, it is not easy to dismiss his apprehension.

Many have pondered the question whether or not a long recessional of American power will succeed the long recessional of British power. They quite rightly fear the consequences, were that indeed to be the case. The continued deterioration of the military balance would ultimately leave the Western world in a position in which its only serious foreign-policy course would be retreat or appeasement.

The bicentennial year should not coincide with a further weakening of our acceptance of our responsibilities to the external world and to ourselves. If we seek to preserve a satisfactory condition for the United States in the world, if we seek the survival of freedom elsewhere than in North America, if indeed we value what our civilization represents, American strength remains indispensable. Without enduring American strength, Western civilization will not survive.

February 1976

The Message from the Gold Market
By MARTIN MAYER

The message from the recent gyrations of the gold market is unmistakable. The ten-year-old U.S. effort to demonetize gold—to make the metal just another commodity, like rubber or tin—is faltering. A monetary system based on paper alone has proved to be inflationary and is increasingly unacceptable to much of the world.

The appropriate response to this message is not quite so clear. The U.S. Treasury acknowledges that its policies happen to *look* bad right now, but believes that everything will be okay if people will only show some patience. But this October, by moving dramatically to increase the cost of lendable funds, the Fed signaled its agreement that the problems of the dollar had reached crisis proportions.

Out in the private sector, as the market testifies—and, secretly, inside many of the finance ministries—economists are beginning to feel that the disarray of the monetary system is structural, and what was described from its beginnings in the mid-1970's as a "non-system" cannot be made to function by any political process now known to man. Eminent figures, far from the "goldbug" lunatic fringe, have begun to call for a complete reversal of policy, for an acknowledged "remonetization," for a dollar once again officially convertible to gold. Not, of course, at the price of $35 an ounce that the U.S. maintained from 1934 to 1971 (while the prices of everything else tripled), but at a price related to what has been paid this year in the markets.

The news stories from the gold markets have stunned many Americans, but they have not really conveyed the sense of astonishment felt by the experts. Nobody ever predicted—nobody ever imagined—the tidal wave that has swept over the gold markets in the wake of demonetization. All the recognized oracles, in fact, had pointed the other way. Testifying before a congressional committee in 1962, the conservative economist Fritz Machlup proclaimed: "The value of gold rests on a mythology which the Congress can destroy whenever it chooses. Gold is nothing but a price-supported commodity."

As late as 1977, after the market price for gold had touched $200 an ounce and then fallen back in the recession, the British economist John Williamson argued that gold would drop further once it was deprived of its monetary status. Two auctions of small amounts of gold by the U.S. Treasury in 1975 had "demonstrated the thinness of the gold market," Williamson observed.

But a message was coming through loud and clear—a message of deep distrust for paper money. Official, presumably final, demonetization of gold was achieved by ratification of the second amendment to the Articles of Agreement of the IMF in early 1978. The amendment assured that no monetary authority would peg its currency to gold or maintain a price for gold. Pressure on the gold market was maintained by auctioning off IMF gold holdings (currently at a rate of 444,000 ounces a month) and U.S. Treasury stocks (currently at 750,000 ounces a month.) Yet instead of dropping, the price of gold went up.

At last August's Treasury auction, the price per ounce crossed the $300 line; at the September auction, the average price reached over $377—and there were bids for more than three million ounces. The supposedly "thin" market was buying at a rate of $450 million a month from official sellers of monetary gold.

"Nobody ever thought," says Federal Reserve Governor Henry Wallich, wonderingly, "what would happen if we went off gold and the price went sky-high." That simply couldn't happen. But it did.

Since the days of Sir Thomas Gresham (who died in 1579), it has been understood that "bad money drives out good"—that whenever people have a choice between two moneys they will tend to spend one of them (the "bad" money, which is expected to lose value over time) and hoard the other (the "good" money, which is expected to retain its value). When Robert Roosa was Under Secretary of the Treasury in the Kennedy Administration, he used to complain about the one-way flow: nations with payments surpluses would take gold from the Treasury in settlement, but when these same nations ran deficits the gold didn't come back.

Whatever the new rules are at the IMF, the world's monetary authorities want to keep gold as the convincing reserve behind their currencies—as the "good" money that everyone will accept in the worst crunch. And if the governments don't trust each other's paper, the world's private hoarders are unlikely to disgorge their gold.

At first, the Treasury took the position that the frenzy in the gold market was irrelevant to the condition of the dollar—after all, gold prices were rising in all currencies, not just dollars. In the end, however, the United States cannot ignore the worldwide gold frenzy, because it can lead to a spiral of dollar depreciation and domestic inflation of disastrous significance.

The danger lies in the fact that the vast majority of the gold purchasers are spending dollars, not other currencies, to buy the metal. They are the same people who last year bought marks and francs, driving down the exchange value of the dollar. And even when the markets finally begin to view gold as "fully priced," the dollar itself may not recover. The world looking at the dollar will see a stock problem (immense holdings in weak hands) as well as a flow problem (American deficits, which may or may not persist through the recession).

In the eyes of a growing number of analysts, an option that we do have is open and aboveboard remonetization of gold. The U.S. could again offer to buy or sell gold for dollars at a certain price, or within certain price ranges.

A return to gold cannot be achieved by the stroke of a pen. The purpose of fixing a price range for gold would now be to discipline a multicurrency system rather than to keep a single currency (the dollar) as a fixed reference point. All the major trading nations are now and would continue to be gold holders, and the price range would have to be set by agreement. What that range should be is a crucial decision: set too low, the gold price might lead to a deflationary drain of gold to private (and Arab government) holders; set too high, it might stimulate rather than repress inflation.

However difficult the remonetization of gold would be, the maintenance of today's international-exchange system, with its demonstrated inflationary bias, seems impossible. The private markets have lost their faith, not just in currencies, but in governments (including international governmental bodies), and now demand some degree of "automaticity" in the system. Whatever its defects, gold seems to offer at least a degree of automaticity. Unless some other credible source of monetary discipline can be found, structuring the system to make central bankers fear the loss of gold will look increasingly attractive.

Perhaps the most persuasive American advocate of a return to convertibillty was the late Milton Gilbert (he died several weeks ago), who had been chief economist of the Bank for International Settlements in Basel. Gilbert liked to tell a story from his early days on the job. Among the assistants he found waiting for him, he recalled, was "a very intelligent young Italian. Once a month he took part of his pay, and bought gold coins for his wife. I remonstrated with him about it once, and he said, 'Look, don't you Americans come over here and try to tell us how to live. I go home and I give that coin to my wife, and I tell her, "If something happens to me, and to the bank and all the governments, you can go into the countryside and give it to a farmer, and with that coin you can eat for a week."' I came around to the opinion that he knew something I didn't know."

November 5, 1979

Corporations in Trouble

Chrysler's Pie-in-the-Sky Plan for Survival

By PETER BOHR

When Lee A. Iacocca, Chrysler's new c.e.o. and Detroit's premier marketing wizard, marched into Treasury Secretary William Miller's office, he carried a request for $1.2 billion in loan guarantees and an extraordinary plan for bringing off Chrysler's recovery. Packed with details normally confined to the secrecy of the boardroom, the plan lays open Chrysler's strategy for all to see. While the whole affair has already provoked considerable debate about whether Chrysler ought to be bailed out, the document itself has largely escaped close critical analysis. The plan makes clear that the company will stick fast to Iacocca's vision of remaining a full-line rival to G.M. and Ford. The chairman intends to reign over an enterprise that can compete in every category from subcompacts to pickup trucks—and reap the glory that was denied him once when Henry Ford refused to name him as his successor.

With a full array of trucks and front-wheel-drive cars, the plan projects, Chrysler can earn an operating profit of nearly $1.3 billion in 1985, with government aid. In the meantime, the company expects to lose a colossal $1 billion this year, and a still staggering $500 million next year, before earning $400 million in 1981.

To Iacocca, the reason for Chrysler's predicament and the justification for turning to the federal trough are simple. "I'll give it to you as clearly as I can. Because of a slight recession, the market shrinks a million cars and that costs us $150 million out of pocket. Second, our market share of 11 percent goes down a point instead of going up from 11 to 12. Now that's a two-point swing that's better than $300 million. It seems that since April, everybody who's been out has been buying G.M.'s X-cars or Japanese cars. Between G.M., the Japanese, and a little Volkswagen, they've got 70 percent of the market, which they are still holding. So volume is our biggest single problem—about $450 million to $475 million worth. But there's more to it than that. Over the next few years we are being forced to rebuild and retool all our products, develop all-new engines and drive trains, develop three-way catalysts and air-bag systems, not to gain a competitive advantage, or to sell more cars, or to put more people to work, but to meet the law."

The chairman points out what "invention on a schedule" means for his company. He contends that the regulations are "regressive" and "always hurt the small the most." The larger companies have more units over which to spread the costs. Furthermore, the companies have been prohibited from collaborating to develop the technology needed to meet the regulations. The result is predictable: General Motors gains the advantage and Chrysler is gradually sapped of its strength. The bottom line, according to Chrysler, is that it is forced to invest twice as much in new-product development and plant modernization as it would if the regulations were not in effect.

The regulatory blues, long a favorite refrain of the auto industry, certainly sound haunting, but the situation is not quite as bad as Iacocca would have one believe. He includes the fuel-economy rules on his list of the regulatory culprits that have done Chrysler in. He seems to ignore the fact that fuel economy has become perhaps the most marketable feature a new car can offer. G.M. is increasing its capital spending by $5 billion between 1980 and 1985 in order to do even better than the standard requires.

Chrysler has a much stronger case when it condemns the exacting emissions and safety standards that are scheduled to go into effect in 1981. The rules that have obtained until now have corrected obvious safety defects and reduced pollutants by 81 percent—all at a bearable cost to the consumer of about $600 a car, or the price of an air conditioner. But the new safety regulations will require passive restraints, which means air bags will be installed in many cars. The device, which is only useful in frontal collisions at speeds in excess of twenty-five miles per hour, will cost some $600 when new and nearly double that if it has to be replaced. By contrast, the simple seatbelt shoulder harness is effective in virtually all types of collisions and costs only about $75.

To satisfy the emissions standards, many autos will be equipped with so-called three-way catalysts, which will help reduce all three of the regulated pollutants to 5 percent of their uncontrolled levels. Ford estimates that it will spend $59 million per percentage point of pollution reduction to meet these standards, compared with $7.7 million per point spent in the years 1968–1977. Since well over three-quarters of all noxious auto emissions have already been eliminated, it must be asked if the new standards will be worth this extraordinary cost.

Chrysler claims that its fixed costs in meeting all government regulations will come to $620 per car, as compared with $340 per car for G.M. But Kenneth Clarkson, professor of economics at the University of Miami and coauthor of the Chrysler-sponsored Wainwright report, which Iacocca frequently quotes, believes that roughly 65 percent of this money will go toward improving fuel economy. G.M. and other automakers now regard such expenditures as mandates of the marketplace rather than the government. Removing this portion from the total leaves a regulatory cost of $217 per car for Chrysler and $119 for G.M. Certainly the $98 difference per car between G.M. and Chrysler is important in the highly competitive auto industry. But when the difference is multiplied by Chrysler's estimated sales for this year ($98 times 1.4 million), the total competitive disadvantage amounts to "only" $137 million. That's a lot of money, but it doesn't begin to explain Chrysler's projected loss of $1 billion.

It isn't the government's responsibility to compensate a company for its skimpy market share.

"Chrysler's main problem has been its product, both the type of product and the quality of it," says David Healy, analyst for Drexel Burnham Lambert. The company has consistently played a "me too" game with Ford and G.M. Time and again, Chrysler copies G.M.'s successful designs two or three years late. It deluded itself into believing that it could flow with the tide, that research and development leading to innovation was an expendable item that had little to do with market share. Healy also notes, "Chrysler's history of launching new models has been horrible."

As recently as last fall, when it introduced its standard-sized St. Regis, the company blew it. Not only was the market unreceptive to large cars, but Chrysler couldn't get the models to dealers in time to coincide with the promotion. By February, the company had an appalling 381-day supply of St. Regises—and there are only 307 days in the sales year! The past is full of similar tales of horror.

Chrysler's forecast for the growth of the auto market in the Eighties ignores the possibility that another gas shortage could absolutely clobber sales.

As a final argument in its plea for federal welfare, Chrysler raises a chilling specter—the complete shutdown of the company. What would happen if that actually occurred has been the subject of two studies, one by Data Resources Inc. and the other by the Department of Transportation. Both indicate that certain parts of the country would be painfully affected. Detroit, already suffering higher-than-average unemployment, could receive a "devastating" blow. The DOT study figures that for every Chrysler production worker who loses his job, two people employed by Chrysler's suppliers and other related enterprises will join the unemployment line. With Chrysler laying off 53,000 factory workers, unemployment in the Detroit area could hit 16 percent.

Even greater hardships would fall on some other areas, the studies predict. Small towns where Chrysler facilities account for 10 percent or more of the factory jobs often lack the diversity to absorb those thrown out of work. Through 1981, the costs of alleviating the hardships of the unemployed, combined with the drop in personal and corporate tax revenues, could cost federal, state, and local governments $16 billion. The loss in G.N.P. could approach twice that figure.

The fate of Chrysler's pension plan would be a further complication in the event of a shutdown. The company's present unfunded vested pension liability is $1.1 billion. Of this, some $250 million is uninsured, so the workers would lose that much in benefits if the plan were to be terminated. The rest is insured by the Pension Benefit Guaranty Corp., a government agency. But the PBGC is already operating at a deficit and simply isn't prepared to confront a major corporate liquidation. That raises the possibility that the workers would lose more than $250 million.

Both the D.R.I. and DOT assessments were clearly designated worst-case scenarios. They assume a breathless sequence of events in which the corporation, having been denied assistance, finds itself closing down or selling off plants one by one until nothing remains but a few hopelessly defeated executives.

Actually, if Iacocca were to find that he had exhausted all possibilities of raising cash on his own, Chrysler could reorganize under the recently revised federal bankruptcy code that went into effect this month. Chrysler could continue profitable operations while shucking off the losers. Liquidation would not be inevitable. As for the towns with Chrysler plants—"Everybody thought that Seattle would never survive the Boeing contraction and that Youngstown could never sustain its loss, but both of them did," says Freda Ackerman, director of Moody's Municipal Bond Department and an authority on local-government finances.

When it's examined closely, even the pension nightmare begins to look less scary. "If Chrysler did terminate its pension plan, the funded portion of the total liability [$1.4 billion] would be sufficient to meet the needs of the beneficiaries for the next seven years," says Henry Rose, general counsel to the PBGC. That would be enough time for the agency to raise its revenues by increasing premiums on other corporate plans. Besides, if Chrysler were to undergo a reorganization that continued operations, the pension plan would probably not be terminated and nobody would lose anything.

Fundamentally, then, Iacocca's apocalyptic talk of liquidation is essentially a bargaining tactic rather than a realistic assessment of the options open to the company. His fear of reorganization may be that it would force Chrysler to hive off some of its parts, leaving it a fragment of its former self. That would shatter his dream of reigning over an enterprise capable of competing across the board with G.M. and Ford.

The trouble is that, even with multi-millions in federal loan guarantees, Chrysler is likely to end up getting downsized anyway. Privately, some bankers believe that to remain a full-line manufacturer, the company could well require additional infusions of aid running as high as $2 billion or $3 billion. So an early restructuring may, in the last analysis, be the most realistic course. The company might then concentrate mainly on assembling cars from parts supplied by others. Or it might take the path of American Motors and become a producer of specialized vehicles. Either way, Iacocca would have to abandon his ambition of going head to head with his old friends at Ford.

October 22, 1979

The Misadventures of Geneen
By CAROL J. LOOMIS

During 1961–71, International Telephone & Telegraph, by acquiring some 250 companies, became a mammoth conglomerate with sales of $7.3 billion. It was confronted then by an antitrust suit, the upshot of which was a consent decreee in 1971 allowing it to keep its largest subsidiary, Hartford Fire Insurance Co., but requiring it to divest itself, most notably, of Avis (rental cars) and Levitt (housing).

Harold Sydney Geneen, the sixty-five-year-old chairman of International Telephone & Telegraph, had no real training for the role he was forced to assume last month at the company's annual meeting, held in Charlotte, North Carolina. Always before, at each of the fifteen previous annual meetings over which Geneen had presided, his was the pleasurable duty of explaining why earnings were up. But earnings were not up in 1974. They were down, by 13 percent, and so Geneen had to make his first run at explaining a decline. The once-over-lightly he gave the details suggested how strongly he must have disliked the job.

Basically, Geneen blamed the company's results on general economic conditions. More specifically, he went on to say, the villains were interest costs, foreign-currency fluctuations, and problems in the property and casualty insurance business. Insurance problems there certainly were, belonging to Hartford Fire, which last year showed a loss of $123 million in its underwriting operations. And Levitt and Avis were still around in 1974 to do some ghostly damage.

The spread of these problems and their number raise the thought that there is behind them a matter more basic: the sheer difficulty of managing a mammoth and diffuse corporation such as I.T.T. Geneen himself seems willing today to acknowledge the magnitude of this problem. His company, he noted at the annual meeting, is active in at least ten major business fields, and has 280 operations in almost ninety different countries. Sounding more like a victim of this creature than its maker, he said, "Your management is charged with one of the more complex management tasks in the business world." There has patently been a loss of self-confidence at I.T.T.

Levitt is a sad story. At the time of the consent decrees, it was a moneymaker; its operating profits in 1971 were about $7 million, on sales of $268 million. I.T.T. had every intention of selling the company publicly, and thought it would go for at least twenty times earnings, and perhaps much more than that.

Unfortunately, in 1972, Levitt's business began to fall apart, for reasons mainly related to steps it had taken after it was bought by I.T.T. in 1968. Levitt had diversified—e.g., into apartment building and factory-built homes. By 1972, these moves were looking disastrous. So was the company's 1969 purchase of a home-building company in Seattle, an area that promptly developed big unemployment problems.

Then the housing market itself turned bad and subsequently horrible. By 1973, Levitt was losing big money and I.T.T. was feeling sick. That year's deficit (figured by accounting rules that had by then become somewhat tougher) came to $14 million. In addition, I.T.T. took a special writedown of $35 million on its Levitt investment. By this time, of course, there was no possibility of a public sale of stock. And in the first nine months of 1974, Levitt added $20 million of new losses.

Obviously, the difficulties of the housing market have been great, but Levitt's problems just as obviously have had a special dimension. One real-estate expert who had had an opportunity to study Levitt closely undertakes to explain that special dimension. Pointing out other instances in which large corporations have bombed in the real-estate business, he says the mistake was for these companies ever to believe in the first place that they had much to bring to the housing business. "Credit, sure. But, basically, housing is not a business that grows more efficient as it grows bigger. It requires too much close, personalized management for that. If you get bigger, all that means is that you have to put in new layers of managers, who don't come cheap. It was never going to work from the beginning, and the buyers should have known that."

And Avis? Well, it qualifies as part triumph, part disaster. In hindsight, it can be seen that I.T.T. got very noble prices—$38 a share in mid-1972, $47 in early 1973—for some Avis stock it sold. So why did it not then sell all it owned? I.T.T. says it was advised by its underwriters that it could not—that the market would not take that much stock. The lead underwriters, Lazard Frères and Kuhn, Loeb, seem to think they were not quite that adamant about the matter, but say they did indeed believe it was best to put the stock out gradually.

Whatever the case, all I.T.T. got by holding on was a migraine. First, the stock market collapsed. Then Avis collapsed. In 1974, with a decade of generally fine performance behind it, Avis made only $4 million, compared with $11.3 million in 1973.

Considering the economic events, it is perhaps none too surprising that Avis had another bad year in 1974, even while its big competitor, Hertz, was increasing its profits 20 percent. The credit for that no doubt belongs much more directly to Hertz's own management than to its owner, RCA. Yet it is almost certainly RCA that I.T.T. has in mind as it gnashes its teeth over this particular defeat. For I.T.T. competes with RCA quite broadly, not only in the car-rental business, but also in international communications, electronics, and frozen foods. And many I.T.T. executives have looked down on RCA, regarding its management, in the rough words of one middle-line I.T.T. executive, as "inept, inefficient, and stupid." So, to Hertz beating Avis, and at a time so important—well, that has got to be bitter stuff indeed for I.T.T.

Considering all that I.T.T. and Geneen have been through in the last few years, it is probably no wonder that Geneen is talking about getting out from under; he appears ready to retire when his current contract expires in 1977.

It is plain that life around I.T.T. the last couple of years has not been too enjoyable. Most of the top executives at I.T.T. concede that those years have been "educational." Geneen will even agree that they have been "humbling."

Which brings us to 1979, and an I.T.T. Rayonier line manager sitting reflecting over coffee in the remote town of Port Cartier, Quebec. "One day," he says, "I'm going to ask somebody in the know at I.T.T. how a giant company gets into these things." The exhibit he had in mind was a very large, five-year-old Rayonier mill sitting three miles away on the banks of the Gulf of St. Lawrence. When open, the mill works at turning wood into chemical cellulose, also known as dissolving pulp, which is the raw material for such products as rayon, acetate, and cellophane. But the mill was not open as the manager talked, and, if it had been, it would surely have been pulping money a lot faster than wood. For the mill has been a total loser and absolute disaster.

The mill has been plagued by labor problems, some a matter of bad luck, some not. It lacks an economical supply of wood, and its engineering is deplorable. Intended originally to produce about 240,000 metric tons of chemical cellulose a year, the mill has in its five years of operation managed to produce only 378,000 tons of product in total, most of that not even chemical cellulose, but rather lower grades of pulp.

It may well have produced its last ton. In September, 1979, Rayonier announced that it would close this brand-new mill forever. I.T.T. announced simultaneously that it would take, in its third quarter, a $320-million write-off on the project. To that wallop may be added other, very large losses that I.T.T. had previously charged off on the mill and additional small losses that will be incurred as the plant is maintained in a mothballed condition. Overall, the pretax damage to I.T.T. can be thought of as about $600 million. Even after taxes, the bill comes to $475 million, enough to make an I.T.T. stockholder suspect that he himself has been reduced to pulp. The people he may blame indisputably include Harold Geneen, who now, after twenty years, is relinquishing the office of I.T.T. chairman.

The clue to how a giant company "gets into these things"—or at least how I.T.T. did—was a meeting held ten years ago. I.T.T. acquired Rayonier, the nation's largest manufacturer of chemical cellulose, in 1968. Its head was Russell F. Erickson, fifty-seven, an engineer by background and a forceful manager in style. Both he and I.T.T. wanted to see Rayonier grow, and they were encouraged by a good market for chemical cellulose that materialized in the late 1960's. So, in 1969, Erickson sent Blanton W. "Buck" Haskell, Rayonier's forty-nine-year-old director of planning, to scout world-wide opportunities for tying up a large tract of timber, beside which Rayonier could put a mill. Haskell returned thinking there were possibilities on the north shore of the St. Lawrence, where there was a vast forest whose exploitation the province might be willing to help finance. But the consensus at Rayonier was that the immediate need was to expand in the U.S., by building a third production unit, with 175,000 tons of annual capacity, at an existing mill in Jesup, Georgia.

When the time came, in the fall of 1969, for Rayonier to present its annual business plan to Geneen and other I.T.T. executives, it was this unit—"Jesup C," an $85-million project—that dominated the discussion and got a go-ahead. Quebec was not even on the formal agenda. But after the Jesup plans were settled, Geneen leaned back and said—as several people remember the gist of his words—"Great!" Pregnant pause. "What else have you got?"

The unmistakable message was "Think big," and Erickson rose to the challenge. "Okay," he is remembered as saying, as if dealing with a greedy kid, "if that's not good enough for you, listen to Haskell."

Haskell, a big Southerner, drawled out the findings of his trip to Quebec. Only one line he delivered seems to have really counted: a description of the provincial woodlands available there as "about the shape and size of Tennessee." Eyes bugged. One man present says Geneen "went gaga." Another: "The juices began to flow." The formal meeting was adjourned, and Geneen huddled with a small group to talk more about Quebec. "I remember thinking," says one man there, "this project is all but approved."

Erickson, now retired, says he himself believed in the timber, but retained doubts, as the feasibility studies wore on, about the ability of Rayonier to handle Jesup C and a Quebec mill all at once. He did not, however, press these opinions on his boss, of whom he says: "There's no point in saying no to Mr. Geneen."

There is a weird reminder of Port Cartier, Quebec, in Rayonier's Stamford, Connecticut, offices. It is displayed, so to speak, on a large globe decorated with bright circles that identify Rayonier's plants, offices, and customers. But there is no circle in Quebec, no hint at all that the company has been locked there in battle with a dragon of a mill.

Rayonier executives say the globe is simply "out-of-date." But a person knowing Port Cartier's history might well fantasize a more dramatic explanation, embodying an emotional scene in which some Rayonier or I.T.T. executive—perhaps even Geneen himself—descended upon the globe in rage and frustration and expunged from it every trace of the mill's existence.

May, June 1975

A&P: Decline of an Institution

By PETER BERNSTEIN

When Jonathan Scott took over as chairman and chief executive of A&P almost four years ago, the company was in desperate straits. It still is. A five-year recovery plan Scott announced in 1975 is a shambles and the company is back in the red. It lost $9.9 million in the first quarter of this year and $6.9 million in the second, and will almost certainly end up with a loss for the year. Concedes one A&P executive: "The company is in the same position today that it was in in 1971."

A couple of points should be made in Scott's defense. For one thing, this is an unfavorable time to be trying to improve the sales and earnings of a supermarket chain. Partly because the huge growth of the fast-food industry has been taking away a lot of business, supermarket sales have been growing only a little faster than inflation in recent years. This slow growth in the real volume of sales has crimped profits. Last year the industry's overall margin came to a thin 0.72 percent. Supermarket chains, in short, have been having a rough time lately. Food Fair recently filed for protection under Chapter 11 of the Bankruptcy Act.

Also, A&P was a very backward company when Scott took over. During the Sixties, Scott points out, there were no borrowings of any kind for investment in growth and little reinvestment of capital in retail facilities. At the same time, Scott notes, the company was paying cash dividends that, in proportion to earnings, ran to nearly double those of other large food retailers. One of the principal beneficiaries of that dividend policy was the John A. Hartford Foundation, set up by a son of A&P founder George

Huntington Hartford (it supports medical research). The foundation, which was then dominated by retired A&P executives, owned one-third of the company's stock (but has since reduced its holdings to about 25 percent). As one observer recently put it, "A&P was being milked."

Jonathan Scott seemed to possess both the business ability and the personal qualities that would be needed to turn A&P around. He had been the chief executive of Idaho-based Albertson's, the country's tenth-largest supermarket chain. Some men reach the top because they marry the boss's daughter; Scott performed the unusual feat of reaching the top in spite of divorcing the boss's daughter. In 1965, after the divorce (he has since remarried), his former father-in-law, J. A. Albertson, named him president of the chain. Albertson's faith in Scott was well placed. Revenues more than tripled in the decade after he became president.

With A&P's condition deteriorating rapidly in February, 1975, there was no question that Scott had to act quickly. One possible strategy was to close down the company's worst operating units, store by store, warehouse by warehouse, plant by plant. A more radical course of action was to shut down entire operating divisions. Scott opted for the first alternative, which was the keystone of a five-year recovery program that Booz, Allen & Hamilton, the management consultants, had formulated for A&P after a year-long study that cost $1 million. It called for the immediate closing of 1,250 unprofitable or marginal stores as well as certain warehouses and manufacturing plants. In retrospect, it is clear that Scott's basic decision was a mistake.

The error was not immediately apparent, however. The "surgery" proceeded smoothly enough. In fact, it did not take as long or cost as much as A&P at first suspected it would. Altogether, the company closed 1,433 stores, more than 40 percent of the number it had when Scott took over, as well as thirty-six food-processing plants and warehouses.

Initially the company seemed to respond. Despite the loss of stores that had accounted for $1.5 billion in annual sales, A&P nearly maintained its volume during the first year of the recovery program. The following year, fiscal 1976, total sales climbed to a record of $7.2 billion, almost 11 percent more than the $6.5 billion the year before. The company was profitable in 1975 and 1976.

It was able to maintain its sales volume partly because the employees felt good about the new management. Spurred on by

Price & Pride, the new corporate-advertising campaign that was directed as much at the employees as it was at the customers, and excited by the plans to make A&P healthy again, the employees rallied around Scott, cleaning up the stores and working harder.

The company also benefited from good will among consumers. When they heard the commercials saying there was a "new" A&P, one that put price and pride together again, they were willing to give the store another chance. After all, the A&P (which employees used to call "Grandma") was something of an American institution. The customers, however, were disappointed by what they found. "The ads featured better-looking stores with very wide aisles and attractive-looking merchandise," laments one A&P vice president, "but the customer who left us two or three years ago would come in and find the same bad situation that she left. A&P simply got ahead of itself in its advertising." Profits sank dismally in fiscal 1977 to the heavy losses in the current fiscal year.

Upper management had failed to perceive the severity of its basic problems. A reconditioning process—retraining of personnel, setting up of basic merchandising programs, among other things—took much longer than Scott had hoped. Some of the new management's remedial measures, moreover, were pretty ineffective. Millions of dollars, Scott admits, were wasted on store-personnel training programs that did not have any impact.

In addition, management's lack of adequate information about store operations made the closing program a somewhat hit-or-miss affair. Because of the absence of detailed profit-and-loss statements, and a cost-allocation system that did not reflect true costs, A&P's strategists could not be sure whether an individual store was really unprofitable.

Even more embarrassing is the poor showing of the program to build new and larger stores. Altogether, the new management planned to spend $500 million in five years. In the first two years alone, A&P announced, it would lay out $230 million to open new stores, remodel and enlarge others, and give more than a thousand stores a face-lift. Some of the financing came from $200 million worth of credit agreements that A&P negotiated with eleven banks. As a result, A&P's long-term debt jumped from $39 million in 1974 to $134 million three years later. But much of the money was badly spent, dispersed somewhat haphazardly, based on area sales volume and what one vice president calls "a certain amount of emotionalism."

The stiffest medicine Scott has administered to A&P has been a massive injection of new people into the corporate management. Of the seventy people in top management (vice president and above), only twenty have been with the company longer than Scott. A mere six have been in their present positions for longer than three years. All of the top ten officers under Scott have come to A&P since he arrived.

In January, 1978, A&P decided to drop the stale Price & Pride campaign. A new one was launched in September, promising that "You'll Do Better at A&P." Still searching for a long-term solution to its many ills, the company has once again turned to management consultants. McKinsey & Co. was hired a year ago to do essentially the same thing Booz, Allen did—work out a new strategy for A&P. The fee: $100,000 a month. Management is currently reviewing the information generated by McKinsey and, in Scott's words, "determining our strategy by area." The changes in the company, he says guardedly, will be "material."

Other members of top management have been less guarded. There is unanimous agreement that A&P will get smaller before it gets bigger. But they are convinced that the old Great Atlantic & Pacific Tea Co. will continue to exist.

November 6, 1978

Why Buildings Are Collapsing
By WALTER McQUADE

The 17,000-seat Kemper indoor arena in downtown Kansas City had no games or political conventions scheduled for the evening of June 4, 1979. The vast empty room, its lights dimmed, was a quiet haven from the wild spring storm raging outdoors.

Shortly after 7:00 P.M., the duty man, Arthur La Master, stood chatting with a security guard in the foyer. Then the two started to stroll through a tunnel into the arena itself. The first thing they noticed was water cascading down the overhead electronic scoreboard. Immediately thereafter, La Master says, he heard a smashing sound, "like the pounding of a sledge on concrete." The scoreboard sagged. He turned in terror and fled as fast as he could:

"The whole place was falling. I thought lightning had struck. . . ." Within a minute the arena's central span lay crumpled on the floor, littered with the debris of the ceiling, an instant ruin.

In the past two years, the mighty steel roof of the Hartford Civic Center Coliseum came crashing down under a heavy snow and ice load; in Chicago, more than 6,500 roofs on garages, stores, and homes collapsed under the weight of the heaviest snows since 1871. The Chicago building code calls for roofs strong enough to support loads of twenty-five pounds per square foot, but the snow piled up in some cases to twice that amount.

Many other famous roofs and walls have failed without actually falling down. Some failures are particularly humiliating. Buildings designed by the best-known American architects have been suffering ignoble ailments. The most notorious of these is the John Hancock Building in Boston.

Hancock commissioned Ieoh Ming Pei, who this year was awarded the American Institute of Architects' gold medal, the top tribute of his fellow architects, to build a skyscraper in the Back Bay. Pei and his principal design partner, Henry Cobb, devised a sixty-two-story tower proportioned as slimly as a fashion model, sequined in reflective-glass panels. Before the building was occupied, hundreds of the glass panels cracked and some fell out, scattering shards below, which made it necessary to cordon off the sidewalks. All 10,344 glass panels were then removed, and the building was rewalled in stronger glass at a cost of $8.2 million. Later, Hancock spent another $17.5 million to stiffen the building's lean frame, and to install two 300-ton adjustable counterweights near the top to help stabilize the structure against the push of wind. Hancock's employees and tenants finally moved into the building in 1976, but some of the new windows have since cracked, too.

The failures are usually attended by much controversy. In the case of the Kemper arena, the city engineer of Kansas City called in engineer James L. Stratta, an experienced investigator from San Francisco, and set him to work to find out what had happened. What attracted Stratta after several weeks of study was a high-strength steel bolt, one and three-eights inch in diameter, used repeatedly in the framing of the building to connect the interior steel truss to the tubular steel frame that protruded above the roof. In one situation, four bolts were relied upon to pick up a downward load of 210,000 pounds and transmit the weight further along the forest of steel. The ultimate capacity of each of these bolts, according to the standard engineering handbook, was 160,000 pounds, or, for four of them, 640,000 pounds. Then why had two of the bolts broken? Stratta suspected that the cause might have been metal fatigue, brought on as the wind rocked the roof from side to side. He checked the handbook and noted that the strength rating of the bolts in question had a footnote warning that there were limitations to the bolts' strength when under "dynamic" loading, that is, subject to varying weights. The bolts' very stiffness could have limited their ability to withstand "racking" without breaking under wind pressure.

Stratta removed two undamaged sections of the frame containing unbroken bolts, tested them under the strains that a fluctuating wind would produce. The bolts failed at approximately one-fifth of the load they should have been able to carry. Stratta declared that the collapse of the roof had been inevitable sooner or later from the day it was put up and that the June 4 gale had been enough to make it sooner. He also charged that the bolts had not been tightened nearly enough when installed.

The municipality of Kansas City—or its insurance company—will probably rely on Stratta's report if either attempts to establish negligence: that the engineers or architects who specified those bolts did not pay attention to footnotes and/or that the members of the contractor's crew who fastened the bolts had their minds on their lunch. The general contractor, the architects, engineers, and bolt manufacturers are not convinced by the Stratta report. They have commissioned their own independent experts to look further for controverting facts that might be just as compelling to an arbiter, or, if it comes to that, to a jury.

The continuing controversy over the other famous fallen coliseum, the Hartford Civic Center, demonstrates how intricate the battles among the experts can become. Travelers Insurance has already paid the city more than $12 million in damages for the collapse, the biggest single liability payment in the company's history, and now is out to recover from the people who put the roof up. A well-known firm of engineers, Lev Zetlin Associates of New York City, bluntly blamed design errors. According to their calculations, based on the original drawings, the roof was under par for the loads it had to expect, with inadequate bracing and an insufficient margin for safety.

Another engineer commissioned by the insurance underwriter for the architect, Vincent Kling & Associates of Philadelphia, has placed the blame on faulty welding, not on design. A group of specialists from four universities—Connecticut, Yale, Hartford, and M.I.T.—has found fault with *both* the design and building procedures.

Even when the cause of a collapse can be established, it is usually difficult to pinpoint the culprit with certainty. Sometimes several parties are involved. Says Paul Weidlinger, a top structural engineer, "The engineer goofs, the contractor goofs, the manufacturer goofs. Most building are quite forgiving, but few buildings can take all of that."

The failures may yet change the shape of architectural and engineering practice in the U.S., and the shape of some future buildings as well. The trend is toward caution and constricting conservatism—hardly the spirit of the most admired American architecture. Architects and structural engineers are turning somewhat cantankerous toward sloppy contractors and boastful manufacturers' salesmen, and even, at times, toward each other and owners: "I get the very best structural engineers I can find," says Vincent Kling, "but for me to be out in front sharing the liability for their specialty is neither fair nor accurate. They are responsible to the owner for their part of the job."

On the other hand, Anthony Grasso, a partner in Weiskopf & Pickworth, one of the nation's largest firms of structural engineers, says, "Architects have to realize that the quality of workmanship on the site is not as good as it once was, and keep things simple. Twenty years ago you could send an inspector out to the job once a week to see how things were going; now you need two or three men on the job watching every day, but owners are unwilling to pay for them. Sometimes, too, architects want to take a quantum leap into the unknown. We have to get them to keep one leg on what already has been done."

Architect Elmer Botsai, a specialist in diagnosing ailing buildings, says most of those that fail do so "because someone has been trying to save cents. Manufacturers bear a large part of the blame. Their specifications are a tragic joke: equating high performance in a wall with withstanding the pressure of a forty-two-mile wind, for example, when we know that almost all cities can have seventy m.p.h. winds on occasion. The force of wind-driven rain can tear paint from a building; I've seen it."

The situation is further complicated for owners and architects by an erosion in architects' control over large projects. Even in immense undertakings the architect was once the client's principal, trusted agent—a combination of buffer and arbiter between him and the contractors, engineers, and a very few other specialists such as landscape architects. During the great building boom after World War II, however, architects were so preoccupied with their design tasks that many other specialists were brought into the act, some of whom worked directly for the owner: land planners, traffic experts, the interiors specialists whom architects call "space cadets," and several others.

By far the most formidable of the new protagonists in commercial and institutional building, interposed between owner and architect, is the construction manager. His role varies. He may simply act as general adviser to the owner, with little or no legal liability, or he may exercise full control, selecting the contractors and suppliers—and sometimes even the architect. The C.M.'s are adept at speeding up the building process by "fast tracking," which means telescoping the processes of planning and construction—putting in foundations, for example, before the building to be set upon them is completely designed—and in cutting other corners to control costs.

The building of the Hartford Civic Center involved one example of corner cutting, architect Kling charges. He had specified that metallurgists be retained to inspect all work done on the framework of the roof while it was being assembled, before it was raised. This substantial exercise in expertise was worth perhaps $100,000, but the construction manager cut the cost to just $15,575 by retaining a former mathematics teacher, who was paid $4.50 per hour to inspect. In contrast, for the new roof that has risen out of that shattered hole—designed much more conservatively, by another architect and engineer—the client is spending between $300,000 and $400,000 to monitor construction. X-ray inspections of the welds are common, and each connection is stamped with the inspector's name.

Part of the blame for the erosion of the architects' control in such situations must be born by architects themselves. They were the first construction managers and might have tried harder to keep that franchise by mastering the increasing complexity of both engineering and construction techniques. Whoever may be at fault, the ironic truth is that we live in an age of great technological talent but waning on-the-job competence.

November 19, 1979

Science

The Second Computer Revolution
By GENE BYLINSKI

Less than thirty years ago, electrical engineer J. Presper Eckert, Jr., and physicist John W. Mauchly, and helpers, laboriously built the world's first electronic digital computer. Their ENIAC (Electronic Numerical Integrator and Computer) was a fickle monster that weighed thirty tons and ran on 18,000 vacuum tubes—when it ran. But it started the computer revolution.

Now under way is a new expansion of electronics into our lives, a second computer revolution that will transform ordinary products and create many new ones. The instrument of change is an electronic data-processing machine so tiny that it could easily have been lost in the socket of one of those ENIAC tubes. This remarkable device is the microcomputer, also known as the computer-on-a-chip. In its basic configuration, it consists of just that—a complex of circuits on a chip of silicon about the size of the first three letters in the word ENIAC as printed here. Yet even a medium-strength microcomputer can perform 100,000 calculations a second, twenty times as many as ENIAC could.

This smallest of all data-processing machines was invented six years ago, but its mass applications are just beginning to explode, setting off reverberations that will affect work and play, the profitability and productivity of corporations, and the nature of the computer industry itself. For the microcomputer provides an awesome amount of computer power in a package that in its simplest form costs less than $10 bought in quantity and easily fits inside a matchbox.

Unlike the familiar older computers that come in their own boxes, the microcomputer is mounted on a small board that can be made to fit easily and unobtrusively into a corner of an electric typewriter, a butcher's scale, a cash register, a microwave oven, a gas pump, a traffic light, a complex scientific instrument such as a gas chromatograph, and any of a myriad other devices whose capabilities already are being enhanced by these slices of electronic brainpower. Soon microcomputers will start replacing wheels, gears, and mechanical relays in a wide variety of control applications, because it's much more efficient to move electrons around than mechanical parts.

To cite these applications and capabilities, as well as many other uses to come in the home, the factory, and the automobile, is to do only pale justice to this marvelous invention. What sets any computer apart from every other kind of machine is its stored and alterable program, which allows one computer to perform many different tasks in response to simple program changes. Now the microcomputer can impart this power, in a compact form and at a low price, to many other machines and devices.

In the most common form of microcomputer, furthermore, a user can change the program simply by unplugging a tiny memory chip and putting a new one in its place. To show off this versatility, Pro-Log Corp. of Monterey, California, built a demonstration apparatus that in its original version is a digital clock; when a program chip that runs the clock is removed and another is put in its place, the thing suddenly starts belting out a tinny version of the theme from *The Sting*.

Besides providing versatility for users, the microcomputer makes possible large economies in manufacturing. Now a manufacturer can buy a standard microcomputer system for many different products and use a different program chip with each. Furthermore, a microcomputer that replaces, say, fifty integrated circuits does away with about 1,800 interconnections—where most failures occur in electronics. The microcomputer, in other words, is one of those rare innovations that at the same time reduces the cost of manufacturing *and* enhances the capabilities and value of the product.

The microcomputer is the logical end result of the electronics industry's headlong drive to miniaturize. The industry has galloped through three generations of components in as many decades. In the late 1950's, the transistor replaced the vacuum tube. Within a few years, the transistor itself gave way to "large-scale integration," or LSI, the technique that now places thousands of microminiaturized transistors—an integrated circuit—on a sliver of silicon only a fraction of an inch on a side. LSI made possible the suitcase-sized minicomputer.

The semiconductor logic circuit, of course, contained the seed of the microcomputer, since the chip had logic elements on it—the transistors. But the individual chips were designed to perform limited tasks. Accordingly, the central processing units of large computers were made up of hundreds, or thousands, of integrated circuits.

Logic chips were also employed for control or arithmetic functions in specialized applications. In what became known as "hard-wired logic" systems, chips and other individual components were soldered into a rigid pattern on a so-called printed-circuit board. The fixed interconnections served as the program.

The electronic calculator, in all but the latest versions, uses hard-wire logic. The arithimetic functions, or the operating program instructions, are embedded in the chips, while the application program is in the user's head—his instructions yield the desired calculations.

A young Intel engineer, M. E. Hoff, Jr., envisioned a different way of employing the new electronic capabilities. In 1969 he found himself in charge of a project that Intel took on for Busicom, a Japanese calculator company. Busicom wanted Intel to produce calculator chips of Japanese design. The logic circuits were spread around eleven chips and the complexity of the design would have taxed Intel's capabilities—it was then a small company.

Hoff saw a way to improve on the Japanese design by making a bold technological leap. In the intricate innards of a memory chip, Hoff knew, it was possible to store a program to run a minuscule computing circuit.

In his preliminary design, Hoff condensed the layout onto three chips. He put the computer's "brain," its central processing unit, on a single chip of silicon. That was possible because the semiconductor industry had developed a means of inscribing very complex circuits on tiny surfaces. A master drawing, usually 500 times as large as the actual chip, is reduced photographically to microminiature size. The photo images are then transferred to the chip by a technique similar to photoengraving.

The central processing unit on a chip became known as the microprocessor. To the microprocessor, Hoff attached two memory chips, one to move data in and out of the CPU and one to provide the program to drive the CPU. Hoff now had in hand a rudimentary general-purpose computer that not only could run a complex calculator but also could control an elevator or a set of traffic lights, and perform many other tasks, depending on its program. The microcomputer was slower than minicomputers, but it could be mass-produced as a component, on the same high-volume lines where Intel made memory chips—a development that would suddenly put the semiconductor company into the computer business.

After other Intel engineers who took over the detailed design work got through with it, Hoff's invention contained 2,250 micro-miniaturized transistors on a chip slightly less than one-sixth of an inch long and one-eighth of an inch wide, and each of those microscopic transistors was roughly equal to an ENIAC vacuum tube. Intel labeled the microprocessor chip 4004, and the whole microcomputer MCS-4 (microcomputer system 4). "The 4004 will probably be as famous as the ENIAC," says an admiring Motorola executive. Despite its small size, the 4004 just about matched ENIAC's computational power. It also matched the capability of an I.B.M. machine of the early 1960's that sold for $30,000 and whose central processing unit took up the space of an office desk.

For logic and systems designers the appearance of the micro-computer brought with it a dramatic change in the way they employed electronics. They could now replace all those rigid hard-wired logic systems with microcomputers, because they could store program sequences in the labyrinthine circuits of the mem-ory chip instead of using individual logic chips and discrete components to implement the program. Engineers thus could substitute program code words for hardware parts.

At first the semiconductor industry showed surprisingly little interest in this great leap in its technology. Semiconductor manu-facturers had made so many extravagant promises in the past that the industry seemed to have become immune to claims of real advances. To speed the adoption of microcomputers, Intel under-took to recast the thinking of industrial-design engineers—the company taught 5,000 engineers to use the microcomputers in the early Seventies and another 5,000 or so later on.

Once these engineers started ordering the tiny computers in some quantity, the big companies rushed to get on board by "second-sourcing" —i.e., copying—Intel's microcomputers. Sec-ond-sourcing is a common practice in the semiconductor industry, widely accepted by the companies involved. It works to the benefit of the user in establishing a competitive source for the component as well as a backup for the original manufacturer. In fact, users normally demand second-sourcing.

Second-sourcing microcomputers proved to be a complex task, however. What's more, Intel kept moving. It followed up the 4004 with a more capacious 8008 model in 1972, and toward the end of 1973 brought out it second-generation microcomputer, the 8080. This was twenty times faster than the 4004. Even then most competitors had no microcomputers of their own to offer. The first real competition to the 8080 was Motorola's 6800, which came a year afterward. The late starters finally began to catch up this year.

They are battling for a market that so far is fairly small—only about $50 million in 1975. But it is expected to reach $450 million by 1980. One estimate is that consumer-product uses will account for about one-third of that market. Microcomputers are expected to start appearing in automobiles. Ford Motor Co. has found that microcomputer-run controls can cut fuel consumption by as much as 20 percent under test conditions. In the home, microcomputer controls could result in savings on electric and heating bills. For the military, the tiny computers promise the evolution of more versatile weapons. In medical electronics, they open up possibilities for compact and less costly diagnostic instruments. There are indications that in conjunction with complex optical and mechanical devices, microcomputers could help restore vision for some of the blind. In one project, a microprocessor chip will be embedded in an eye-glass frame to decode visual information from artificial "eyes" and send it to the brain.

There seems to be little disagreement that the microcomputer is close to being an ultimate semiconductor circuit and that it now sets the direction for semiconductor technology. Everyone agrees, furthermore, that there will be a whole spectrum of microcomputers aimed at different applications, with many companies sharing the anticipated big market.

The ability of users to operate a whole hierarchy of computers, from a big host machine to the microcomputer far down in the organization, will speed the trend toward "distributed" computer power. Texas Instruments, one of the late starters in the game, sees as a result a computer world polarized into giant machines and huge numbers of microcomputers, with medium-sized computers diminishing in importance. Some specialists see computers of the future evolving into modular processor systems based on microcomputers, with many of their programs embedded in microcomputer memories, replacing expensive software.

In its impact, the microcomputer promises to rival its illustrious predecessors, the vacuum tube, the transistor, and the integrated-circuit logic chip. So far, probably no more than 10 percent of the tiny computer's potential applications have reached production stage. Today, nearly thirty years after the debut of the ENIAC, there are about 200,000 digital computers in the world. By 1985, thanks to the microcomputer, there may be 20 million.

November 1975

Shiva, Next Step to Fusion Power
By GENE BYLINSKI

In the dun-colored hills thirty-five miles southeast of San Francisco, where jackrabbits frolic after dark, stands a vision of what the twenty-first century holds. Inside a somber rectangular building, an intricate steel latticework painted a dazzling white supports the world's most powerful laser. Its twenty beams home in on a metallic chamber which looks, perhaps, like a captured UFO or a piece of hardware left over from *Star Wars*.

This is the Shiva laser-fusion facility at the University of California's Lawrence Livermore Laboratory, where within the next few weeks scientists will begin blasting slabs of laser lights at tiny hydrogen pellets inside that target chamber. Their aim: to demonstrate the scientific feasibility of laser fusion. In earlier experiments some ignition of the thermonuclear fuel has already been achieved. Shiva, named after the multi-armed Indian deity, is designed to make those spheres, no bigger than a grain of salt, blaze like miniature suns for a billionth of a second. If the Shiva scientists are lucky, they may be able to achieve "scientific breakeven," that magic moment when the energy output from one of those man-made suns will equal the energy needed to fire the laser.

Completing this $25-million project tested the skills of more than 100 companies over the past four years.

A shot sequence with Shiva will resemble a rocket launch, complete with a countdown. Five minutes before the firing, the shot director will press a button in the control center, initiating a computer-controlled sequence that starts with safety checks. Next, the huge capacitor—a short-term storage battery—is charged with electricity from the power grid. The shot director will then press the "fire" button, releasing the lightning-like charge into the 2,000 flash lamps in the amplifiers. A thousandth of a second later, a laser pulse races through the system. The pulse is split by mirrors into twenty beams that speed toward the target chamber through long pipes. As they near the target, these slabs of laser light are focused into cones.

In less than a billionth of a second, the points of the cones of light hit the fuel pellet from twenty different angles and with a force twenty-five times that of all the electric power generated in the U.S. The tremendous compression, to a hundred times the density of lead, implodes the fuel sphere, forcing the hydrogen to ignite and producing energetic neutrons that can be ultimately harnessed to make electricity.

Unlike a rocket launch, a Shiva shot will be almost silent. In the basement, a slight pop may be heard as the capacitor discharges. Inside the target chamber the fuel ignites with a brilliant burst of green light and a noise no louder than a firecracker. "No one in San Francisco will know anything has happened," says John L. Emmett, the young physicist who directs laser research at Livermore. "It will be done with a whimper rather than a bang."

But those shots will be heard by scientists around the world. Competition is keen to be the first to reach the energy breakeven point. The 375-man team at Livermore appears to have the best chance of winning. Behind them lie years of experience derived from studies of fusion inside hydrogen bombs and the design of a remarkable computer code for laser fusion. Called LASNEX, it has been so accurate in its predictions that it has enabled the Livermore scientists to march confidently from one predicted milestone to the next—a performance unheard of in a complex applied-science program. John H. Nuckolls, who supervises target design at Livermore, likens LASNEX to "the breaking of an enemy code. It tells you how many divisions to bring to bear on a problem."

Ironically, Shiva's most likely fate is to become in a few years just another dot on the proud chart of advances helped along by the oracular LASNEX code. For impressive as it is, Shiva is scheduled to be swallowed up as a component within an even larger laser, called Nova, which is supposed to be the final experimental facility before the big jump into fusion reactors.

Nova will try to compress the fuel pellets to a density twenty times as great as that achieved by Shiva. Both temperature and density would exceed that of the sun's interior and approach that of the super-hot stars known as "white dwarfs." At that point, the release of energy would be great enough, in theory at least, to make fusion reactors commercially feasible. Such reactors would ignite those man-made miniaturized suns in rapid succession, firing as many as ten per second. Fusion power—safe, clean, and virtually inexhaustible—is envisioned toward the end of the century. Flushed with their success so far, the cocky scientists from Livermore are now talking about achieving this goal at least a decade ahead of schedule.

January 1978

End of an Era

The Bottom Revisited

By DANIEL SELIGMAN

Could it ever happen again? The antecedent of that pronoun is, of course, Black Thursday, October 24, 1929, a day on which millions of investors lost their shirts, socks, and spats, and whose golden anniversary has recently given the nation's financial commentators, ever on the lookout for portentous questions, an occasion for raising yet another one.

Our own view is that it can happen again. We will go further: it *has* happened again. If "it" is defined as the clobbering taken by investors, not just on Black Thursday—which was actually not the worst of 1929's down days—but as the percentage loss between that year's high and low, then it has happened in spades. The only difference is that it has taken somewhat longer this time around.

From the summer high in the Dow Jones industrials (381.17) to the fall low (198.69), the 1929 loss was 48 percent. On an inflation-adjusted basis, the Dow has fallen by about as much during the past decade. It has recently been lurking around the low 800's, precisely where it was a decade ago. During that decade, the consumer price index has just about doubled. Therefore, the real value of the Dow has declined by around 50 percent.

Perhaps you are resisting the idea of comparing short and dramatic declines with long, boring erosions of value. However, there is another, and perhaps more significant, sense in which one might argue that "it" has already happened. People who ask questions about such possibilities are ordinarily thinking of the 1929 decline as a disastrous episode from which we have long since recovered. But we have not recovered—not, at least, on an inflation-adjusted basis. *In October, 1979, the Dow in real terms was probably lower than it was after the 1929 crash.* Consumer prices have risen by about 4.3 times since the late fall of 1929, the Dow by 4.1 times. So if the question is whether we need to worry again about anything as awful as the 1929 bottom, the answer is all too clear. Friends, we are there right now.

November 19, 1979

A Modestly Cheerful Mr. Greenspan
By WILLIAM BOWEN

With the end of the Seventies nearly at hand, it is natural to ask whether the Eighties will be any better. The short answer is "Yes—maybe." The yes part, distilled into one essential number on a chart, is a projected growth rate of 3.4 percent a year for real G.N.P. over the decade—not as good as the Sixties, but distinctly better than the Seventies.

The 3.4 figure comes from Townsend-Greenspan, the New York economic consulting firm headed by Alan Greenspan, who was chairman of President Ford's Council of Economic Advisers. His 3.4 figure is not a prediction of what the G.N.P. growth rate in the Eighties will actually be, nor does it represent a middle path between an optimistic projection and a pessimistic one; 3.4 indicates the *best* that we can reasonably expect.

It involves some assumptions, which is where the "maybe" comes in. The underlying one is that we won't encounter any severely damaging disruptions of our oil supply. And it is assumed that oil prices won't rise much faster than prices generally. There is also an assumption that "we do things right," as Greenspan puts it, that the federal government will adopt and carry out effective policies to bring about a substantial reduction in the underlying rate of inflation.

These assumptions could be considered optimistic. That's all right: when it comes to making assumptions about the future, optimism is not necessarily less realistic than pessimism—it only seems that way when things have been going badly. The assumptions are *rationally* optimistic—they are on the cheerful side, but they do not presuppose anything that is inherently improbable. It is reasonable to assume, as Greenspan does, that in matters beyond our control we will not suffer serious bad luck, and that for the rest, as he puts it, "we won't shoot ourselves in the foot."

If the cheerful assumptions do work out and we do get 3.4 percent real growth, the nation's output indeed will still not be expanding fast enough to meet all the demands on it. We will still see the same sort of pushing and shoving over shares that we have seen in the Seventies.

The huge rise in oil prices; government regulations that imposed large and increasing costs to bring us cleaner air, cleaner waterways, safer cars, safer workplaces; expanding social-welfare programs—all created ever-larger claims upon output without adding anything to output. This made it impossible for working people, or most of them, to obtain the increases in real income that came to be expected in the Fifties and Sixties. The result has been an intense, inflation-fanning chase for larger increases in money income to bring real income up to expectations.

In the Eighties, two other big claimants will be taking heftier shares of the nation's output than they took in the Seventies. Capital spending has to start absorbing a larger share of G.N.P. if real economic growth is ever to catch up with the demands. And the Eighties will undoubtedly see a rise in the share going to defense.

So while 3.4 percent growth would not be enough to satisfy all the claims upon G.N.P., it would nevertheless by pretty robust. Compounded over ten years, 3.4 percent real growth will mean a

40 percent rise in real G.N.P. With population growth of just under 10 percent, there will be 28 percent more real G.N.P. per American in 1989 than in 1979. We won't get price stability during the Eighties, but if we adhere to sensible economic policies, there should be a lot less inflation than during the Seventies. In the Townsend-Greenspan projections, the inflation rate will get down to below 6 percent in the second half of the decade.

Rising productivity, of course, is the fundamental source of gains in real income. And productivity and inflation interact in important ways. Inflation affects productivity mainly by retarding capital investment. Severe inflation, moreover, impairs the efficiency of markets. Also, continued inflation as bad as we've seen in the Seventies is bound to erode the satisfaction and morale of many employees, to the point of affecting their work. Productivity, for its part, affects inflation directly through labor costs, which amount to two-thirds of total business costs. The rise in labor costs over any period can be thought of as the rise in compensation minus the gain in productivity.

So a huge vicious circle has been at work in the economy of the Seventies. Inflation has weakened productivity growth. Weak productivity growth has contributed to the inflation.

There seems to be something like a consensus out among the people (if not among economists) that in order to slow the rise in prices we have to cut federal spending. This is a correct perception. A reduction in the federal government's share of G.N.P. is a necessary ingredient in any effective program to reduce the underlying rate of inflation.

The most valuable benefit of a reduction in federal budget deficits would be that we could then proceed with a deliberate and sustained slowing in the growth of the money supply.

Big budget deficits tend to induce inflationary increases in the money supply. Economist Edgar R. Fiedler, a former assistant secretary of the Treasury for economic policy, explains the matter this way: "The most specific reason for inflationary monetary policy is that the Federal Reserve often finds itself caught by the 'deficit dilemma.' Any time the economy is at or close to full utilization and the budget is in substantial deficit . . . it becomes difficult, if not impossible, for the Federal Reserve System to keep the growth of money within noninflationary bounds."

In other words, we can't slow inflation effectively just with monetary policy. It takes a combination of fiscal *and* monetary policy, working together.

Unfortunately, reduction in the growth of the money supply would reduce not only the rate of inflation, but also the level of demand in the economy, with some increase in unemployment. Otherwise, the policy would be noncontroversial—something for nothing. In reality, of course, there's a lot of ideological or sentimental aversion to fiscal-monetary restraint as a means of slowing inflation. Those who don't like it argue that the payoff is meager compared to the pain. As evidence they often point to the supposed fact that recessions are ineffective at slowing inflation.

In truth, bringing the rate of inflation down is one thing that recessions seem to be able to do. Look at the most recent example, the recession of 1974–75. It was a bad one, but it did slow inflation quite a lot, a fact that was too little noted at the time and has been too widely forgotten since. The yearly rise in consumer prices (December to December) dropped from 12.2 percent in 1974 to 4.8 percent in 1976. The reason recessions *seem* to fail at slowing the rise in prices is that usually the hard-won gains against inflation are thrown away in a swing to overly hasty reflation—as happened in 1977.

With an optimal mix of government actions, including measures to encourage capital investment, it should be possible to avoid severe costs in either increased unemployment or reduced output. To those who insist that the costs would still be too high, Greenspan replies: "Is there an alternative? We don't have either the option of doing nothing or the option of applying a painless cure."

Inflation such as we have seen in the Seventies is hostile to growth, and over a span of years, a lasting reduction in the rate of inflation will mean more real growth, not less. Opponents of fiscal and monetary restraint often complain about "lost output," but continued inflation involves "lost output" too. We certainly have lost output galore in the inflationary Seventies.

Persistent inflation at high rates badly retards capital investment. It pulls up interest rates, as we know all too well, and therefore increases borrowing the costs. It reduces the true rate of return on invested capital, because depreciation allowances come nowhere near matching the inflated costs of replacements. So corporations appear to be earning more than they really are, and therefore pay too much tax on their reported profits. The worse the inflation and the longer it continues, the wider the gap becomes.

But when inflation slows down and inflationary expectations begin to recede, there could be a major revival of capital investment in the middle Eighties—a revival of such large dimensions that it may qualify as an investment "boom." There is plenty of investing to be done, once borrowing costs come down and confidence is reborn: investments in alternative-energy sources, in energy conservation, in public transportation, replacement of industrial equipment made obsolescent by high energy costs, and replacement of aged plants and equipment.

But waging a sustained and resolute campaign against inflation has so far proved to be extremely difficult for the U.S. The eminent economist Paul Samuelson, for one, doesn't think we will succeed in conquering it—he doesn't think we will be willing to pay costs.

Everything depends upon credibility. Economists of the "rational expectations" school believe that if a credible anti-inflation policy is established, Americans will respond to it. Herbert Stein, Greenspan's predecessor as CEA chairman, is inclined to agree. "How quickly the inflation does slow down," he says, "will depend in part on how much businesses and individuals believe that the policy will be carried through to a successful conclusion. If they do believe that, they will adapt their own wage and price decisions to the expectation of a lower inflation rate, and the process of disinflation will go fairly quickly."

And despite all the gloom about energy, the U.S. has resources that would make it possible to reduce our dependence on OPEC considerably without technological breakthroughs or grandiose crash programs. By reducing energy use per unit of output, switching as many factories and utilities as possible from oil to coal, and completely freeing up domestic oil production, we could achieve a significant reduction in dependence on OPEC within a short span of years. We probably won't do that, but we *could* if we had the will.

With its domestic resources of coal, natural gas, and petroleum, the U.S. is in a much better position to reduce its dependence on imported oil than are Japan and most nations of Western Europe. What the U.S. is most seriously short of is not energy resources, but strength of will, clarity of goals, and sense of shared national purposes.

Economists tend to underestimate the importance of purpose in the economic performance of nations. One exceedingly impressive performance was the sustained industrial development of Germany in the fifty years or so prior to World War I. Looking back on that achievement, a British writer observed that "the Germans succeeded in what they did because it was their intention to do so" —in short, because they wanted to.

If those economic overachievers of our day, the Japanese, have any secret, it is their sense of shared purpose, translated into national economic goals and policies to which everyone can feel he is contributing. Why do the Japanese compete so successfully in world markets? Because they want to.

Implicit in those "rationally optimistic" Greenspan assumptions is a belief that we can respond more effectively than we have in the recent past, if we want to.

October 8, 1979

The Past Is Prologue
By WALTER GUZZARDI

The pages of this book have carried glimpses of the past half-century as contemporary *Fortune* writers saw it—still photographs of history's rapidly unfolding action. We have seen the panorama—the sweeping rise and the ensuing ebb of the power of America over those fifty years. It was an epoch of enormous achievement, when centuries of change, coming on with breathtaking velocity, were compressed in the span of a man's lifetime. By the simple act of striding out into the world, Americans seemed to change its size, its shape, and even the speed at which it spun.

As the era began, the U.S. stood depressed, bewildered, unsure of its role and purpose. Americans who shortly before had held jobs and supported families were roaming the countryside searching for food and shelter. From there, we burst forth angrily to become victors in a great war and authors and enforcers of as decent a peace as history can recall. History's precedent called for sowing occupied lands with salt, but America made the enemy's soil fertile; there we planted the seed of democracy, and there, surprisingly, it flourished. Out of magnanimity as well as self-interest, we distributed bounty to defeated enemy and exhausted ally. Resisting the tug of isolationism, we stayed abroad with a military presence to check the advance of the new totalitarianism, and we made ourselves purposeful leaders of a grand alliance.

While we were doing so much for so many beyond our shores, we achieved a different miracle at home. In an atmosphere of individual liberty, heady after the disciplines of Depression and war, we spread abundance throughout our society, so that the two—liberty and abundance—seemed marvelously in gear. We knew that no man impoverished by society could be free (our memory of the hard years was fresh enough for that), and we came to believe that no man in a free society need be impoverished.

Now at the close of the fifty years, disillusionment and discouragement have overtaken us once more. The economic growth that supported our achievement abroad, that replaced misery with prosperity at home, that allowed us to extend social guarantees to the needy, is jeopardized by virulent inflation. Once the world depended upon us; now our dependence on foreign oil renders us strategically vulnerable, imposes great and uncontrollable costs, and makes us appear helpless, plethoric profligates. Now we are better at wringing our hands than working with them, better at pounding our heads than using them.

Our crisis is largely one of the spirit, and only intelligence (we are among the best-educated countries on earth) and will (the characteristic that carried us across frontiers) can help us. No inevitable force has brought us down, nor does decline have to presage fall. In the paramount years, we stretched to do everything for everybody, granting social demands that burst apart our democratic forms and put an intolerable load on our economic system, just as external adversaries stepped up their threats. History tells us that democracy is a quest. The *quest* for the 1980's and beyond is to use the intelligence and the will to choose between all the commitments made over the past decades, and get them to a size we can afford. Then we can tackle the external factors, and resume the growth that pays the bills for the betterments we shall always want. The *quest* is also the *test* for our democractic system of governance.

The chief beneficiary of this redemptive effort will be the U.S. economy, which was the principal victim when we allowed success and openhandedness to bring on overcommitment and prodigality. Fifty years ago, the economy was slipping into near coma. It emerged slowly in the 1930's under the New Deal's ministrations, which left the ineradicable view that, in crisis, the government must act in place of an inadequate private sector. The insurance that the New Deal took out for the old and the poor positioned government centrally in our economic life, and it has never significantly retreated. But its role was relatively diminished during the Eisenhower years, as the economy rolled along, gathering momentum and breadth, and the rising tide lifted all boats. Later, mistaking strength for omnipotence, the Great Society was to rewrite those insurance policies with clauses so grand that even we could not pay for them.

While the economy was booming, though, the boom was the loudest in history. The great propellant came from science and technology, which had been the great symbols of hope in the 1930's. Spurred hotly by the exigencies of war, supported strongly by government afterward, technology radically altered American life. New alloys, chemicals, plastics, and synthetic fibers transformed industrial processes. Electronics and high-speed computers rendered obsolete the old, and put together revolutionary new methods of mass production and distribution. Put to terrible use in war, nuclear fission promised cheap, abundant energy in peacetime.

From war's destruction, too, came a beneficent family of "miracle drugs," first penicillin, then its children, the broad-spectrum antibiotics, and later the steroids, all effective against hitherto untreatable diseases. Preventive vaccines were discovered for tetanus, diphtheria, and polio. Thirteen years were added to life expectancy at birth in the U.S. between 1930 and 1976. In that field, blessings were easy to count.

Ever-flowing technology also transformed transporation and communications. By 1930, only twenty-seven people had flown across the Atlantic, a trip that took about thirty hours in piston-driven propeller aircraft. Last June, 299,000 Americans made the trip to Great Britain by jet plane in a few uncomfortable hours. The world shrank further when space exploration began, and Americans bounced like balloons across the surface of the moon; no one who saw on television those bizarre stuffed figures, free-floating across a wild chaos of cold sterile rock, will ever forget the sight. The revolution in transporation and communications made us into one nation, and the one nation became tied inextricably to the world economy.

The vehicle carrying scientific and technological change to the marketplace was the business enterprise, meaning more and more the big corporation. Old-style bosses and owner-managers gave

way to professionals bred in business schools. Corporations became multidimensional. Conglomerates took on high debt to
acquire strings of companies in unrelated fields—sometimes
through peaceful purchase, sometimes after jarring takeover
fights. American companies were the first to go en masse beyond
their national borders to search for new markets. As the big
multinational corporations transferred their capital, technology,
and management skills around the world, responsible to no single
national sovereignty, they stirred up nationalistic fears that those
wealth-laden Americans were gobbling up all of Europe.

With new technology and markets, with the organizing force of
corporations, the U.S. indeed became the land of plenty in the
Fifties and Sixties. Living out the American dream, middle-income
families experienced enormous increases in their standard of
living. A house in the suburbs, lots of kids, then second homes
and boats and gadgets, became their way of life.

But on a deep level explicated by Daniel Bell, the Harvard
sociologist, all that consumption cut with eversharper edge against
the grain of some cherished American beliefs. Prodigality and
display, made easier by the installment buying that brings instant
satisfaction—no need to save and wait; stretch out on those golden
sands now; fly today, pay tomorrow—contradicted the familiar
ethos of work, achievement, and self-restraint. In that way, Bell
explains, "materialistic hedonism" became rampant, and liberal
capitalism lost "moral grounding."

That disjoining of our economic system from its basic values
coincided with other sad partings. Many Americans parted from
their religions. Young people parted in angry rebellion from their
parents. More people got divorces. The traditional ways in which
families are formed came apart, and so did sexual conventions.
Literature parted from moral purpose, and deified transient sensa-
tions; music was reduced to orgiastic spasms. A President parted
from our standards of decent behavior.

This crisis of the spirit was joined to arrogance and overreaching.
In a burst of social scientism, we succumbed to the illusion that we
could fine-tune the economy, banish recessions, and have growth
forever. We could save Vietnam for democracy, but give up not a
whit of what we wanted at home. Instead, we added the tasks of
eradicating society's blemishes, which increasingly scandalized us:
poverty, racial inequality, environmental pollution. Intolerable
weights were added one by one to our democratic system.

This destructive process was epitomized in the programs of the Great Society. As rising affluence lighted up the flames of rising expectations, so the outpouring of federal largesse detonated what Daniel Bell called "the revolution of rising entitlements." Starting with the New Deal, society rightly accepted the responsibility to aid the poor, the old, and the afflicted. But now anyone in any way disadvantaged had a proper claim to have the disadvantage erased.

More than any other nation, the U.S. was built on an aspiration to equality, and, Alexis de Tocqueville wrote, God gave Americans the means of achieving that ideal "by placing them on a boundless continent." But now, at a time of limitations, distinctions had to be made: Just what was the nature of this ideal we aspired to? That all should stand equal before the law was written into the Constitution. Just as indisputable was the ideal that all should have equal access to education, and an equal chance for self-improvement.

But now, unexpectedly, there entered a third kind of equality—"equality of outcome," which carried with it the notion that our society should redistribute wealth and other favors to everyone who, for whatever reason, might have lagged in the race for success (the numbers of laggards increased promptly). The American scholar Martin Diamond called this notion "a vast inflation of the idea of equality."

The pursuit of that kind of equality set off the most costly chase in American history. "Transfer payments," which include money piped from those who work for it to those who do not, rose to altitudes that boggled minds even in the age of space. The federal budget went into perpetual deficit. And the engine for all the payments, our enterprise system, lost part of the motive energy that it derives from offering rewards for work and risk-taking.

For all of those tangible and intangible costs, most federal programs failed far more than they succeeded. From the moment of its christening, "the war on poverty" was a monument to excess. It was generously conceived, deceptively entitled, and wastefully pursued. The argument over how much poverty the "war" has eliminated is waged now with volleys of numbers fired off by opposing statisticians, leaving, in the end, a reasonable inference that some of the truly poor have been truly helped. But where have all the billions gone? Where pockets of rural poverty are shrinking, as in Appalachia, the workings of the economy are bringing the improvement; elsewhere, urban slums and crime have not declined, and crowds of demoralized welfare dependents remain abandoned to a vast bureaucracy. In the minds of many Americans, the poor have been transformed from people we want to help to a special-interest group whose claims to entitlements are looked on with suspicion.

The question of race intertwines with that of poverty, and excess shows up there, too. No group ever came before society with more authentic grievances than the blacks. In its 1954 decision in *Brown* v. *Board of Education of Topeka,* the Supreme Court specified that an equal education for blacks meant an education in the presence of other Americans. Since then, the courts and the Equal Employment Opportunity Commission have gone beyond the idea of integration to one of preferential treatment for blacks as restitution for historic injustices.

The results of that judicial activism today are ambiguous. Education and job opportunities now open to blacks have remarkably improved, although all racial handicaps have been by no means eliminated. But mandatory busing has re-inflamed racial hostility. And the need to discriminate against other people in order to place blacks throughout society—in jobs, schools, politics, government—precisely in proportion to their numbers disturbs even those who are otherwise sympathetic to the black cause.

Our modern economy created neither poverty nor racial disparities, but as it dug out the raw materials for production and disposed of waste, it *was* the leading agent of damage to the environment. Government moves to curb the damage, however, started without regard for costs, which have leaped beyond anyone's expectations. The steel and automobile industries are able to attribute many current troubles to the cost of pollution controls. By posing a choice between preserving the environment and preserving jobs, they are likely to get some controls relaxed—a small adjustment to reality that may stand as forerunner to the conviction that the regulation of business has gone too far. But the professional and managerial class of regulators remains powerfully positioned in the cluster of new agencies established early in the 1970's. These people have a vested interest in regulating, and seek to transcend markets in the name of social policy. They will resist any lessening of governmental powers.

Support for their exertions will come from those in academe and elsewhere who believe in the old pastoral dream of America the beautiful, which has been stirred up by our awareness that technology has its darker side. Chemicals that bring the harvests that feed the world (and jack up our balance of payments) also pollute water and kill wildlife; poison from tail pipes can choke cities; nuclear power carries with it threats as great as its promise. The dangers are real, and the next task of technology will be to meet them, as in some ways it already appears to be doing. But Utopian yearning to make America a bucolic paradise only makes the task harder.

Though it is true that environmental and other government regulations have been hampering American corporations in international markets, the corporations themselves have also been losing their competitive burn. Many have chosen the easier path of seeking tariff protection, as steel has done (its higher costs now cascade through American industry), or of getting government handouts, as Chrysler has done, rather than sharpening their competitiveness. American industry has slipped from the technological heights, and Japanese high-quality high-technology products—color TV sets, stereos, cameras, watches, and all the rest—are taking over world markets.

We have the capacity to reverse this process, with wise trade policies, with our huge domestic market (still by far the biggest in the world), our natural resources, and our educated population. The first step is to repeal the view of government and business as polarities, and think of them more properly as two members of the American household. We need an understanding by which business and government would stop acting as though each were invented precisely for the purpose of exasperating and winning victories over the other.

Both sides have a contribution to make. The challenge to management is to do some hard thinking about how to develop a broader base for understanding. Right now, nothing seems too extreme for politicians to say about business, and they seem to take pleasure in making oil-company executives squirm in the public spotlight. Those gratifying little dramas do not promote progress on the energy issue.

Even in the matter of energy, where so much lies beyond our control, a revived will to act can have sweeping effects. American enterprise developed those huge reserves of once-cheap Middle Eastern oil, and in our profligate use of it, we laid the groundwork for the dependence that debilitates us today. Now, the vocal advocates of price controls notwithstanding, we know what we have to do: cease shielding ourselves from market mechanisms that fix the value of each energy source, use government research funds to develop new sources, and supply incentives to private investment. Above all, we must free ourselves of the illusion, fostered in Washington, that energy policy can be effective without being painful to anyone.

The other great externality that threatens us is the might of the Soviet Union. Wildly unpredictable power lodges in that country, and it may act in ways that no policy of ours could forestall. Yet our own aberrations explain some of our present dilemma. After Vietnam, we starved the defense budget and let our arsenal deteriorate. Now we are mustering the resolve to restore balance. But as more goes for defense, other government expenditures will have to be slashed, and we shall have to make hard choices. Some cherished causes will have to turn out losers.

The heavy penalty that we are paying for thinking only of powers and never of limits is reflected precisely and painfully in our current inflation rates. But inflation is only a symptom—the high fever that runs when excessive social demands cannot be contained. The mass movements that began in the late 1960's under the flag of "participatory democracy" smashed up the political apparatus, which, for all its bumbling and venality, managed to transpose interest-group demands into compromises and ad hoc majorities. Platoons of activists now roam political battlefields, and placards that read NO NUKES (thus simplifying the most complex issue that science, politics, and morality ever offered mankind) bump against those carried by born-again, hot-blooded patriots demanding NUKE THE AYATOLLAH. What Edmund Burke called "rival follies" wage unrelenting war on one another. Burke also called society a partnership of the dead, the living, and the as yet unborn: in our right-to-it-all, get-it-all, keep-it-all querulousness, we have broken that pact.

To cry for leadership is to beg the question. A democracy gets the leadership it deserves. Our dilemma, as political scientist Benjamin Barber of Rutgers tells us, is "not an absence of leaders but a paucity of values that might sustain them."

Rising material wealth started this erosion of old values and ideals, and it will never invent their replacement. Immediately, the task for American intelligence and will is to construct a balanced polity that will redirect liberal capitalism to its earlier path—to yield steady growth, to bring in the rising tide once more, to earn enough to pay for defense and welfare without bankrupting ourselves. Behind that polity must stand a reconciliation of values—a new paradigm of what we want to become, and the price we are willing to pay. The past half-century stands as prologue to that quest.

February 11, 1980